THE REVELS PLAYS

General Editor: Clifford Leech

THE CHANGELING

The Changeling

THOMAS MIDDLETON
& WILLIAM ROWLEY

EDITED BY

N. W. BAWCUTT

THE REVELS PLAYS

Manchester University Press

Oxford Road Manchester M13 9PL

This edition first published 1958
Reprinted 1961 and 1970
ISBN 0 416 60130 8

First published as a University Paperback 1970
Reprinted 1973
Reprinted 1975
ISBN 0 416 18480 4

Introduction, Apparatus Criticus, etc.
© 1958 N. W. Bawcutt
Type set by The Broadwater Press Ltd.
Reprinted by lithography in Great Britain
by Whitstable Litho Ltd., Whitstable, Kent

Distributed in the U.S.A. by
HARPER & ROW PUBLISHERS INC
BARNES & NOBLE IMPORT DIVISION

TO

MY MOTHER AND FATHER

General Editor's Preface

The aim of this series is to apply to plays by Shakespeare's predecessors, contemporaries, and successors the methods that are now used in Shakespeare editing. It is indeed out of the success of the New Arden Shakespeare that the idea of the present series has emerged, and Professor Una Ellis-Fermor and Dr Harold F. Brooks have most generously given advice on its planning.

There is neither the hope nor the intention of making each volume in the series conform in every particular to one pattern. Each author, each individual play, is likely to present special problems—of text, of density of collation and commentary, of critical and historical judgment. Moreover, any scholar engaged in the task of editing a sixteenth- or seventeenth-century play will recognize that wholly acceptable editorial principles are only gradually becoming plain. There will, therefore, be no hesitation in modifying the practice of this series, either in the light of the peculiarities of any one play or in the light of growing editorial experience. Nevertheless, in certain basic matters the plan of the series is likely to remain constant.

The introductions will include discussions of the provenance of the text, the play's stage-history and reputation, its significance as a contribution to dramatic literature, and its place within the work of its author. The text will be based on a fresh examination of the early editions. Modern spelling will be used, and the original punctuation will be modified where it is likely to cause obscurity; editorial stage-directions will be enclosed in square brackets. The collation will aim at making clear the grounds for an editor's choice in every instance where the original or a frequently accepted modern reading has been departed from. The annotations will attempt to explain difficult passages and to provide such comments and illustrations of usage as the editor considers desirable. Each volume will include either a glossary or an index to annotations: it is the hope of the editors that in this way the series will ultimately provide some assistance to lexicographers of sixteenth- and seventeenth-century English.

But the series will be inadequately performing its task if it proves acceptable only to readers. The special needs of actors and producers will be borne in mind, particularly in the comments on staging and stage-history. Moreover, in one matter a rigorous uniformity may be expected: no editorial indications of locality will be introduced into the scene-headings. This should emphasize the kind of staging for which the plays were originally intended, and may perhaps suggest the advantage of achieving in a modern theatre some approach to the fluidity of scene and the neutrality of acting-space that Shakespeare's fellows knew. In this connection, it will be observed that the indications of act- and scene-division, except where they derive from the copy-text, are given unobtrusively in square brackets.

A small innovation in line-numbering is being introduced. Stage-directions which occur on separate lines from the text are given the number of the immediately preceding line followed by a decimal point and 1, 2, 3, etc. Thus the line 163.5 indicates the fifth line of a stage-direction following line 163 of the scene. At the beginning of a scene the lines of a stage-direction are numbered 0.1, 0.2, etc.

'The Revels' was a general name for entertainments at court in the late sixteenth and seventeenth centuries, and it was from the Master of the Revels that a licence had to be obtained before any play could be performed in London. The plays to be included in this series therefore found their way to the Revels Office. For a body of dramatic literature that reached its fullest growth in the field of tragedy, the term 'Revels' may appear strange. But perhaps the actor at least will judge it fitting.

CLIFFORD LEECH

Durham, 1958

Contents

Preface

My aim in this edition of *The Changeling* has been to supply an accurate text based directly on the 1653 quarto, and to add to it all the information so far discovered which is relevant to an appreciation of the play. The critical section is perhaps more detailed than is usual in editions of this kind, but *The Changeling* has not received a great deal of critical attention, and it seems to me that several important aspects of the play have not been adequately treated in what has so far been written about it.

Most of the work on the book was done with the aid of postgraduate awards from the University of Liverpool, including the William Noble Fellowship. The University also supplied me with photostats of part of Reynolds's *God's Revenge*. My thanks are due to Professor Kenneth Muir, and to the late Dr A. K. McIlwraith, who read and criticized parts of the book in an early form; to Miss Inga-stina Ekeblad, who has helped me in a variety of ways; and above all, to the General Editor, who has been unfailingly generous with advice and encouragement.

N. W. B.

Liverpool,
   November, 1956

Additional Notes

Introduction, p. xxx, l. 13. In his review of the first edition (*Journal of English and Germanic Philology*, LVIII, 1959, p. 694), G. Blakemore Evans points out that three short drolls from *The Changeling* may be found in *The Marrow of Complements* (1655). It seems unlikely, however, that these were intended to be acted.

Ibid., l. 19. The earliest revival of the play in England appears to be that by the First Folio Theatre Club, at the Interval Club theatre, London, on 3 May 1950. The recent production at the Royal Court theatre, with Mary Ure as Beatrice and Robert Shaw as De Flores, ran from 21 February to 18 March 1961.

Page 9, I. i. 122. Cf. Psalm civ. 15.

Page 66, III. iv. 170–1. Cf. Jonson's masque *Hymenaei*, ll. 453–4:

> Shrinke not, soft *Virgin*, you will loue
> Anon, what you so fear to proue.
>
> (Jonson, VII, 225)

Page 70, IV. i. 63–4. Cf. Juvenal, *Satire* x, 168–72.

Abbreviations

The following abbreviations are used in the Introduction, Commentary, and Glossary:

(C) COLLECTED EDITIONS OF DRAMATISTS' WORKS

Bullen	*The Works of Thomas Middleton*, edited by A. H. Bullen (1885).
Chapman, *Comedies*	*The Comedies of George Chapman*, edited by T. M. Parrott (1914).
Chapman, *Tragedies*	*The Tragedies of George Chapman*, edited by T. M. Parrott (1910).
Dekker	*The Dramatic Works of Thomas Dekker*, edited by R. H. Shepherd (1873).
Fletcher	*The Works of Francis Beaumont and John Fletcher*, edited by Arnold Glover and A. R. Waller (1905-12).
Jonson	*The Works of Ben Jonson*, edited by C. H. Herford and Percy Simpson (1925-52).
Webster	*The Complete Works of John Webster*, edited by F. L. Lucas (1927).

In the Commentary and Glossary the titles of Shakespeare's plays are abbreviated as in Onions, *Shakespeare Glossary*, p. x. The line-numbering is that of the Globe edition. The phrase 'See G.' in the Commentary directs the reader to the Glossary.

Introduction

The Changeling, no. 712 in Sir Walter Greg's *Bibliography*, was entered by Humphrey Moseley in the Stationers' Register on 19 October 1652 (where it is described as 'a Comedie . . . written by Rowley'),[1] and published in 1653, in quarto, with the following title-page:

> THE / CHANGELING: / As it was Acted (with great Applause) / at the Privat house in DRURY-LANE, / and *Salisbury Court.* // Written by { *THOMAS MIDLETON,* and *WILLIAM ROWLEY.* } Gent'.
> // *Never Printed before.* // LONDON, / Printed for HUMPHREY MOSELEY, and are to / be sold at his shop at the sign of the *Princes-Arms* / in St *Pauls* Church-yard, 1653.

A variant exists with a different imprint:

> //*Never Printed before.* // LONDON, / Printed in the Year, 1653.

In other respects the two issues are identical, and it is impossible to tell which has priority; Greg suggests that the second may have been intended for private circulation.[2] The large ornament on B1^r seems to indicate that the printer was Thomas Newcomb.[3] The play was reissued in 1668 with a cancel title-page:

> THE / CHANGELING: / As it was Acted (with great / Applause) by the Servants of His / Royal Highness the Duke of *York*, at / the Theatre in *Lincolns-Inn* Fields. // [ornament] // LONDON, / Printed for *A.M.* and sold by / *Thomas Dring*, at the *White Lyon*, over against / the Inner *Temple-Gate* in *Fleet-street.* 1668. // Where you may be Furnish'd with / most sorts of *Plays.*

---

[1] Greg, *Bibliography*, I, 60.   [2] *Ibid.*, II, 828.
[3] See C. W. Miller's article on Newcomb, *University of Virginia Studies in Bibliography*, III (1950–1), 164 (Ornament I).

$A_1{}^v$ has a reset '*Drammatis Personæ*' and a publisher's advertise-
ment, probably Dring's. An examination of the text shows clearly
that the sheets are those of the first edition.

The text of the present edition is based on photostats of the
Huntington Library copy of the first of the 1653 quartos described
above. Collation with the British Museum and Bodleian Library[1]
copies of the play has revealed evidence of proof-corrections on the
outer formes of gatherings B and D, notably on $D_1{}^r$, though only
two of these (II. i. 149 and II. ii. 131) could be considered as anything more than corrections of obvious misprints. Uncorrected
sheets can be found in the 1668 issue, so it would seem to follow
that there was only one printing of the play. One set of running-
titles was used throughout. The source of the printed text was
probably a transcript from theatrical prompt-copy. This could
conceivably have been a private transcript made some years before
the play was printed, though it seems much more likely that Moseley had the play transcribed immediately before sending it to the
printer. Most of the features of the text point to prompt-copy: exits
and entrances are usually clearly marked, and one or two of the
stage-directions hint at prompt-copy,[2] though none of them give
any definite proof.

The quarto text offers few problems to the editor. Misprints are
slight and for the most part easily corrected, and though much of
the verse is mislined it is not usually very difficult to rearrange it.
Editors have suggested that the text as we have it is incomplete:
E. H. C. Oliphant[3] considers that in the original there was probably
at least one scene in which preparations were made for the introduction of Antonio and Franciscus into Alibius's madhouse, and he
also points out that the preparations for a wedding-masque in IV.
iii come to nothing. But a hypothetical opening scene involving
Antonio or Franciscus is hardly necessary,[4] and the dance of fools

---

[1] The Rawlinson copy in the Bodleian is heavily annotated with notes
and comments of various kinds, apparently the work of a late 17th-century
private reader. None of it appears to be of any real value, and some is sheer
gibberish.

[2] Cf. III. iii. 89, v. i. 11, and v. i. 73.1.

[3] *Shakespeare and his Fellow Dramatists* (1929), II, 903.

[4] See below, p. lxiii, n. 1.

and madmen at the end of IV. iii does away with the need for a scene
which would have been very difficult to fit in to the later part of the
play. Hazelton Spencer[1] notices that the quarrel between Antonio
and Franciscus is not brought to a conclusion, but this again may be
a deliberate omission, made in order not to impair the effect of the
last act. Act II is somewhat shorter than the average of the other
four acts, but there is little need to suppose that the quarto is substantially deficient.

The play has been reprinted in the following collections and
editions:

Old English Plays [edited by C. W. Dilke], 1815, IV, 219–324.
The Works of Thomas Middleton, edited by the Rev. Alexander
Dyce, 1840, IV, 205–300.
The Works of Thomas Middleton, edited by A. H. Bullen, 1885,
VI, 1–112.
Thomas Middleton (*The Mermaid Series*), edited by Havelock Ellis,
with an introduction by A. C. Swinburne, 1887, I, 83–167.
The Chief Elizabethan Dramatists, edited by W. A. Neilson, 1911,
pp. 715–40.
Thomas Middleton (*Masterpieces of the English Drama*), edited by
M. W. Sampson, 1915, pp. 291–376.
Representative English Plays, edited by J. S. P. Tatlock and R. G.
Martin, 1916, pp. 383–419.
Typical Elizabethan Play, edited by F. E. Schelling [1926], pp.
587–626.
Shakespeare and his Fellow Dramatists, edited by E. H. C. Oliphant,
1929, II, 901–46.
English Drama 1580–1642, edited by C. F. Tucker Brooke and
N. B. Paradise, 1933, pp. 911–77.
Elizabethan Plays, edited by Hazelton Spencer, 1934, pp. 1015–50.
Elizabethan and Stuart Plays, edited by C. R. Baskervill, V. B.
Heltzel, and A. H. Nethercot, 1934, pp. 1317–54.

Most of the necessary alterations in the text were made by Dilke
and Dyce, and later editors owe much to their work, the editions of
Bullen and Ellis being virtually reprints of Dyce. On points of
detail, however, modern editors have tended to revert to quarto
readings. The present text aims to follow the quarto as closely as

[1] *Elizabethan Plays* (1934), p. 1016.

possible, and many of the small but quite unnecessary changes made by earlier editors have been removed from the text. The punctuation is taken from the quarto wherever possible, but fuller or heavier punctuation has been freely inserted where it seemed needed to make the sense more immediately evident. The lineation is largely Dyce's, though at some points the quarto lining has been retained, or what appeared to be a more natural reading introduced. Asides are an important feature of the play, and have therefore been clearly marked as such, though the quarto gives no indication of any kind. When a speech continues after an aside, the change to direct address is indicated by a stage-direction such as 'to him' or 'to De F.'; all these have been added in the present edition, and they are not recorded separately in the collation. Contractions in the quarto stage-directions have been silently expanded. Stage-directions inserted into the text where the quarto is deficient are enclosed in square brackets. Most of them are taken over from earlier editors, but at several points their wording has been slightly altered to bring it in line with the wording of the stage-directions surviving in the quarto. None of these changes alter the effect of the stage-directions, and the details of them have not been recorded in the collation.

2. MIDDLETON AND ROWLEY

Much of our present knowledge of the lives of Thomas Middleton and William Rowley, the joint authors of *The Changeling*, has come to light only in recent years, and there are many problems yet to be solved in their biography, the canon of their works, and their connexions with the stage and with each other. Thomas Middleton, the more famous of the two, was born in London in 1580 and christened at St Lawrence in the Old Jewry on 18 April of that year.[1] His father, William Middleton, a bricklayer and citizen of London, died on 20 January 1585/6, and on 7 November 1586 his widowed mother, Anne, was married to Thomas Harvey at St Lawrence.[2] Unfortunately Harvey proved to be something of an adventurer,

[1] Mark Eccles, 'Middleton's Birth and Education', *R.E.S.* VII (October 1931), 431.
[2] *Ibid.*, p. 431.

and during the early years of Middleton's life there were frequent quarrels and law-suits between his mother and stepfather, which also affected Middleton himself and his sister Avice.[1] He was educated, as Mark Eccles has shown, at Queen's College, Oxford, where he subscribed on 7 April 1598.[2] On 28 June 1600 Middleton sold his share in certain property left by his father, in return for an allowance of money

> . . . for my advauncement & p[re]ferment in the Vniv[er]sity of Oxford where I am nowe a studient.[3]

But the family quarrels pursued him even to Oxford, and at least once he was forced to return to London to defend his own and his mother's interests. In one law-suit the deposition of a certain Anthony Snode, dated February 1600/1, gives the impression that by that time Middleton had given up his university career: '. . . nowe he remaynethe heare in London daylie accompaninge the players.'[4] There appears to be no record of any degrees awarded to him, and it is very probable that he was forced to leave Oxford without taking a degree. Some time in the next two years he married Mary Marbeck, or Morbeck, daughter of Edward Morbeck, a Clerk of Chancery, and granddaughter of the famous musician John Merbeck. His only son, Edward, was born in 1604.[5]

Middleton's first publication was a metrical paraphrase, *The Wisdom of Solomon Paraphrased* (1597), followed in 1599 by *Micro-Cynicon, Six Snarling Satires*, and in 1600 by *The Ghost of Lucrece*.[6] Two other non-dramatic works, *The Black Book*, a prose pamphlet, and *Father Hubburd's Tales, or The Ant and the Nightingale*, a mixture of prose and verse, were published in 1604.

---

[1] See M. G. Christian, 'A Sidelight on the Family History of Thomas Middleton', *S.P.* XLIV (July 1947), 490–6.

[2] Eccles, *op. cit.*, pp. 436–7. See also M. G. Christian's note in *N. & Q.* CLXXV (October 1938), 259–60.

[3] M. G. Christian, 'Middleton's Residence at Oxford', *M.L.N.* LXI (February 1946), 90.

[4] P. G. Phialas, 'Middleton's Early Contact with the Law', *S.P.* LII (April 1955), 192.

[5] See the pedigree quoted by Dyce, *The Works of Thomas Middleton* (1840), I, Introduction, xii, and Eccles, *op. cit.*, pp. 440–1.

[6] First discovered in 1920. There is a facsimile edition by J. Q. Adams (1937).

It has been suggested that Middleton helped to write *The Meeting of Gallants at an Ordinary*, a pamphlet also published in 1604.[1] His earliest dramatic activities are indicated by various entries in Henslowe's diary. On 22 May 1602 he received payment, together with Munday, Drayton, Webster '& the Rest', for a play called 'sesers ffalle',[2] and on 29 May, with Dekker, Drayton, Webster, and Munday, for a play called 'too shapes'.[3] Greg argues that the closeness of the dates and the similarity of authorship must mean that the two titles refer to one play.[4] Nothing more is known about it. On 21 October he received payment for a play called simply 'Chester',[5] and a further payment on 9 November for 'Randowlle earlle of chester'.[6] It has not survived. On 14 December 1602 he was paid for a prologue and epilogue for 'the playe of bacon' (i.e. *Friar Bacon and Friar Bungay*),[7] and at some time before 14 March 1604 he and Dekker wrote 'the pasyent man & the onest hore' (i.e. *The Honest Whore, Part I*).[8] All these entries refer to the Admiral's men, though on 3 October 1602 he received payment in earnest of an unnamed play for Worcester's men.[9]

Middleton's career as an independent playwright covers the first quarter of the seventeenth century. His early plays were mostly lively comedies of intrigue set against a background of London life; later, his interest turned more to tragi-comedy and tragedy,[10] several of the later works being written in collaboration with Rowley. His famous political satire, *A Game at Chess*, caused a minor sensation when it was performed in 1624. Many of his plays were not published until long after their first performance, and the exact order of the plays is uncertain.[11] The canon of Middleton's works is equally

---

[1] See F. P. Wilson's edition of *The Plague Pamphlets of Thomas Dekker* (1925), pp. xix–xx.

[2] *Henslowe's Diary*, edited by W. W. Greg, I (1904), 166.

[3] *Ibid.*, p. 167.   [4] *Ibid.*, II (1908), 222.   [5] *Ibid.*, I, 171.

[6] *Ibid.*, p. 171.   [7] *Ibid.*, p. 172.   [8] *Ibid.*, p. 175.   [9] *Ibid.*, p. 182.

[10] Evidence has been discovered that he wrote a tragedy called 'The Viper and her Brood' in 1606 or earlier, though the play is lost and nothing is known about it. See H. N. Hillebrand, 'The Viper's Brood', *M.L.N.* XLII (January 1927), 35–8.

[11] R. C. Bald has drawn up a chronology of the plays, *M.L.R.* XXXII (January 1937), 33–43, though some of his suggested dates have not been accepted by later scholars.

undetermined: scholars have claimed to detect his hand in plays as various as *Timon of Athens*, *The Puritan*, *The Bloody Banquet*, *The Second Maiden's Tragedy*, *Wit at Several Weapons*, and *The Revenger's Tragedy*, and in the opposite direction the influence of such dramatists as Dekker and Ford has been detected in plays normally assigned to Middleton. Certainly some of these attributions are rather far-fetched, though the whole question is so complex that it would be impossible to deal with it except at considerable length.[1]

In the later part of his life, much of Middleton's time was spent in the writing and production of various kinds of masques and pageants. His earliest work of this kind, the *Masque of Cupid*, written for the marriage of the Earl and Countess of Somerset, and played on 4 January 1613/14, has not survived. From 1613 onwards he wrote many of the pageants that were given yearly by one or other of the London Companies to welcome the new Lord Mayor, beginning with *The Triumphs of Truth* in 1613 and ending with *The Triumphs of Wealth and Prosperity* in 1626. In 1616 he wrote *Civitatis Amor*, a civic pageant celebrating the assumption by Prince Charles of the title of Prince of Wales. He also wrote a number of 'Entertainments', complimentary speeches and songs for banquets and civic occasions. His *Inner-Temple Masque* was given on New Year's Day, 1619, and *The World Tossed at Tennis*, written with Rowley, probably early in 1620. On 6 September 1620 he was appointed City Chronologer, to record the memorable events in the City of London, and he seems to have carried out the task conscientiously.[2]

By 1623 Middleton was living at Newington Butts, as Dyce discovered,[3] and his burial on 4 July 1627 is recorded in the Parish Register.

Nothing is known of William Rowley's date of birth and early

---

[1] In the most recent study of some of these problems, *Middleton's Tragedies* (1955), Samuel Schoenbaum has argued, not entirely convincingly, that both *The Revenger's Tragedy* and *The Second Maiden's Tragedy* are by Middleton.

[2] For a fuller account see R. C. Bald, 'Middleton's Civic Employments', *M.P.* xxxi (August 1933), 65–78, and his edition of Middleton's *Honourable Entertainments*, *M.S.R.*, 1953. [3] Dyce, *op. cit.*, i, xxxviii.

life, and virtually all the biographical information that survives concerning him derives from his connexions with the stage. He first appears as an actor in the Duke of York's, later the Prince's, company, which began to function in 1608,[1] though it did not receive its patent for playing in London until 30 March 1610. From 1610 until about 1617 Rowley was one of the leading members of the company, which travelled widely in the provinces, returning to give performances at Court during the winter months. Rowley's name is to be found on several of the financial and other agreements made by the company,[2] and his play *Hymen's Holiday, or Cupid's Vagaries*, which has not survived, was performed at Court on 24 February 1612. His association with Middleton appears to have begun in 1616 or 1617, for *A Fair Quarrel*, the first play they wrote together, was published in 1617 with a declaration on the title-page that it had been performed by the Prince's company, and early in 1619 Rowley played the part of Plumporridge, in Middleton's *Inner-Temple Masque*, together with other members of the Prince's company. His activities for the next two or three years are difficult to establish with any certainty. He played the part of Jacques, 'a simple clownish Gentleman', in his own play *All's Lost by Lust*, which was certainly performed before 1620, and Bentley suggests that it was first performed by the Prince's company in 1619 or 1620, though this is no more than conjecture.[3] In 1621 Rowley wrote an elegy on his fellow-player Hugh Attwell, who had died on 25 September,[4] and this may mean that he was still a Prince's man at that date.

There is definite evidence, however, that for the last few years of his life Rowley was a member of the King's company. He is mentioned in the cast of *The Maid in the Mill*, a play of which he was joint author, which was licensed by Herbert for the King's company on 29 August 1623.[5] He also appears to have played the Fat Bishop

[1] *Eliz. Stage*, II, 242.

[2] The details of these transactions and other incidents affecting Rowley are given in *Eliz. Stage*, II, 243–6, *M.S.C.*, Vol. I Part III (1909), p. 273, Vol. I Parts IV, V (1911), p. 372, and in *Henslowe Papers*, edited by W. W. Greg (1907), pp. 90–1, 93, and 126.

[3] The problem is discussed in Bentley, I, 215.

[4] Quoted in Bentley, II, 352–3.   [5] Adams, *Herbert*, p. 25.

in Middleton's *A Game at Chess*, which the King's company first performed on 6 August 1624.[1] On 20 December 1624 he was one of eleven signatories to a submission given to Herbert by the King's company for having acted an unlicensed play called *The Spanish Viceroy*.[2] His was the eighth name in the licence given to the King's players on 24 June 1625,[3] and the title-page of his play, *A New Wonder, A Woman Never Vexed*, published in 1632, describes him as '*one of his Maiesties Servants*'.

Rowley was one of a number of actors who were given a grant of black cloth by the Lord Chamberlain for the funeral of James I on 7 May 1625.[4] He is, however, described in the list as one of the Prince's company, and not, as we might expect, as a King's man. Bentley accounts for this

> ... by the assumption that Rowley had not yet been sworn as a King's man, and that since he still appeared in the Lord Chamberlain's records as a Prince's player it was thought better to grant him livery as a member of that organization than to omit him altogether.[5]

Further information about the last years of Rowley's life is contained in the evidence in a lawsuit provoked by a lost play called *Keep the Widow Waking, or the Late Murder in Whitechapel*, written by Rowley, Ford, Webster, and Dekker, and licensed by Herbert in September 1624.[6] It would appear from Dekker's deposition that Rowley died before 24 March 1625/6, and this probability is strengthened by an entry in the Parish Register of St James, Clerkenwell, which records the burial of 'William Rowley housekeeper' on 11 February 1625/6.[7] On 16 February 1625/6 'Grace relict of William Rowley' appeared before a public notary and renounced administration of his estate.[8]

Rowley's non-dramatic works include the elegy on Hugh Attwell mentioned above, an elegy on the death of Prince Henry, and a

---

[1] See R. C. Bald's letter in *T.L.S.* (6 February 1930), 102.
[2] Adams, *Herbert*, p. 21.   [3] *M.S.C.*, Vol. I Part III, p. 282.
[4] *M.S.C.*, Vol. II Part III (1931), p. 326.   [5] Bentley, II, 556.
[6] See C. J. Sisson, *Lost Plays of Shakespeare's Age* (1936), pp. 114–15, and Adams, *Herbert*, p. 29.
[7] Sisson, *op. cit.*, p. 102.
[8] M. J. Dickson, 'William Rowley', *T.L.S.* (28 March 1929), 260.

prose pamphlet, *A Search for Money* (1609). Most of his plays were written in collaboration, and partly because of this the canon of his writings is very difficult to establish. According to D. M. Robb there are nearly fifty plays in which various scholars have claimed to detect his work.[1] As information about Rowley is not very easily accessible, it may be of use to give a list of the extant plays most generally accepted as his, or partly his: the first four are by Rowley alone, the remainder the result of collaboration. The dates are those suggested by Robb.[2]

> *A Shoemaker a Gentleman* (c. 1608)
> *A New Wonder, A Woman Never Vexed* (c. 1610)
> *All's Lost by Lust* (c. 1619)
> *A Match at Midnight* (c. 1622–3)
> *The Travels of the Three English Brothers* (1607) (with Day and Wilkins)
> *Fortune by Land and Sea* (c. 1608–9) (with Heywood)
> *The Old Law* (c. 1615) (with Middleton and Massinger)
> *A Fair Quarrel* (1615–16) (with Middleton)
> *The World Tossed at Tennis* (early 1620) (with Middleton)
> *The Birth of Merlin* (c. 1620) (collaborator uncertain)
> *The Witch of Edmonton* (1621) (with Dekker and Ford)
> *The Changeling* (1622) (with Middleton)
> *The Spanish Gipsy* (1623) (with Middleton)
> *The Maid in the Mill* (1623) (with Fletcher)
> *A Cure for a Cuckold* (1625) (with Webster)

3. STAGE-HISTORY

Sir Henry Herbert's licence for *The Changeling* survives only in the form of a manuscript note by Malone in his copy of the 1653 quarto:

> Licensed to be acted by the Lady Elizabeth's servants at The Phoenix, May 7, 1622. by Sir Henry Herbert Master of the Revels.[3]

---

[1] D. M. Robb, 'The Canon of William Rowley's Plays', *M.L.R.* XLV (April 1950), 129.
[2] *Ibid.*, pp. 135–40.
[3] Bodleian Mal. 246(9); first noted by W. J. Lawrence, 'New Facts from Sir Henry Herbert's Office-Book', *T.L.S.* (29 November 1923), 820.

The earliest record of an actual performance dates from 4 January 1623/4, when the play was produced at Court:

> Upon the Sonday after, beinge the 4 of January 1623, by the Queene of Bohemias company, *The Changelinge*, the prince only being there. Att Whitehall.[1]

According to G. E. Bentley, Herbert's licence for *The Changeling* is the earliest evidence we have of a new and reorganized Lady Elizabeth's company of players, formed in 1621 or 1622 to play at the Phoenix theatre, and substantially different from any earlier company of the same name.[2] Among the leaders of the troupe was Christopher Beeston, the owner of the Phoenix, and the subsequent stage-history of *The Changeling* shows that the acting rights of the play were vested in Beeston himself rather than in the various companies that occupied his theatre. The company appears to have disintegrated, or at any rate to have stopped playing at the Phoenix, at some time during 1625, probably because of a severe outbreak of plague which kept the theatres closed for the greater part of that year.[3] From the summer of 1626 onwards the theatre was occupied by Queen Henrietta's company, again organized by Beeston. The title-page of *The Changeling* states that the play was performed at the Salisbury Court playhouse (built in 1629) as well as at the Phoenix, and Bentley comments:

> Mention of these two theatres normally indicates a Queen Henrietta's play, for no other company occupied both houses.[4]

An entry in the diary of John Greene records that he saw the play in March 1634/5,[5] though he does not specify the theatre or company concerned.

Bentley presents evidence to suggest that Queen Henrietta's company had broken apart by the end of 1636, to be replaced at the Phoenix by a new company, the King and Queen's Young Company, or, as they were often called, 'Beeston's Boys'.[6] Christopher

---

[1] Adams, *Herbert*, p. 51.   [2] Bentley, I, 183.
[3] *Ibid.*, I, 186–7, II, 654–7.   [4] *Ibid.*, I, 254.
[5] 'The Diary of John Greene (1635–59)', edited by E. M. Symonds, *The English Historical Review* XLIII (July 1928), 386.
[6] Bentley, I, 237–8.

Beeston died in the autumn of 1638, his son, William Beeston, becoming leader of the company, and *The Changeling* is one of a substantial number of plays which the Lord Chamberlain protected for William Beeston on 10 August 1639 by forbidding other companies to perform them.[1]

Much of the success of the play during the period preceding the closing of the theatres in 1642 seems to have come from the comic sub-plot centred on Antonio, the Changeling. In *The Spanish Gipsy*, licensed on 9 July 1623, another Lady Elizabeth's and Queen Henrietta's play by Middleton and Rowley, there is a passage which suggests that the actor playing Pretiosa had also acted the part of the Changeling:

> Do not thou move a wing; be to thyself
> Thyself, and not a changeling.
>   *Pret.* How? not a changeling?
> Yes, father, I will play the changeling;
> I'll change myself into a thousand shapes,
> To court our brave spectators; I'll change my postures
> Into a thousand different variations,
> To draw even ladies' eyes to follow mine;
> I'll change my voice into a thousand tones,
> To chain attention: not a changeling, father?
> None but myself shall play the changeling.[2]

There is a similar, though much less elaborate, reference to 'playing the changeling' in Middleton's *Anything for a Quiet Life*; it is very unlikely, however, that an allusion to *The Changeling* is intended.[3]

---

[1] *M.S.C.*, Vol. II Part III (1931), pp. 389–90.

[2] II. i. 103–12 (Bullen, VI, 139). In *A Biographical Chronicle of the English Drama 1559–1642* (1891), II, 102, F. G. Fleay has suggested that Roderigo speaking of 'too sad a tragedy' (III. i. 79) is really Middleton himself thinking of *The Changeling*. This is too fanciful to deserve much consideration; the 'tragedy' is clearly Roderigo's rape of Clara at the beginning of the play. It should perhaps be mentioned that H. D. Sykes (*Sidelights on Elizabethan Drama*, 1924, pp. 183–99) has argued strongly, on stylistic grounds only, that *The Spanish Gipsy* was actually written by Ford. Bentley, however, regards the play as a normal Middleton–Rowley collaboration (Bentley, IV, 895).

[3] See II. i. 71–3 (Bullen, V, 263) Fleay (*op. cit.*, II, 340) finds an allusion to *The Changeling* in Scene IV of *The London Chaunticleres* (ed. 1659, p. 9): 'If I don't act my part well, may I be a changeling indeed, and be beg'd for the City fool'. If there is an allusion it hardly seems very pointed.

Three contemporary writers give an indication of Antonio's popularity. In the anonymous pamphlet *A Key to the Cabinet of the Parliament* (1648), there is a brief reference to '*Robins* the Changeling'.[1] This is almost certainly William Robbins, an actor of comic parts who belonged to Queen Henrietta's company and later to the King's company, and died in October 1645 in a skirmish in the Civil War.[2] In the Praeludium to Thomas Goffe's *The Careless Shepherdess*, printed in 1656, certain characters sit on the stage of the Salisbury Court discussing their taste in plays:

Landl. Why I would have the Fool in every Act,
   Be't Comedy, or Tragedy, I'ave laugh'd
   Untill I cry'd again, to see what Faces
   The Rogue will make: O it does me good
   To see him hold out's Chin hang down his hands,
   And twirle his Bawble. There is nere a part
   About him but breaks jests. I heard a fellow
   Once on this Stage cry, *Doodle, Doodle, Dooe*,
   Beyond compare; I'de give the other shilling
   To see him act the Changling once again.
Thri. And so would I, his part has all the wit,
   For none speaks Craps and Quibbles besides him:
   I'd rather see him leap, laugh, or cry,
   Then hear the gravest Speech in all the *Play*.
   I never saw Rheade peeping through the Curtain,
   But ravishing joy enter'd my heart.[3]

A little later we have:

Spar. Nay, ne're fear that, for on my word you shall
   Have mirth, although there be no Changlings part.[4]

Bentley, in his biographical account of Timothy Rheade, or Reade, concludes that

Landlord had seen Reade, Robbins's successor as comedian of Queen Henrietta's company, play the part of the Changeling for

---

[1] The passage is quoted by Leslie Hotson, *The Commonwealth and Restoration Stage* (1928), p. 37, and in Bentley, II, 549.

[2] Bentley, II, 547–9.

[3] Ed. 1656, pp. 4–5; also Bentley, II, 541. The Praeludium itself is almost certainly not by Goffe, who died in 1629; it was probably added to the play in 1638, and may have been written by Richard Brome (see Bentley, IV, 503–4).

[4] *Ed. cit.*, p. 5.

the Queen's company on the stage of the Salisbury Court some time in 1637 or later.[1]

Finally, Edmund Gayton mentions the play in his *Pleasant Notes upon Don Quixot*, published in 1654:

> ... it is not out of most mens observation, that one most admirable Mimicke in our late Stage, so lively and corporally personated a Changeling, that he could never compose his Face to the figure it had, before he undertook that part.[2]

Bullen suggests that the 'admirable mimic' is Robbins,[3] though it could equally well be Reade.

The popularity of *The Changeling* survived the closing of the theatres. In 1659 John Rhodes brought together a company of actors to play at the Phoenix theatre, and *The Changeling* was one of several pre-Restoration plays revived by them, according to Downes, who mentions two members of the company, Betterton and Sheppey, whose fame was due in part to the success with which they acted their roles in the play:

> *Mr. Betterton*, being then but 22 Years Old, was highly Applauded for his Acting in all these Plays, but especially, For the Loyal Subject; The Mad Lover; *Pericles*; The Bondman: *Deflores*, in the Changling; his Voice being then as Audibly strong, full and Articulate, as in the Prime of his Acting.
>
> *Mr. Sheppy* Perform'd *Theodore* in the Loyal Subject; Duke *Altophil*, in the Unfortunate Lovers; *Asotus*, in the Bondman, and several other Parts very well; But above all the Changling, with general Satisfaction.[4]

In November 1660 Sir William D'Avenant gained control of the company, which took the name of 'The Duke's Company', and transferred it temporarily to the Salisbury Court, or Whitefriars, theatre, where Pepys saw a performance of the play:

> Feb. 23 1660/1. Then by water to Whitefriars to the Play-house, and there saw *The Changeling*, the first time it hath been acted these twenty years, and it takes exceedingly.[5]

---

[1] Bentley, II, 540.　[2] Ed. 1654, p. 144; also quoted in Bullen, VIII, 347-8.
[3] Bullen, VIII, 348.
[4] John Downes, *Roscius Anglicanus* (1708), edited by Montague Summers [1936], pp. 18-19.
[5] *Pepys on the Restoration Stage*, edited by Helen McAfee (1916), p. 120.

If Pepys' 'the first time' is correct, Downes, who wrote many years later and from memory only, must have been mistaken in thinking that the play was first revived while the company was at the Phoenix, even though he makes a definite statement to that effect.[1] 'These twenty years' suggests that the play held the stage up to the closing of the theatres in 1642.

In June 1661 D'Avenant's new theatre, built on a site in Lincoln's Inn Fields,[2] was taken over by his company, and evidence that The Changeling was performed there is to be found on the title-page of the 1668 reissue of the quarto, which claims that the play was

> . . . Acted (with great Applause) by the Servants of His Royal Highness the Duke of York, at the Theatre in Lincolns-Inn Fields.

A further performance of the play is recorded in a manuscript volume in the British Museum, Sir Edward Browne's Memorandum Book, 1662, containing among other items a substantial list of plays seen at various theatres, together with the prices paid for admission. One entry reads:

> At the Cardinalls cap in Cambridge.
> Changeling — — — 1—6[3]

(Three other plays are mentioned with The Changeling.) As Greg points out,[4] the authorship and exact dating of these entries are somewhat uncertain, and no company is mentioned. The Cardinal's Cap was a Cambridge inn standing near to Pembroke Hall.[5]

One final point should be mentioned in connexion with the seventeenth-century stage-history of the play. The frontispiece to The Wits, or Sport upon Sport, a collection of drolls published by Francis Kirkman in 1672, shows the stage of a theatre which many scholars have taken to be the Red Bull theatre, even though the original has no caption or description, and it is not by any means

---

[1] Op. cit., p. 18. [2] See Hotson, op. cit., pp. 120ff.
[3] MS. Sloane 1900, fol. 60b.
[4] 'Theatrical Repertories of 1662', The Gentleman's Magazine N.S. CCI (July 1906), 69.
[5] It is mentioned in Randolph's poem 'On the Fall of the Mitre Tavern in Cambridge' (Poems, ed. Thorn-Drury, 1929, p. 161).

certain that it is intended to represent the Red Bull.[1] One of the figures on the stage is entitled simply 'Changeling', and M. W. Sampson identifies it as Antonio in *The Changeling*:

> Antonio's costume is a long-skirted coat and high pointed cap. The object dangling from the right wrist may be a horn-book.[2]

Elson, however, is less confident:

> The figure of the "Changeling" adds a further riddle, for no such personage appears in the *Wits* drolls. He is presumably taken from Middleton and Rowley's play of the same name; but what is he doing here? Can there have been a droll about the Changeling, acted by Cox or merely abridged for reading, which for some reason was omitted from all the published collections?[3]

There appears to be no evidence surviving to settle this problem.

No record exists of any performance of *The Changeling* during the eighteenth and nineteenth centuries. William Hayley, the patron of Blake, wrote a plagiarized version of *The Changeling* which he called *Marcella*. It was performed three times in November 1789, but for various reasons met with little success.[4]

The play has been revived in recent years. On 20 November 1950 an abridged version, with the sub-plot omitted, was broadcast by the B.B.C.; on 16 May 1954 a single performance was given at

---

[1] See J. J. Elson's edition of *The Wits* (1932), pp. 424–6. Elson reproduces the frontispiece, and it has frequently been reprinted elsewhere.

[2] *Thomas Middleton* (*Masterpieces of the English Drama*), 1915, p. 399. See also Leslie Hotson, *Shakespeare's Motley* (1952), pp. 62–3.

[3] *Op. cit.*, p. 427.

[4] It is printed in volume VI of *Poems and Plays* (1785), by William Hayley. Hayley's preface (*ed. cit.*, pp. 3–5) is a dishonest piece of work that gives no indication of the real origin of his play. Dilke (*Old English Plays* (1815), IV, 221–2) noted the striking resemblances in plot between *Marcella* and *The Changeling*, but it was Genest (*Some Account of the English Stage* (1832), VI, 579–86) who went into the matter in detail and proved conclusively that the later play was a plagiarism. It is a very bad play, and deserves little attention, though it might perhaps be of interest to quote one example of what *The Changeling* undergoes at the hands of Hayley. 'Think what a torment 'tis to marry one . . .' (II. i. 131ff) becomes:

> Think what it is to press the nuptial couch,
> When, for the roses Love should scatter there,
> The fiend Antipathy has form'd its pillow
> Of sharpest thorns, that lacerate the brain!

Wyndham's theatre by the Pegasus Society; and in November 1956 the play was produced at Oxford by the Experimental Theatre Club.

4. SOURCES

It was first pointed out by Langbaine[1] that the principal source of *The Changeling* is John Reynolds's *The Triumphs of God's Revenge against . . . Murther*,[2] a collection of thirty 'Tragicall Histories' divided into six books. All the stories follow the same pattern: greed and adultery lead to murder and from there to the inevitable punishment of death. Book I was entered in the Stationers' Register on 7 June 1621, and published in the same year; it contains five histories, the fourth of which is the main source of *The Changeling*.

Reynolds's narrative falls into three distinct sections.[3] In the first, Beatrice and Alsemero meet in the church and fall in love; Beatrice arranges for her unwanted suitor Alonzo to be murdered by De Flores, a 'Gallant young Gentleman' in attendance on her father, who receives nothing more than a few kisses as his reward for the murder; and the section closes with the marriage of Beatrice and Alsemero. In the second, Alsemero suddenly becomes violently and unreasonably jealous of Beatrice, who resents his jealousy and loses her affection for him. When her father sends De Flores to her as a messenger she welcomes him and eventually becomes his mistress; but Alsemero traps them both in the act of adultery and kills them. In the final section Alonzo's brother Tomazo challenges Alsemero, who meets him at the appointed place and kills him by means of a cowardly trick. Alsemero tries to flee, but is captured and executed.

Each of the three sections is virtually complete in itself, and Rey-

---

[1] *An Account of the English Dramatick Poets* (1691), p. 371.

[2] The full title reads: *The Triumphs of Gods Revenge against The Crying and Execrable Sinne of Wilfull and Premeditated Murther*. Reynolds must have been accused by some of his contemporaries of having translated his stories from French or Italian originals, for later editions contain a 'Readvertisement To The Ivdiciovs Christian Reader', strenuously denying the charge of plagiarism and claiming that all the narratives were discovered and collected by the author during his travels.

[3] What follows is a very condensed summary: the relevant parts are quoted in full in Appendix A.

nolds's technique seems to be to let the action run down to a stop and then galvanize it into life through some quite fortuitous cause or event. Alsemero's jealousy is quite inexplicable, and he could easily have avoided the duel with Tomazo by telling him that Beatrice and De Flores, who are now both dead, had been responsible for the death of Alonzo. Reynolds has accordingly been criticized for the clumsy construction and unconvincing motivation of his story, but it must be remembered that he wrote as a moralist, not as a novelist, and his jerky and episodic technique gave him many opportunities to moralize on the deceptiveness of fate and the inevitability of retribution. The dramatists, however, are more concerned with continuity of effect, and transform their source into a single uninterrupted narrative. The events in Act II, for example, which are immediately consecutive in *The Changeling*, have large intervals of time between them in Reynolds. The most important borrowings, taken chiefly from the opening section of Reynolds, occur in the first half of the play, and from III. iv onwards its main development is independent of Reynolds, though it incorporates a few incidents from him.

Undoubtedly the most significant difference between the play and the source lies in the treatment of the characters. It would not be unfair to Reynolds to say that his characters are mere puppets, moved about according to the demands of a heavily didactic theme. The dramatists not only alter their attributes, making Alsemero a man of honour and integrity, and De Flores a repellent and ugly villain instead of a handsome young man; they create in them all the force and vividness and human plausibility which have given the play its reputation. In Reynolds morality is a purely external force, that waits for the characters to make a mistake and then strikes them down; in *The Changeling* it works through the characters, who are morally responsible for themselves, and are forced to experience intimately the consequences of their own actions.

Many of the incidents in the second half of the play are obviously not derived from Reynolds, and one of the most important of these is the substitution of Diaphanta for Beatrice. The particular combination of circumstances in *The Changeling*—the heroine's loss of virginity prior to marriage, the use of a substitute on the wedding night, and the subsequent murder of the substitute partly because of her unreliability—forms a situation which occurs repeatedly in legends and folk-tales, and E. G. Mathews has made an exhaustive survey of what he calls 'The Murdered Substitute Tale' with *The Changeling* in mind.[1] Various scholars have pointed out analogues to the situation contained in *The Changeling*—G. P. Baker a version in Old French,[2] and Karl Christ a story to be found in an English manuscript of the *Gesta Romanorum*[3]—and have postulated a comparatively late English version which was the immediate source of *The Changeling*. This was first identified by Bertram Lloyd as a novel published in 1622 by Leonard Digges, *Gerardo The Unfortunate Spaniard*, a translation from the Spanish of G. de Cespedes y Meneses.[4] Digges's book was entered in the Stationers' Register on 11 March 1621/2, and *The Changeling* was licensed on 7 May 1622, so that the play must have been written in a comparatively short time, unless Middleton read the book in the original Spanish. Two extracts from Digges's version are given in Appendix A, and bear an obvious relationship to the development of Acts IV and V of *The Changeling*, though it must also be remembered that many of the details of the Cespedes-Digges version occur in the earlier analogues cited by Mathews.[5] Digges's book, however, may have had a greater importance to the dramatists than such detailed borrowings would indicate. The earlier part of the story of Isdaura (who corresponds to Beatrice) describes how she was left in the charge of 'an old trusty seruant . . . a loyall *Biscayner* by birth', while her father sailed to the West Indies to make his fortune. On his return her father decided to marry her to Roberto, the son of an old

---

[1] 'The Murdered Substitute Tale', *M.L.Q.* VI (June 1945), 187–95.

[2] 'A New Source of *The Changeling*', *The Journal of Comparative Literature* I (1903), 87–8.

[3] *Quellenstudien zu den Dramen Thomas Middletons* (Leipzig, 1905), pp. 97–8.

[4] 'A Minor Source of *The Changeling*', *M.L.R.* XIX (January 1924), 101–2.

[5] C. R. Baskervill (*M.P.* XIV (December 1916), 488) has argued that *The Changeling* is not based primarily on Reynolds, but on 'some old drama, probably in English', containing a version of the Murdered Substitute tale. But the absence of any evidence that such a play existed and the detailed similarities between *The Changeling* and Reynolds make it difficult to allow the argument much weight.

friend. The Biscayner was bitterly disappointed at this decision, for he passionately loved Isdaura and had hoped to win her through his devoted care of her. One evening shortly before the wedding he went to Isdaura's room, revealed his love for her, and threatened to kill her with a dagger if she did not promise herself to him. Terrified, she did so, and even gave him her hand; but his passion was so strong that he took her in his arms, and finally ravished her. When he had fallen asleep, she stabbed him several times with his own dagger, wrapped his body in a sheet, and put it in the street. The murder was not traced to Isdaura, but the loss of her virginity led to the events which occurred on the wedding night.

Mathews argues that this part of the story, which can also be paralleled in earlier tales and narratives, probably influenced the dramatists' conception of the character of De Flores:

> In Reynolds' tale, De Flores had performed a much more hellish service than rearing his beloved. But this De Flores . . . is a mere shadow in lavender. Why, the dramatists speculated, should not their villain make the same demand as the Biscayner? To do so, and to survive so as to take his part in the later action, he must be as much more powerful than the Biscayner as his earlier service is the more hellish. So, out of the weak original De Flores and the love-crazed Biscayner came a third thing, the villain of the play, loathesome and passionless in his crimes, but tender to Beatrice, and fascinating both to her and to his audience.[1]

It must be made clear, however, in justice to Middleton and Rowley, that though Digges's (or Cespedes') Biscayner may well have helped to shape the character of the De Flores of *The Changeling*, his power and vividness are entirely the creation of the dramatists; Digges's Biscayner is no more a real figure than Reynolds's De Flores.

There can be little doubt that Middleton was acquainted with Shakespeare's plays, and it has been suggested that the character of De Flores owes something to Shakespeare's villains, notably Richard III and Iago.[2] Certainly De Flores is physically repulsive

---

[1] *Op. cit.*, pp. 192–3.
[2] See A. W. Ward, *A History of English Dramatic Literature* (1875), II, 82, Hugo Jung, *Das Verhältnis Thomas Middletons zu Shakspeare* (Leipzig, 1904), pp. 84–7, and K. Christ, *op. cit.*, pp. 99–100.

like Richard III, and he is called 'honest' De Flores (IV. ii. 37 and
57, V. ii. 9–10) just as Iago is repeatedly called 'honest Iago', but in
other respects there is little similarity. Hugo Jung detects three
other Shakespearian echoes in the play, though none of them is of
much importance.[1] *The Changeling* comes at the end of the great
period of Elizabethan–Jacobean drama, and it is not surprising that
it contains echoes of earlier plays.[2] Yet there is nothing which we
could reasonably call plagiarism, and the play is not derivative in
the way of so much of the later Caroline drama. The dramatists undoubtedly learned much from their predecessors, but they used
their knowledge to achieve a fresh and independent creation.

It will perhaps place the sources of the main plot of *The Changeling* in clearer perspective if we remember that the situations contained in them had already been utilized by Middleton and Rowley
in various forms before they wrote *The Changeling*. Rowley, for
example, had used a version of the murdered substitute device in
All's Lost by Lust, III. iii and IV. ii, and the famous scene (III. iv) in
which De Flores demands his reward from Beatrice, which is not
to be found in any of the sources, is anticipated with remarkable
similarity by part of a scene from *A Fair Quarrel*.[3] Middleton and
Rowley were probably attracted to Reynolds's story because of the
potentialities it offered for development rather than for its own
sake, for it does not by any means stand out among Reynolds's
other narratives, and they compress, alter, and select from their
source with the boldness of skilled dramatists.

The sources of the sub-plot are less easily indicated than those of
the main plot, partly because the sub-plot is made up of a number
of elements which may derive from widely-differing sources. The

---

[1] *Op. cit.*, pp. 85–6. Jung considers that the appearance of Alonzo's ghost
in v. i imitates Banquo's ghost in III. iv of *Macbeth*; Tomazo's lines to De
Flores (IV. ii. 42–3) echo *Richard III*, I. iv. 239; and Beatrice's 'Oh my presaging soul!' (V. i. 109) is virtually a quotation of Hamlet's 'O my prophetic
soul!' (I. v. 40).

[2] See the Commentary on III. iv. 121 and 167, V. ii. 54–5, and v. iii. 164.

[3] See especially III. ii. 29–141 (Bullen, IV, 216–21). This part of the play
is usually assigned to Rowley, and the corresponding part of *The Changeling* to Middleton; E. Engelberg, however, has argued not very convincingly that both are by Middleton (*N. & Q.* CXCVIII (August 1953),
330–2).

theme of the jealous elderly husband attempting to guard his young and attractive wife from unwelcome attentions is so common in the literature of the period that there is little point in looking for a particular source. In their handling of this theme, however, Middleton and Rowley add certain distinctive features that are perhaps more directly derivative.

The action of the sub-plot is set throughout in the mad-house of Alibius. *The Changeling* is not unique in this respect, for Dekker and Middleton's *The Honest Whore, Part I*, Dekker and Webster's *Northward Ho*, and Fletcher's *The Pilgrim* all contain scenes set in a lunatic asylum. It has long been assumed that Alibius's mad-house is a private asylum, but recently Robert Reed, developing a suggestion of O'Donoghue,[1] has argued that in fact it represents Bethlehem Hospital, the actual 'Bedlam' of the Jacobean period.[2] Like Bethlehem Hospital, it admits 'daily visitants' (I. ii. 52), and Lollio's references to fools on one side of the stage and madmen on the other (III. iii. 33–4, 204–5) suggest an allusion to the fact that Bethlehem Hospital was built in two parallel wings which may have housed separately the fools and madmen. Alibius and Lollio, according to Reed, are satirical portraits of Dr Hilkish Crooke and his steward. Crooke was appointed keeper of Bethlehem in April 1619, but in 1632 he and his steward were discharged from their posts for various offences including fraud, neglect of duty, and the acceptance of bribes. Reed sees hints of much of this in *The Changeling*:

> Alibius (whose name means 'being in another place') spends most of his time in drumming up profitable trade on the outside, while Lollio is portrayed as accepting bribes and favouring certain more well-to-do inmates within the hospital. Both are constantly concerned about private profit, and the successful Alibius, returning from business outside the hospital, is able to observe, 'We shall have coin and credit for our pains' (IV. iii. 214).[3]

---

[1] E. G. O'Donoghue, *The Story of Bethlehem Hospital from its Foundation in 1247* (1914), p. 156.

[2] 'A Factual Interpretation of *The Changeling*'s Madhouse Scenes', *N. & Q.* CXCV (June 1950), 247–8. In his book, *Bedlam on the Jacobean Stage* (1952), pp. 34–5, 47–8, Reed puts the same arguments forward in a more tentative form.

[3] Reed, *N. & Q.* (June 1950), 248.

It is difficult not to feel, however, that Reed is overstating his case. All the mad-house scenes mentioned above, in whatever country they may nominally be placed, have strong generic resemblances, and must all owe a good deal to Bethlehem Hospital, a place of resort so celebrated in the early seventeenth century that the dramatists themselves are bound to have visited it at some time or other. All these mad-houses, real or fictitious, admit 'daily visitants', and have a governor with one or more assistants. In all the plays mentioned it is quite customary, when a new patient is brought to the asylum, for the keeper to be given or promised a sum of money to look after him;[1] and in any case, it is extremely doubtful whether a Jacobean audience would have been shocked when those patients who could afford it bought themselves extra comfort and attention. Money used in this way can hardly be regarded as a 'bribe', and there is no suggestion anywhere in *The Changeling* that Alibius or Lollio mis-spend the money entrusted to them. When Franciscus and Antonio give money to Lollio later in the play to further their pursuit of Isabella, he is fully aware that neither is a genuine patient, and his acceptance of their bribes has nothing to do with professional etiquette. It is never hinted that the outside activities of Alibius (which are not specified) are as disreputable as those of Crooke, and his name, as Karl Christ points out,[2] may well have been borrowed from Reynolds's story of Alibius and Merilla (Book I, History v), which comes immediately after the source of the main plot. He is not noticeably rapacious, and on the whole appears to regard his mad-house as a kind of business venture which will yield a reasonable living to himself and his wife if he fosters it carefully. The physical resemblance that Reed detects between Alibius's mad-house and the historical Bethlehem Hospital is interesting, but there is virtually no evidence surviving to make his argument conclusive. It is hard not to feel, in short, that the mad-house of *The Changeling* is not so very much closer to

[1] Reed has not apparently noticed a detail in Stow's account of Bethlehem Hospital: 'In this place people that bee distraight in wits, are by the suite of their friendes receyued and kept as afore, but not without charges to their bringers in', John Stow, *A Survey of London*, edited by C. L. Kingsford (1908), I, 165.

[2] *Op. cit.*, p. 99.

Bethlehem Hospital than the other mad-houses of Jacobean drama, and that if Middleton and Rowley had intended to satirize a contemporary institution and its officials, they would have done so much more plainly.

As yet no very definite source has been discovered for the incidents which occur in the sub-plot. The disguise of fool or madman had been used before in several plays,[1] though nowhere at such length as in *The Changeling*. Certain of the incidents in the sub-plot bear some resemblance to parts of an earlier play by Middleton alone, *The Family of Love*. In the earlier play two rival gallants, Lipsalve and Gudgeon, enlist the help of Dr Glister in their pursuit of Mistress Purge. Glister, however, is their secret and successful rival, and plays them off against each other. In III. iv they meet and give each other a thrashing, upon which they realize that they have been duped and determine to cuckold Glister by way of revenge. In v. i they gain admission to the doctor's house by pretending to be patients, but he is aware of the deception, and uses his medical knowledge to thwart them. In *The Changeling* the two gallants are of course Antonio and Franciscus, and though Alibius plays a much less important part than Glister in *The Family of Love*, the two plots are decidedly similar. Antonio and Franciscus, attracted by Isabella, pretend to be mad in order to become patients in Alibius's mad-house, and in IV. iii Lollio arranges for the rivals to meet and thrash each other. In both plays the gallants are told that the thrashing given to the rival will earn them the lady's love. In *The Changeling* this device is not carried to a conclusion, but in both plays the two gallants fail ludicrously in their purposes. It is generally agreed that Rowley was responsible for the actual writing of the sub-plot, but it may well be that Middleton suggested some incidents for it which had perhaps proved successful in an earlier play of his own.

---

[1] The most subtle uses are obviously those in *Hamlet* and *King Lear*; we might also compare *The Honest Whore, Part I*, where Bellafronte pretends to be mad in order to gain Matheo, Marston's *Antonio's Revenge* and Ford's *Love's Sacrifice*, which is later than *The Changeling*.

5. COLLABORATION

All the evidence seems to show that *The Changeling* was the result of an unusually close collaboration. The play has a remarkable consistency and continuity, and there is a complete absence of the discrepancies in detail between one part and the next which are often the sign of a work written by several authors. When there is such a close collaboration it is usually extremely difficult to distinguish the respective share of each author, but in the case of *The Changeling* there is a striking unanimity of opinion among scholars and critics as to the division of scenes between Middleton and Rowley. It is generally agreed that Rowley wrote the sub-plot and the opening and closing scenes of the play, and Middleton the remainder of the main plot. This gives us the following division:

I. i, I. ii — Rowley
II. i, II. ii — Middleton
III. i, III. ii — Middleton
III. iii — Rowley
III. iv — Middleton
IV. i, IV. ii — Middleton
IV. iii — Rowley
V. i, V. ii — Middleton
V. iii — Rowley

Stork expresses uncertainty about v. ii,[1] while Oliphant finds some touches of Middleton (which he does not specify) in I. i and assigns the first sixteen lines of IV. ii to Rowley.[2] Otherwise, all scholars and editors from Dyce and Bullen onwards accept this basic division of the play. It might at first sight appear too clear-cut to be fully convincing, but a careful study of the play, using the various methods developed by modern scholars to isolate a given author's share in a particular work, leads to a conviction that it is substantially correct.

Parallels between the text of *The Changeling* and other plays by Middleton and Rowley are quoted in full in the Commentary, and

[1] *William Rowley: his All's Lost by Lust and A Shoemaker a Gentleman*, edited by C. W. Stork (1910), Introduction, p. 44.
[2] *Shakespeare and his Fellow Dramatists* (1929), II, 907 and 931.

there is no need here to give more than a brief reference to them.[1] Most of these examples are of comparatively important themes and metaphors which appear to have attracted the two dramatists, but there is a great deal more evidence in the form of minute habits of vocabulary and patterns of speech which would require a disproportionate amount of space to be fully illustrated. Middleton, for instance, is noticeably fond of the ejaculation 'Push', which Rowley never uses, and it occurs six times in his share of the play.[2] He frequently uses certain abstract words in the plural—'comforts', 'sweets', 'joys'—a usage reflected in the main plot of *The Changeling*. Rowley too has certain verbal characteristics. His love of puns and similar ambiguities shows itself clearly in his share of *The Changeling*, and he also uses a related device to which D. M. Robb has given the term 'cue-catching',[3] in which one character repeats a word or phrase of the previous speaker in such a way as to alter the meaning:

Then you know not where you are.

| *Als.* | Not well indeed. |
| *Jas.* Are you not well, sir? | (I. i. 22–3) |

I am old, Lollio.

Lol. No, sir, 'tis I am old Lollio.   (I. ii. 19–20)

Middleton's use of puns is far less frequent, and his particular form of playing upon words is a biting irony, found several times in his section of the main plot, which is quite beyond the range of Rowley.[4] Stork points out a tendency towards latinized vocabulary in Rowley,[5] and a few illustrations of this can be given from his share

---

[1] For Middleton, see the Commentary on II. i. 15, II. ii. 6–7, 44, 66–7 and 126, III. ii. 1–2, III. iv. 25–6, 90, 94, and 170, and v. i. 71; and for Rowley, on I. i. 119 and 150, I. ii. 69–70, III. iii. 113 and 173–5, IV. iii. 177–9, v. iii. 36–9, 116–17, 118, 119, and 165.

[2] See P. G. Wiggin, *An Inquiry into the Authorship of the Middleton-Rowley Plays* (1897), p. 38.

[3] *Op. cit.*, p. 133. Rowley uses this device with the following words: 'well', I. i. 22–3, v. iii. 15–16; 'state', I. i. 140–2; 'bound', I. i. 218; 'figure', IV. iii. 100–1; 'hand', IV. iii. 177–9; 'meet', IV. iii. 190–1; 'ground', v. iii. 41–4; and 'commend', v. iii. 91–3.

[4] Compare II. ii. 135–7, III. ii. 1–2, IV. ii. 48–9, and v. i. 79–81 and 110–12. Rowley can create quite powerful dramatic irony, especially in I. i, but not the pungent verbal irony of Middleton.   [5] *Op. cit.*, p. 25.

of the play, words such as 'odoriferous' (I. i. 120), 'Iulan' (I. i. 175), 'participate' (III. iii. 18), and 'Mare Mortuum' (V. iii. 119). Such minor idiosyncrasies may not amount to much when taken separately, but their cumulative effect is highly convincing.

A comparative study of the versification of Middleton and Rowley also tends to support the division of the play made above. The comparison is not easy to make, as very few of Rowley's plays are available in accurate and reliable editions. There is, however, sufficient material for us to make fairly reliable conclusions. Middleton has far more virtuosity as a writer of blank verse than Rowley, and in the fluency of his verse and the high proportion of feminine endings, many of them of two syllables, he resembles Fletcher, though at their best his lines have a strength and incisiveness which is rare in Fletcher. His natural medium is verse, and *Women Beware Women* and *A Game at Chess* show that in the later part of his career his technique as a writer of verse had matured to the point at which it was fully adequate to the demands made on it, and could convey information or irony or subtle implications naturally and easily. Rowley never seems to have attained a similar maturity, and a certain rigidity and stiffness of movement is to be found throughout his plays. Even in his later work lines of verse occur which can only be considered rough and clumsy, and as Robb points out,[1] he has none of Middleton's structural ability at building up long passages of blank verse. This should not be taken to mean, however, that Rowley was incapable of writing powerful and effective verse; Robb notes the mixture of strength and weakness in his work, and argues that he improved considerably under the influence of greater contemporaries.[2] If, for instance, we accept the division of the play given above, it follows that Rowley was responsible for the most famous lines in the play, Beatrice's speech at V. iii. 149ff.

The differing characteristics described above are reflected in the verse of *The Changeling*. In Act I, the proportion of feminine endings is low, and there is something of monotony in the movement of the blank verse, as in Jasperino's speech at I. i. 25–34. Clumsy lines are found embedded in longer passages, as in the fourth line of the following quotation:

[1] *Op. cit.*, p. 134.　　[2] *Ibid.*, p. 135.

> ... one distastes
> The scent of roses, which to infinites
> Most pleasing is, and odoriferous;
> One oil, the enemy of poison;
> Another wine, the cheerer of the heart,
> And lively refresher of the countenance.
>
> (I. i. 118–23)

Several lines in Act I may be either rough verse or a kind of rhythmic prose, and there is one passage, I. ii. 86–90, printed as verse in the quarto, which all editors change to prose.

The verse of Act II is noticeably different. Feminine endings, sometimes of two syllables, are frequent:

> Though my hard fate has thrust me out to servitude ...
> Perfect your service, and conduct this gentleman ...
> As much as youth and beauty hates a sepulchre ...
>
> (II. i. 48; II. ii. 54, 67)

The Act opens with two blank verse soliloquies, each over twenty lines long, of a type which occurs repeatedly in Middleton's plays, though far less frequently in Rowley's.

In III. iii there is a return to the characteristics of Act I— a higher proportion of prose, a crudity of verse, and a number of utterances which might be either rhythmic prose or a very irregular kind of verse, and this distinct alternation of styles persists throughout the play. Act V does perhaps offer a certain amount of difficulty, though the style of the third scene as compared to the first two appears to identify it as definitely Rowley's. It is, of course, extremely improbable that in such a close collaboration Middleton and Rowley did not look over each other's work, and we cannot exclude the possibility that passages or revisions by one writer may be found in a section assigned as a whole to the other. There do not appear to be any traces of Middleton's hand in the parts of the play given to Rowley.[1] It is, however, possible that one or two short passages in the main plot are by Rowley, though such attributions are almost entirely a matter of personal opinion.

---

[1] This refers only to the actual writing; it has already been suggested that some of the details of the sub-plot were taken from Middleton's *The Family of Love*, and he may also have supplied the incident at v. iii. 95–9 (see the Commentary on this passage).

A further piece of evidence exists to support Rowley's authorship of the sub-plot. The character of Lollio, Alibius's steward, has, in its mixture of naïveté and shrewdness, some affinity with the Shakespearian clown, and this particular type of humorous figure can be found repeatedly in the plays Rowley wrote or helped to write. The Clown in *The Birth of Merlin*, Jacques in *All's Lost by Lust*, Compass in *A Cure for a Cuckold*, Bustofa in *The Maid in the Mill*, Cuddy Banks in *The Witch of Edmonton*—all these have much in common with Lollio, and it is extremely probable that Lollio is entirely Rowley's creation. It might also be suggested that Antonio and Franciscus are nearer to this type of character than to any of Middleton's comic creations.

The effects of a collaboration can reveal themselves in more subtle ways than those discussed above, and there have been considerable differences of opinion among scholars as to the mutual influence that Middleton and Rowley may have had upon each other, even though it is generally acknowledged that Middleton was the more skilful dramatist of the two.[1] It is sometimes suggested that the greatness of *The Changeling* owes much to Rowley's influence. Miss Wiggin, for example, considers Middleton to be a cynical realist lacking in charity or sympathy, and argues that Rowley, with a more humane and genial outlook, made up this deficiency even in parts of the play he did not write himself.[2] But it is doubtful whether the differences between the two dramatists can be expressed simply in these terms, and a different theory of their relationship might be suggested.

In his outlook Rowley seems to belong with popular dramatists like Dekker and Heywood. Much of the material in his plays, even details of imagery and humour, seems part of that common stock of dramatic material that all Elizabethan and Jacobean playwrights could draw upon, and his moral outlook, without being any more

---

[1] For discussion of this aspect of collaboration, see Wiggin, *op. cit.*, pp. 52ff, Oliphant, *op. cit.*, 11, 12, and E. N. S. Thompson, 'Elizabethan Dramatic Collaboration', *Englische Studien* XL (1909), 44, 45–6. W. D. Dunkel's argument (*P.M.L.A.* XLVIII (September 1933), 800–2) that Rowley merely revised a work originally written solely by Middleton has virtually nothing to support it.

[2] *Op. cit.*, pp. 55–8.

tolerant or sympathetic than Middleton's, is comparatively simple and straightforward. Middleton, on the other hand, is more sophisticated, more of an individualist. He has a wider awareness of the curiosities of human psychology, and is particularly fond of the ironies which result when one character in a play is ignorant of the true nature of another character. But we sometimes have the impression that Middleton's subtlety fails to reveal any profound insight into human character; it works, as it were, in a moral vacuum, and some of the plays, the comedies especially,[1] fail to be as impressive as their sophistication would lead us to expect.

These differences might be related to *The Changeling* in the following way. Both dramatists were fully aware of the rich dramatic potentialities of their material. Middleton, the more skilful of the two, took the scenes in which the psychological tensions were at their greatest, notably the two magnificent scenes (II. ii and III. iv) between Beatrice and De Flores. He also developed the web of intrigue and deceit surrounding the virginity tests and the events that take place on Beatrice's wedding night. Rowley took the opening and closing scenes of the play, and used them to set the whole plot against a firm and rigorous moral background.[2] He also took the comic sub-plot. It is likely that Middleton's influence helped to give his verse, especially in v. iii, a power and vividness that it rarely shows elsewhere. In this way the two dramatists were able to use their gifts to the fullest effect, and to support and reinforce each other.

---

[1] See L. C. Knights's essay on the comedies, *Drama and Society in the Age of Jonson* (1937), pp. 256–69.

[2] We should notice how Rowley makes a deliberate allusion at v. iii. 72–6 to I. i. 1–12; the end of the play fulfils the beginning. It is certainly true that Middleton's moral awareness is deeper in *The Changeling* than in any of his other plays; III. iv in itself is proof of that. But it would be difficult to say whether this is due to Middleton's natural development or to the influence of Rowley; many scholars have pointed out that neither Middleton nor Rowley achieves anything as profound and penetrating as *The Changeling* in his own unaided work.

6. THE PLAY

Criticism of *The Changeling* did not begin until the nineteenth-century revival of interest in Elizabethan drama. Scott refers to the play in a note to his edition of *Sir Tristrem*, a mediaeval romance:

> The barbarous ingratitude of the queen of Cornwall resembles that of the heroine in Middleton's *Changeling*, an old play, which contains some passages horribly striking.[1]

and in his remarks on Middleton Leigh Hunt comments:

> There is one character of his (De Flores in the *Changeling*) which, for effect at once tragical, probable, and poetical, surpasses anything I know of in the drama of domestic life.[2]

Modern criticism has tended to confine itself to the main plot of *The Changeling*, and in particular to the two scenes (II. ii and III. iv) between Beatrice and De Flores. Magnificent though they are, however, they should not be considered in isolation, for the play is a unity, and its full meaning is revealed only at the end of the last scene.

The Changeling is basically a study in sin and retribution, expressed in terms of sexual relationships, and it develops the subject with a maturity and balance rarely found in Elizabethan drama. Love in *The Changeling* is not an absolute value to which all others are subordinate, nor is it mere lust or sensuality. It is a force of immense potentiality for good or evil, that can radically alter human character and conduct. It needs, therefore, to be guided and controlled by wisdom and intelligence, and on one level the play illustrates the disastrous results which occur when these controls fail to operate. Much of this aspect of the play, as Miss Bradbrook has shown,[3] is expressed by a series of themes or concepts which underlie and prompt a good deal of the play's imagery and vocabulary. One of the most important of these themes is that of sight and outward appearance. The lover is attracted by the woman's beauty, and his difficulty is to judge this beauty at its true worth, to deter-

---

[1] *Sir Tristrem*, edited by Walter Scott (1806), p. 304.
[2] *Imagination and Fancy* (1844), edition of 1891, p. 199.
[3] *Themes and Conventions of Elizabethan Tragedy* (1935), pp. 214ff.

mine what lies behind it. He is influenced in this by two opposing
sides of his character. One is his 'will', a term that appears to signify
a stubborn and reckless selfishness.[1] It is used in the opening scene
by three characters—Vermandero, Beatrice, and De Flores—and
the remainder of the play shows how several of the characters are
dominated, even to the point of disaster, by their intense egotism.
The other is his 'judgment', his maturity and wisdom, which must
not be deceived by the senses or perverted by the will. It is perhaps
ironical that the fullest statement of the 'sight' and 'judgment'
theme is by Beatrice herself, and it sums up the play as fully as any
single quotation can do:

> Our eyes are sentinels unto our judgments,
> And should give certain judgment what they see;
> But they are rash sometimes, and tell us wonders
> Of common things, which when our judgments find,
> They can then check the eyes, and call them blind.
>
> (I. i. 72–6)

Both here and in Alsemero's reply (I. i. 77–9), the eyes are personified as active agents, able to deceive or even take over the function
of the judgment. In the discussion between Beatrice and Alsemero
on unreasonable likes and dislikes (I. i. 108–28) the terms used to
describe the topic are of barely qualified disapproval ('infirmity',
'frailty', 'imperfection') as though to suggest that feelings which are
not sanctioned by the 'judgment' are a liability, a weakness of
character. The theme is carried a stage further in Beatrice's long
soliloquy at the beginning of Act II. She too needs to test her skill
as a judge of character, her 'intellectual eyesight', in order to find
out which of her suitors is the 'true deserver', and on this basis she
must choose which one to trust and depend on. The need for this
ability, and the terrible effects of its failure, are clearly shown in the
later part of the play, in her dealings with De Flores, Diaphanta,
and Alsemero himself.

Closely linked with the theme of appearance and reality is the
concept of change or transformation. The word 'change' occurs

---

[1] Miss Bradbrook (*op. cit.*, p. 214) defines 'will' as 'instinctive desire,
often . . . sensual desire'. But the play's term for the latter is 'blood', as at
II. ii. 146 and v. i. 7.

nineteen times in the play, and it has a variety of implications. In the first place, the change may be one of character. Alsemero, for example, is transformed by his love for Beatrice from a hardened traveller and soldier, indifferent to women, to a courtier and gallant, a change so striking that his friend Jasperino comments on it almost with amazement. Secondly, the change may relate to appearance. That which was seen at first as ugly or repellent becomes acceptable or even attractive, and the beauty which inspired love comes to be seen as a mask for spiritual ugliness. Finally, the change may be of a more physical nature, a substitution of one person for another. Alsemero replaces Alonzo as Beatrice's lover, and is in his turn supplanted by De Flores; Diaphanta takes the place of Beatrice on Alsemero's wedding night. The word is used several times in the opening scene, and one of its effects is to suggest that those concerned, particularly Beatrice and Alsemero, are beginning a period of uncertainty and instability: new and disturbing forces have entered their lives, and they have not yet worked out their best course of action.

The last major theme is the expression of attraction or repulsion, usually sexual, in terms of food or poison. This is particularly noticeable in connexion with De Flores; he thinks of love as an appetite to be satisfied, and is himself described as a poison or poisonous reptile—viper, toad, and serpent—several times by Beatrice.

When stated as simply as this, the themes of the play may appear commonplace, and indeed there is no attempt in *The Changeling* to modify or redefine conventional ways of thought. The play is based entirely upon traditional attitudes, and its originality lies in the power and consistency with which they are applied to a particular situation. The dramatists' interest, in other words, is psychological rather than philosophical: the close inter-relationships of a small group of characters are explored with a fine and penetrating insight.

The opening scene is important in other respects. Many of the details in it combine to generate an atmosphere of tension without which the later scenes would lose much of their power. The first sixty lines in particular are full of omens and premonitions which can be ambiguously interpreted, and phrases like 'hidden malady' (I. i. 24) and 'this smoke will bring forth fire' (I. i. 50–1) give the impression of an impending evil that Alsemero is powerless to escape. Such words as 'speed', 'haste', and 'violence' echo each other throughout the scene, and prepare us for sudden and violent reactions, for extremes of emotion, from characters too engrossed in their own purposes to see clearly what is before them.

In Act II the action moves to the more confined setting of Vermandero's castle, and the speed of events quickens considerably. The soliloquies by Beatrice and De Flores that open II. i are both extremely revealing. Beatrice is quick and self-confident, her thoughts forming themselves into aphorisms which would appear almost trite if the audience did not suspect that the real truth contained in them was to be brought out very sharply in the later part of the play. The last eight lines of her speech (II. i. 19–26) are a good illustration of the sudden and abrupt transitions in the pattern of her thoughts, the 'snipe-like darts of her mind', as Miss Ellis-Fermor puts it.[1] Her ideas are disconnected, provoked by sudden spurts of memory and emotion, and it is not surprising that she should grasp at a plausible way out of her difficulties without stopping to work out its full implications. De Flores' soliloquy, and indeed all his speeches in I. i and II. i, reveal the extent to which he is obsessed by the thought of Beatrice, her attitude towards him, and the overwhelmingly compulsive desire that drives him to see her on every possible occasion. His mind, however, is more logical than Beatrice's, and he analyses her behaviour and his own in an attempt to see the situation as clearly as he can. As Miss Bradbrook puts it:

> He has a certain self-knowledge which sets him above the others, if it does not give him self-mastery.[2]

He acknowledges his own ugliness, and the loathing Beatrice has for him, but refuses to abandon his pursuit of her. His soliloquy at II. i. 76–88, after he has been contemptuously snubbed by Beatrice,

[1] *The Jacobean Drama* (1936), p. 146. Professor Ellis-Fermor's account of the play contains some illuminating comments on the working of Beatrice's mind.
[2] *Op. cit.*, p. 216.

shows that he sees love as 'beyond all reason', a force governed by
caprice; he endures Beatrice's hatred in the hope that ultimately
her resistance will collapse, either through an inexplicable change
of feeling on her own part or through his own dogged persistence:

> Wrangling has prov'd the mistress of good pastime;
> As children cry themselves asleep, I ha' seen
> Women have chid themselves abed to men. (II. i. 86–8)

Beatrice's reaction is characteristic:

> The next good mood I find my father in,
> I'll get him quite discarded . . . (II. i. 92–3)

Miss Ellis-Fermor describes her as a 'spoilt child',[1] and the phrase
explains a good deal of her behaviour, her complacent self-assur-
ance, her belief in her own skill in handling other people, and her
assumption that others exist only to further her own purposes.

At the end of II. i Tomazo warns Alonzo that Beatrice has no real
affection for him, but Alonzo's attitude is one of almost contemptuous self-confidence. His manner is normally courteous, but it is
obvious from several of his remarks that he is another of the play's
self-willed, obstinate characters who refuse to recognize any ob-
stacle to their desires, and he is determined to see Beatrice as what
he wants her to be and not as she really is.

Middleton's use of the aside is particularly noticeable in the
scene that follows, II. ii. It has two main functions. One is to reveal
the effect and inner significance of each remark with an intimacy
and fullness of detail that we might otherwise expect only from a
novelist. The other is to show in varying degrees the extent to
which the characters are isolated from each other, withdrawn into
a private world of reverie and preoccupation. When, for example,
Beatrice rejects Alsemero's offer to challenge Alonzo, and then, by
a sudden flash of perception which is one of the most brilliantly
ironic strokes in the play, persuades herself that De Flores is the
ideal instrument to rid her of Alonzo, she becomes increasingly
unaware of Alsemero in her mounting excitement and self-con-
gratulation, until he is forced to protest, 'Lady, you hear not me'
(II. ii. 48). Confident, however, in her own ability to manage the

[1] *Op. cit.*, p. 147.

affair single-handed, she conceals her plan from Alsemero, and quickly gets him out of the way in order to carry it out. Her love for Alsemero is utterly selfish; she refuses his offer solely because it will involve him in danger, and abandons Alonzo to his fate without a trace of pity or compunction.

In the interview that follows between her and De Flores, Beatrice begins her pretence of liking De Flores by telling him that his looks have improved:

> Y'have prun'd yourself, methinks, you were not wont
> To look so amorously.   (II. ii. 74–5)

Her remarks fit into the theme of appearance and reality, and also give a significant hint of the real alteration that later takes place in her attitude. De Flores is sceptical at first, but when she persists he can only assume that the long-awaited change of feeling has come about, that at last Beatrice 'dotes' on his 'pick-hair'd face' (II. i. 39–40). Beatrice's hint of 'employment' (II. ii. 94) is enough to start De Flores begging to serve her with an intensity that Beatrice takes to be the result of greed and poverty. Miss Bradbrook describes the scene as one of 'ironic comedy'[1] and there is certainly a comic note in the way in which both characters become more and more excited at what seems to be the fulfilment of their wishes, though each is deceived about the real intentions of the other. As they part, Beatrice congratulates herself on her skill (II. ii. 144–6), while De Flores muses cynically on the unpredictable appetites of women (II. ii. 150–3).

In III. i and ii the murder is swiftly and efficiently carried out, and in III. iv, the most famous scene in the play, De Flores returns to claim his reward. Immediately before his entry, Beatrice meditates in her usual vein of moralizing and self-praise:

> I have got him now the liberty of the house:
> So wisdom by degrees works out her freedom . . .
>
>   (III. iv. 12–13)

and she looks forward eagerly to the death of Alonzo. De Flores' aside at his entrance (III. iv. 18–20) illustrates both the coarseness of his mind and the absolute perversity of his moral values: his lust

---

[1] *Op. cit.*, p. 217.

for Beatrice matters more than anything else. Both of them see the death of Alonzo solely as a means of achieving their own desires, though De Flores is aware of the 'deed' and its implications in a way that Beatrice is not. From this point onwards, however, Beatrice is forced, step by step, to understand and acknowledge the meaning of an act for which she is fully as responsible as De Flores.

Beatrice is shocked when De Flores produces Alonzo's finger, but his reply (III. iv. 29–32) exposes the shallowness and hypocrisy of her attitude. She offers him the ring as a reward, stressing its value, but De Flores accepts it grudgingly:

> 'Twill hardly buy a capcase for one's conscience, though,
> To keep it from the worm, as fine as 'tis.   (III. iv. 44–5)

Beatrice notices that he looks 'offended' (III. iv. 52), and tries to reassure him that she realizes her responsibilities:

> 'Twere misery in me to give you cause, sir. (III. iv. 58)

but she is almost certainly unaware of the ominous twist his reply gives to her sentence:

> I know so much, it were so, misery
> In her most sharp condition.   (III. iv. 59–60)

Then, a little condescendingly, she offers him the final reward of three thousand florins. This might well be considered the turning-point of the scene and of the play as a whole. De Flores perceives that it is indeed with money only that Beatrice intends to pay him, and his perverted sense of honour, by which murder for lust is acceptable but murder for money is not, is deeply offended. He tries to make Beatrice understand him by stressing exactly what it is he has done, but his references to the 'life-blood of man', 'murder', and 'conscience' (III. iv. 66–70) only bewilder Beatrice, who is willing to give him an unlimited sum of money to get rid of him.[1] He refuses to fly without her, and when she fails to understand him, his explanation is significant:

[1] Her supposition that he may be too 'modest' to name the sum he wants is of course deeply ironical, and it also prepares us for her own 'modesty' later in the scene (III. iv. 125).

> Why, are not you as guilty, in (I'm sure)
> As deep as I? And we should stick together.
>
> (III. iv. 83–4)

They are now equals, accomplices in crime who should 'stick together', and the remainder of the play illustrates the gradual
deepening of their relationship. Beatrice, however, still tries to
maintain an attitude of dignified superiority, repulsing De Flores'
attempts to kiss her, until he works up to a totally unambiguous
declaration:

> And were I not resolv'd in my belief
> That thy virginity were perfect in thee,
> I should but take my recompense with grudging,
> As if I had but half my hopes I agreed for.
>
> (III. iv. 116–19)

Beatrice's reply superbly illustrates her character. Surprise,
horror, indignation, and hurt pride all combine in what Swinburne called 'a touch worthy of the greatest dramatist that ever
lived':[1]

> Why, 'tis impossible thou canst be so wicked,
> Or shelter such a cunning cruelty,
> To make his death the murderer of my honour!
> Thy language is so bold and vicious,
> I cannot see which way I can forgive it
> With any modesty.   (III. iv. 120–5)

She is plainly living in the world of values and relationships that
existed before the murder took place, and it is one of De Flores'
functions to strip this pretence from her:

> A woman dipp'd in blood, and talk of modesty?
>
> (III. iv. 126)

Beatrice at last begins to perceive the 'misery of sin' (III. iv. 127),
but tries to keep De Flores at bay by stressing the gap between
them: creation intended them to live in different worlds. Once
again, De Flores undeceives her; she has placed herself in his world,
and is now 'the deed's creature', whom 'peace and innocency' have

---

[1] *Thomas Middleton (The Mermaid Series)*, 1887, I, Introduction,
p. xxxvi.

rejected (III. iv. 132–40). Beatrice still struggles against the new relationship, and kneels to De Flores as he had kneeled to her in II. ii, but her last desperate attempt to buy him off is met with the famous lines 'of which Shakespeare or Sophocles might have been proud':[1]

> Can you weep fate from its determin'd purpose?
> So soon may you weep me.   (III. iv. 162–3)

Beatrice, forced to yield, recognizes the power of morality, and the scene closes with what Miss Bradbrook calls 'one of Middleton's most daring and most perfectly managed modulations of feeling',[2] De Flores' final speech at III. iv. 167–71. But even in the comparative tenderness there is an ominous note: her 'peace' is to yield to him; she is now dependent on him, and will come to love what she once hated.

Certain aspects of III. iv need perhaps to be stressed. In the first place, the mutual deception of Beatrice and De Flores is equally strong on both sides. Even though De Flores always sees through their illusions and pretences more quickly than Beatrice, to describe him as a kind of Iago plotting the downfall of a superior being hardly accords with the development of III. iv; De Flores is plainly not prepared for Beatrice's attitude, and the length of time it takes him to make a direct statement of what he wants indicates the depth of his deception: he makes no attempt to be explicit at first because he assumes that he has no need to. The exact degree to which he believes Beatrice willing to give herself to him is not easily determined, but several of his speeches in III. iv reveal the pain, disillusionment, and anger of an ugly man, intensely susceptible to women's beauty, who has felt with delight that his desire was about to be satisfied, only to realize that he had been deceived. His ability to blackmail Beatrice makes it impossible for her to defy him, but she puts herself in his power solely through her own actions, and not through any manœuvring on his part.

It is plain that from III. iv onwards Beatrice is a creature of evil, a spiritual partner of De Flores, but the exact nature of the process

---

[1] T. S. Eliot, 'Thomas Middleton', *Selected Essays* (1932), p. 164.
[2] *Op. cit.*, p. 219.

she has undergone in becoming this is a matter of some dispute.[1] William Archer takes the extreme view that the whole plot of *The Changeling* is totally implausible: Beatrice is a clever woman, aware of De Flores' feelings towards her, the emotions given her in III. iv are 'naive to the point of ludicrousness', and she could have responded to the situation in various ways, not merely the one shown.[2] These objections are clearly based on misreadings of the play. Beatrice is not a particularly intelligent woman. She is a poor judge of characters, including her own, and the play gives repeated instances of her clumsiness in handling other people. Her plans of action, which seem wonderful to her, though they always end in disaster, or near-disaster, come to her as sudden flashes of inspiration, and not from any steady perception of the situation as a whole. When her inspirations fail her, she is far from perceptive or quick-witted; until he becomes brutally plain, she completely fails to understand De Flores, and it is quite in keeping with her character that, shocked and bewildered, totally unable to see any escape from what appears to be De Flores' unanswerable logic, she should yield herself to him. Miss Ellis-Fermor describes her plotting as that of a 'clever child', and sees an 'essential innocence' in her soliloquy at III. iv. 10–17 anticipating the death of Alonzo.[3] According to T. S. Eliot, *The Changeling* is

> . . . the tragedy of the not naturally bad but irresponsible and undeveloped nature, caught in the consequences of its own action. . . Beatrice is not a moral creature; she becomes moral only by becoming damned.[4]

Even these accounts, it might be argued, are not completely accurate. Beatrice is not innocent in any fine or worthy sense: it is the innocence of selfishness, of ignorance, of one who has failed to realize that she is as much subject to the laws of morality as anyone

---

[1] The question is discussed by T. S. Eliot and Miss Ellis-Fermor, in the essays already mentioned, and in Miss Helen Gardner's interesting article, 'Milton's "Satan" and the Theme of Damnation in Elizabethan Tragedy', *English Studies 1948*, collected by F. P. Wilson, pp. 56–8.

[2] *The Old Drama and the New* (1923), pp. 96–100. Apparently Middleton could have written a fine play 'had he taken the trouble to think the thing out'.

[3] *Op. cit.*, pp. 146–7.   [4] *Op. cit.*, p. 163.

else. But it would not be right to say that she is unaware of morality.[1] She rebukes De Flores as self-righteously as any blameless heroine, and there is a note almost of cruel comedy in the way in which she appeals to the traditional maidenly virtues—'honour', 'modesty'— as a defence against 'wicked' De Flores, the 'villain', completely unaware that by her act she has struck at the roots of morality and destroyed the protection it gave her. Mr Eliot claims that she is not 'naturally bad', but her speech at v. iii. 149–61 suggests a different interpretation: the tragedy of Beatrice is that at the decisive moment in her life, the testing time of her character, she comes to discover that she is evil, that she belongs with the wicked. This may seem unnecessarily harsh, but there is a danger of sentimentalizing her character. She is, of course, beautiful, wealthy, and of high social standing, but none of these qualities relate to character, and in many ways she is distinctly unamiable. She could be described as selfish, proud, self-righteous to the point of complacency, and in the later scenes hard and unscrupulous. She is completely unaware of the real significance of the deed she instigates because in her egotism she is aware of morality only as it protects her and not as it restrains her, and one of the lessons of the play is that these two aspects of morality are inseparable.

De Flores' function in all this is to act as a symbol of the world to which Beatrice has committed herself, to be her 'evil genius',[2] the 'conscience'[3] reminding her what she is. He is both a man, willing to sacrifice even his salvation to gratify his lust, and a representative of evil. In certain respects his function might be compared to that of Mephistophilis in Marlowe's *Dr Faustus*; Mephistophilis can hardly be said to tempt Faustus: invoked by Faustus, he serves him, and ultimately claims his soul.[4] Similarly, De Flores has no power over Beatrice until she summons him of her own volition, and some of his force and strength could be attributed to the tra-

[1] Ironically, she makes more speeches of a somewhat moralizing kind than any other character in the play.

[2] The phrase is used by Fredson Bowers, *Elizabethan Revenge Tragedy* (1940), p. 205.

[3] He uses the word five times, usually applying it to himself.

[4] See Miss Gardner's comparison of *The Changeling*, *Macbeth*, and *Dr Faustus*, *op. cit.*, pp. 47ff.

ditionally implacable and inevitable power of the forces of evil claiming their own. Beatrice's early loathing of him springs from an affinity she will not allow herself to recognize. De Flores consciously proclaims his own character; Beatrice has to be forced to look into herself, with agonized reluctance, to see clearly what she is, and in the later scenes of the play she struggles desperately to prevent others making the same discovery of herself that she has made.

The moral world which surrounds the characters of *The Changeling* is the orthodox Christian universe of sin and punishment, in which our 'choices' are of fundamental importance, and must not be guided by wrong and selfish desires. Two aspects of it are reflected in the vocabulary of the play. One is the continual use of words with definite religious overtones, such as 'heaven', 'creation' and 'creature', 'bless' and 'blessed',[1] 'devotion', 'holy', and 'reverence'. Their chief effect, particularly in the speeches of De Flores in II. ii, is to suggest that the person using them has perverted beliefs and worships false gods; in the case of De Flores it is lust, and for Tomazo it is revenge (v. ii. 63–7). The second aspect is rather different. Certain of the more explicitly religious references hint at a parallelism between *The Changeling* and the story of Adam and Eve. Alsemero thinks of marriage in terms of the creation (I. i. 7–9); Beatrice is 'that broken rib of mankind' (v. iii. 146) and she loses her 'first condition' and is turned out by 'peace and innocency' (III. iv. 138–9) just as Eve loses her innocence and is forced to leave the garden of Eden. De Flores is, of course, the 'serpent' (I. i. 225), and Alsemero's remark towards the end of the play:

> Did my fate wait for this unhappy stroke
> At my first sight of woman?   (v. iii. 12–13)

might be said to contain a hint of Adam's experience: his attempt to create a paradise on earth by means of marriage has been frustrated by Beatrice's discovery of evil.

From IV. i to V. ii the play moves forward on the level of plot and

---

[1] Beatrice, who has most need of blessing, uses the expression 'bless me' four times.

intrigue, and it is sometimes suggested that in these scenes there is a deterioration in the quality of the play. But this development is a natural one, from Beatrice's initiation into evil in Acts II and III, to the deepening involvement in trickery and deception which follows from it, and it is hard to see how the play could have been kept on a purely psychological level once the relationship between Beatrice and De Flores has been cleared of misunderstandings. Further, the last two acts of the play, as Miss Gardner shows,[1] point out the hollowness of what Beatrice has gained by the murder, the emptiness of a temporal benefit from commerce with evil.

Much of Act IV is taken up with the virginity tests that Beatrice and Diaphanta undergo. Some of the older critics find this device in bad taste; a modern reader is perhaps more likely to consider it totally unconvincing.[2] It might be best to regard it as symbolic of the kind of problem Beatrice has constantly to face now that she has committed herself to evil. At IV. i. 4–8 Beatrice dreads the penetration and intelligence of Alsemero that she praised at the beginning of II. i; he is now an adversary, a clever opponent to be cheated if necessary, and she is forced into an elaborate system of deceit. The sight of Diaphanta gives her another sudden inspiration, and she deals with her as she had dealt with De Flores, developing the topic in such a way that in the end Diaphanta herself offers her services. In IV. ii she fakes the effects of the virginity test, to the intense relief of Alsemero, whose suspicions have been aroused by Jasperino, and who is clearly prepared to judge even her with an inflexible moral rigour (IV. ii. 105–7). The beginning of the same scene reintroduces Tomazo, now dedicated to the revenge of his brother. Unlike earlier revengers, such as Vindice in *The Revenger's Tragedy*, he is not at the centre of affairs, planning the downfall of others; he hardly knows even the basic facts, and by a supreme irony appeals for information to De Flores himself, to receive in reply what is probably the most caustic single touch of irony in the play:

[1] *Op. cit.*, pp. 57–8. She compares the mock wedding-night in *The Changeling* to the banquet in *Macbeth*.

[2] The fantastic nature of the virginity test makes us wonder whether Middleton himself took it very seriously.

> 'Las, sir, I am so charitable, I think none
> Worse than myself.   (IV. ii. 48–9)

Beatrice's soliloquy opening v. i shows that she has learnt little from her experience with De Flores. She is shocked and indignant that Diaphanta should selfishly put her in danger, but this time her reaction is to become brutal and threatening:

> No trusting of her life with such a secret,
> That cannot rule her blood to keep her promise.
>   (v. i. 6–7)

Her selfishness is exposed by the unconscious hypocrisy of her attitude; it is she, Beatrice, who has failed to 'rule her blood' (her love for Alsemero) to 'keep her promise' (her betrothal to Alonzo), and she has lost any right to condemn Diaphanta.

One of the effects of the murder has been to bring Beatrice and De Flores close together, as fellow-conspirators, and he now speaks to her with the casual familiarity of a social equal. v. i. 23–35 is a brilliant piece of characterization: Beatrice's attempts to assert herself, with something of her former imperiousness, are decisively overruled by De Flores, and inertly, almost despairingly, she leaves the control of affairs in his hands. His cold-blooded efficiency rouses her admiration, and even her affection; as he predicted at the end of III. iv, her loathing is slowly turning to love:

> How heartily he serves me! His face loathes one,
> But look upon his care, who would not love him?
>   (v. i. 70–1)

The remainder of v. i contains some of the finest touches of irony in the play, culminating in Beatrice's suggestion that De Flores should be rewarded for his care in attending to the fire he has started, a device that arouses even De Flores' cynical admiration.

The main function of the closing scene, which is probably by Rowley, is to pass judgment on the characters, to make plain and explicit the significance of what has happened. The involved system of deceit and intrigue built up by Beatrice proves to be its own destruction; her familiarity with De Flores has not escaped notice, and Alsemero's suspicions are stronger than ever. The imagery of the early part of the scene makes substantial use of the appearance

and reality theme: Alsemero realizes that he has deceived himself
about the true characters of Beatrice and De Flores, and when she
confesses to the murder he thinks of her as 'deform'd' (v. iii. 77).[1]
The motives that prompt her to confess illustrate both the consistency of her character and her inability to judge others. For her
the murder of Alonzo was of negligible importance compared to
her love for Alsemero, and she imagines that he will judge the
matter in the same way. There is almost a pathetic note in her asser-
tions that she has not been unfaithful to him, as though she considers adultery a far more serious offence than murder. He, of
course, is horrified, and when De Flores confirms the very thing she
wanted to conceal, he throws the pair together in a speech that
mingles anger and loathing. His reference to the 'black audience'
(v. iii. 116) is explicit: Beatrice and De Flores are damned.

De Flores resolves the situation by stabbing Beatrice and bringing her on to the stage. Vermandero's bewildered appeal to her is
answered by the most famous lines in the play:

> Oh come not near me, sir, I shall defile you ...
>
> (v. iii. 149ff)

Without self-pity or sentimentality, apology or excuses, Beatrice
sees herself as corrupt and defiling, the evil child of a good father.
She has proved to be a 'common thing', worthy only to be thrown
away 'regardlessly', to lose her identity in the filth of the common
sewer. At last she acknowledges the destiny that bound her fate in-
escapably to De Flores, and sees the prophetic nature of her early
loathing for him. Alsemero learns the truth about his wedding
night, though even here the final touch comes from De Flores:

> Yes; and the while I coupled with your mate
> At barley-brake; now we are left in hell.
>
> (v. iii. 162–3)

The end has come for both of them. Beatrice is glad to die because
it is now a 'shame to live' (v. iii. 179); De Flores egotistically
glories in the fulfilment of his ambition, and his last words (v. iii.
175–7) are appropriately addressed to Beatrice, the woman from
whom he will not be parted.

---

[1] Compare Beatrice's 'deformity' at v. iii. 32.

The play concludes with an assessment of the whole course of events. Alsemero will not allow Vermandero to reproach himself; justice has been done, the guilty have been punished, and the innocent vindicated (v. iii. 182–7). His words to Tomazo:

> Sir, you are sensible of what truth hath done;
> 'Tis the best comfort that your grief can find.
> (v. iii. 188–9)

show that the play's morality, though rigorous, is not inhuman; genuine 'comfort' comes from the knowledge of truth, not from the satisfaction of blind and selfish passions. In a calmer and more reasonable manner than in his earlier speeches, Tomazo acknowledges a superior power that will punish the evil-doers far more severely than he can. Alsemero, and the characters from the sub-plot, sum up the 'changes' that have taken place. The lines addressed to Tomazo:

> Your change is come too, from an ignorant wrath
> To knowing friendship. . .   (v. iii. 202–3)

illustrate once more the mature and human moral scheme behind the play: 'friendship' is based on truth and knowledge; 'wrath' springs from ignorance and leads to moral blindness and isolation. On this note the play ends:

> *Als.* Sir, you have yet a son's duty living,
>   Please you, accept it. . .   (v. iii. 216–17)

Alsemero offers Vermandero the duty as a son that was lacking in Beatrice as a daughter, and moral order is finally re-established.

The verse-style of *The Changeling* is surprisingly difficult to criticize, for it does not rely, as Miss Bradbrook points out,[1] on strikingly rich imagery and vocabulary to make its effect, and much of the verse, taken in isolation, would not perhaps seem very distinguished to a reader unfamiliar with the play. These qualities, however, are not such a liability as might appear at first. *The Changeling* is conspicuous among Elizabethan plays for the naturalness of its characters, for its plausibility as an account of a particular human situation, and it is entirely in keeping with this that the

---

[1] *Op. cit.*, pp. 238–9.

play's vocabulary should be that of ordinary life, that its imagery, though at times brilliantly effective, should be sparse and carefully controlled, always subordinate to the pressure of meaning behind it. There are no displays of poetic virtuosity, no irrelevancies or digressions: every part is related to what precedes and follows it, and this consistency and continuity is the main strength of the play. Individual lines or speeches derive their power from their relationship to the play as a whole, and taken from their context often seem to do no more than state an emotion or reaction in firm, but somewhat colourless, verse. A good example of this is Beatrice's speech at III. iv. 120–5 (quoted on p. lii). Virtually the only metaphorical touch ('To make his death the murderer of my honour') is a barely perceptible personification, and in itself the passage seems no better than verse which a number of Middleton's contemporaries could produce. When we see it, however, in its context, with a full knowledge of the characters involved and the events which have preceded it, one word after another springs to life—'impossible', 'wicked', 'honour', 'modesty'—and takes on great richness and subtlety of implication. The same applies to the ironies which fill the play. Lines such as:

> *Bea.*   Hie quickly to your chamber;
>   Your reward follows you.
> *Dia.*   I never made
>   So sweet a bargain.   (v. i. 79–81)

are effective only if we are fully aware of the treachery and self-deception that lie behind them. The dramatists' interest is concentrated on implications of plot and character, and the verse is a clear medium which is handled so unobtrusively that its effect is one of complete spontaneity and naturalness.

Compared to the blank verse of Shakespeare's great plays the verse of *The Changeling* may seem abstract or even prosaic, but this does not mean that it lacks strength. Its particular strength, however, might be termed a muscular strength, and takes the form of an energy of movement, a discreet placing of stress at the right point for emphasis. In the famous line:

> Can you weep fate from its determin'd purpose ? (III. iv. 162)

the four heavy beats that open the line combine with the rhyming stress on the last two words ('determin'd purpose') and the skilful positioning of 'determin'd' to produce an extraordinarily powerful effect. In another passage:

> De F.   Push, you forget yourself!
> A woman dipp'd in blood, and talk of modesty?
>   (III. iv. 125–6)

the curt, rapid speech-rhythm and the verse-rhythm combine so naturally as to be almost indistinguishable. But such effects rarely become noticeable, and the verse does not often rise to such heights as Beatrice's superb speech at v. iii. 149ff, with its unusual vigour of imagery.

The sub-plot of *The Changeling* has been dismissed very briefly by the great majority of critics. T. S. Eliot, for example, speaks of its 'nauseousness',[1] and uses the play as an illustration of Sidney's dictum:

> So falleth it out, that having indeed no right Comedy, in that comical part of our Tragedy we have nothing but scurrility, unworthy of any chaste ears, or some extreme show of doltishness, indeed fit to lift up a loud laughter, and nothing else.[2]

Miss Ellis-Fermor even considers that the sub-plot might have been omitted from the play without serious loss.[3] It is, of course, much inferior to the main plot, and parts of it, especially in I. ii, are crude and trivial. But the sub-plot as a whole is far from being worthless, and some at least of the objections that have been made to it spring from misconceptions of its nature and purpose.

The sub-plot may best be defined as a comedy of sexual intrigue which has its setting in a mad-house. It is neither mere 'comic relief' nor a travesty of madness which twentieth-century taste is bound to find offensive. In a variety of ways it echoes or reflects the main plot, as several modern critics have pointed out,[4] and at the

---

[1] *The Use of Poetry and the Use of Criticism* (1933), p. 41.

[2] *An Apology for Poetry*, in G. Gregory Smith, *Elizabethan Critical Essays* (1904), I, 199.

[3] *Op. cit.*, p. 144.

[4] The sub-plot is analysed by William Empson, *Some Versions of Pastoral* (1935), pp. 48ff, M. C. Bradbrook, *op. cit.*, pp. 221ff, and Karl

end of the play the connexion between the two plots is clearly and
deliberately stated. No doubt there is an element of buffoonery in
the sub-plot which appears to have been one of the main reasons for
the play's popularity; but we are not forced to accept the contemporary judgment if we can find convincing evidence for a more
intelligent appreciation.

The use of madness in the sub-plot can be seen in its true light
only if we remember that virtually all the mad speeches are given
to two characters, Antonio and Franciscus, who are not genuine
madmen at all. The contemporary audience probably recognized
almost immediately that Antonio and Franciscus were would-be
lovers in disguise, and a good deal of what appears to be gibberish
consists of ambiguous references to their purpose in entering the
mad-house.[1] This aspect of the sub-plot is emphasized in IV. iii,
where Isabella herself pretends to be a madwoman and completely
deceives Antonio. The humour is not at the expense of real madness, which Isabella does not seem to find very amusing; it is
directed at the absurdity of the lovers in disguise, at the 'madness'
of love itself and the fantastic behaviour it provokes.

In its treatment of sexual intrigue the sub-plot is linked to the
main plot in a variety of ways. There are, of course, several cross-
references between the two plots, and in V. ii and especially in V. iii
characters from both parts are brought together. There are also
similarities of plot. As William Empson points out,[2] Isabella corresponds to Beatrice, both women being key figures in their respective parts of the play. Each is surrounded by a set of would-be
lovers, and has to make her choice among them, the choice being
between an illicit love and duty, in Isabella's case to her husband
and in Beatrice's to her father and the man she has promised to
marry. The theme of blackmail, of rewards demanded for services
given, is equally important in both parts. In III. iii Lollio overhears
Antonio revealing his love to Isabella, and with that knowledge

---

Holzknecht, 'The Dramatic Structure of *The Changeling*', *Renaissance
Papers*, edited by A. H. Gilbert (University of South Carolina, 1954),
pp. 77–87.
    [1] This makes unnecessary a preliminary scene in which they plot their
entry into the mad-house.
    [2] *Op. cit.*, p. 49.

attempts to coerce her as De Flores in III. iv successfully coerces Beatrice. But Isabella is too strong for him, and counters him, as Miss Bradbrook shows,[1] by threatening to have Antonio treat him in exactly the way De Flores treated Alonzo:

> . . . be silent, mute,
> Mute as a statue, or his injunction
> For me enjoying, shall be to cut thy throat . . .
>
> (III. iii. 240–2)

A variant of the same theme occurs twice later in the sub-plot, first with Antonio (IV. iii. 145–57) and then with Franciscus (IV. iii. 188–202); each gallant is told by Lollio that he can earn Isabella's love by ridding her of the unwelcome attentions of his rival. All these incidents parallel in some way the relationship of Beatrice, Alonzo, and De Flores.

The imagery of the sub-plot provides a further link with the main plot. Some of the themes that recur in the latter—sight and outward appearance, and the transformation of appearances—are equally important in the sub-plot, particularly in Antonio's speeches:

> This shape of folly shrouds your dearest love,
> The truest servant to your powerful beauties,
> Whose magic had this force thus to transform me.
>
> (III. iii. 119–21)

The theme is most fully expressed in IV. iii, where Antonio's inability to see through Isabella's disguise parallels the 'blindness' of the characters in the main plot:

> Have I put on this habit of a frantic,
> With love as full of fury to beguile
> The nimble eye of watchful jealousy,
> And am I thus rewarded ?   [*Reveals herself.*]
> *Ant.* Ha! Dearest beauty!
> *Isa.*   No, I have no beauty now,
> Nor never had, but what was in my garments.
> You a quick-sighted lover ? Come not near me!
> Keep your caparisons, y'are aptly clad;
> I came a feigner to return stark mad. (IV. iii. 127–35)

---

[1] *Op. cit.*, p. 221.

There are other, though less important, similarities: Antonio's 'deformity' at III. iii. 186 anticipates v. iii. 32; both Beatrice and Isabella use metaphors derived from the legend of the labyrinth, at III. iv. 71 and IV. iii. 106–8; and De Flores' reference to plucking 'sweets' at II. i. 46 is echoed by Antonio's:

> Shall I alone
> Walk through the orchard of the Hesperides,
> And cowardly not dare to pull an apple?
>
> (III. iii. 173–5)

The main plot itself provides certain links. 'As Miss Bradbrook points out,[1] Tomazo's comment on his brother:

> Why, here is love's tame madness . . .   (II. i. 154)

reminds us of the sub-plot, and when Alsemero hears Beatrice confess the murder of Alonzo, he locks her into the closet with the comment, 'I'll be your keeper yet' (v. iii. 87), much as Lollio has to lock up the madmen when they become out of control.

All these parallels, however, point to a very real difference in tone and intention between the two plots. Though the sub-plot contains potentially tragic material, and such a speech as Isabella's in III. iii:

> . . . would a woman stray,
> She need not gad abroad to seek her sin,
> It would be brought home one ways or other . . .
>
> (III. iii. 213–15)

would not be out of place in the main plot, all the situations which parallel the main plot are turned to comic effect, and certain points in the sub-plot almost suggest a deliberate parody of the main plot. When Franciscus, at IV. iii. 188–99, is told of the rival he must meet, he cries 'He's dead already', which seems to echo De Flores' 'His end's upon him' (II. ii. 134); but whereas De Flores' speech is eagerly accepted by Beatrice, and a tragic situation begins to develop, in the sub-plot any possibility of tragedy is cut short by Lollio's naive common-sense:

> Will you tell me that, and I parted but now with him?
>
> (IV. iii. 193)

[1] *Op. cit.*, p. 217.

Similarly, Lollio's attempt to ape De Flores in III. iii is an almost pathetic failure, and it is as though one character after another in the sub-plot tries to expand into a heroic figure, a sinner of tragic dimensions, only to be abruptly deflated. As Isabella puts it:

> When you are weary, you may leave the school,
> For all this while you have but play'd the fool.
>
> (III. iii. 145-6)

Antonio wishes to be the gallant and seducer, the master of intrigue, but succeeds only in making a fool of himself, both literally and metaphorically.

At two points in the sub-plot there are passages which appear to be satirical commentary on the main plot. The dialogue on honour between Lollio and Antonio at IV. iii. 90-9 bears the same relationship to the somewhat brittle 'honour' of Beatrice as Falstaff's speech on honour in *Henry IV, Part I* does to that of Hotspur. In the same scene Alibius's fear that the madmen in the wedding entertainment may alarm the ladies present, who are 'nice things, thou know'st', and Lollio's reply:

> You need not fear, sir; so long as we are there with our commanding pizzles, they'll be as tame as the ladies themselves.
>
> (IV. iii. 61-3)

both reflect ironically on the behaviour of Beatrice and Diaphanta.

A further difference between the two plots might be summed up by saying that what is implied in the main plot becomes literal in the sub-plot. The deceptive appearances which are suggested by imagery in the main plot become actual disguises in the sub-plot, and the madness of love which is no more than hinted at in the main plot moves much closer to real madness in the sub-plot. The first of these two ideas is developed explicitly near the end of the play:

> *Ver.* Beseech you hear me; these two have been disguis'd
> E'er since the deed was done.
> *Als.*   I have two other
> That were more close disguis'd than your two could be,
> E'er since the deed was done.   (V. iii. 126-9)

In the main plot, the woman's outward appearance is deceptive because it provides no index to the true nature of her character, and this theme is developed metaphorically at some length. In the sub-plot, the whole matter is put much more simply and literally:

> . . . I have no beauty now,
> Nor never had, but what was in my garments.

(IV. iii. 131–2)

In the one case, the lover is unable to judge the woman's character because of her beauty, in the other he cannot even see that beauty for what it is. Indeed, one of the functions of the sub-plot is to enable the audience to grasp the essential themes of the main plot—the madness of love, the deceptiveness of appearances, the transformations men and women undergo through love—by isolating and enlarging them to the point of literalness, and some effect of this sort is probably felt even by those critics who dismiss the subplot as valueless.

The total effect of all these different kinds of relationship between the two halves of the play is not easily assessed. Possibly a deliberate and symbolic contrast is intended by the dramatists. Two sets of characters are portrayed, one group living in a world of normal human relationships, the other in a fantastic environment of madness which might be expected to have a damaging effect upon conduct. Yet the first group behaves with a real and terrible madness that leads to the death of four people, while in the world of apparent madness sanity always manages to assert itself, so that no real damage is done. Beatrice becomes entangled in her own intrigues and is destroyed; Isabella retains her sanity and integrity through her own strength of character. It may be, as Empson suggests,[1] that her surroundings force Isabella to see the problem more clearly than Beatrice; Antonio's attempt to seduce her is interrupted by the sudden appearance of madmen dressed as birds and beasts, a symbolic presentation of the bestiality that is released when human actions cease to be governed by reason and sanity.

The final connexion of the two parts comes in the last scene of the play. As Empson points out,[2] De Flores' reference to 'barley-brake' (V. iii. 162–3) echoes the madmen's cries at III. iii. 165, but the most important link occurs some lines later, after Alsemero has made his speech beginning:

---

[1] *Op. cit.*, p. 50.   [2] *Ibid.*, p. 52.

What an opacous body had that moon . . .

(v. iii. 196ff)

Alsemero sums up the events of the main plot, and then, one after
the other, each in terms of the transformation imagery we have
come to recognize as characteristic of the play, the leading figures of
the sub-plot acknowledge their mistakes, and Alibius pledges himself to wiser conduct in future. All that has happened is now seen in
its true light. The two halves of the play have followed a similar
pattern: sexual passion has led to a series of complicated intrigues
which have now worked themselves out, in the one part in tragic
disaster, in the other in ludicrous failure on the part of the in-
triguers. The normal tenor of life has been interrupted by a sudden
crisis; at the end of the play the crisis is resolved, and normality
finally reasserts itself.

THE CHANGELING

DRAMATIS PERSONÆ.

VERMANDERO, *father to Beatrice.*
TOMAZO DE PIRACQUO, *a noble lord.*
ALONZO DE PIRACQUO, *his brother, suitor to Beatrice.*
ALSEMERO, *a nobleman, afterwards married to Beatrice.*   5
JASPERINO, *his friend.*
ALIBIUS, *a jealous doctor.*
LOLLIO, *his man.*
PEDRO, *friend to Antonio.*
ANTONIO, *the changeling.*   10
FRANCISCUS, *the counterfeit madman.*
DE FLORES, *servant to Vermandero.*
Madmen.
Servants.

BEATRICE-JOANNA, *daughter to Vermandero.*   15
DIAPHANTA, *her waiting-woman.*
ISABELLA, *wife to Alibius.*

The Scene: *Alicant.*

15. *Beatrice-Joanna*] Dilke; *Beatrice* Q.   18. *Alicant*] Dyce; *Allegant* Q.

The Scene. Alicant, or Alicante, is a Valencian seaport on the east coast of Spain. I. i takes place near the harbour of the city, and the remainder of the main plot in the rooms of Vermandero's castle; the sub-plot, from I. ii to IV. iii, is set in the mad-house of Alibius.

The Changeling

Act I

Enter ALSEMERO.

Als. 'Twas in the temple where I first beheld her,
    And now again the same; what omen yet
    Follows of that ? None but imaginary;
    Why should my hopes or fate be timorous ?
    The place is holy, so is my intent: 5
    I love her beauties to the holy purpose,
    And that, methinks, admits comparison

Act 1] *Dilke, Dyce;* ACTUS PRIMUS. *Q.*

Q is divided into Acts, but not Scenes, which were first added by Dyce.
   The Title. 'Changeling' had various meanings in the 17th century. It
referred in the first place to the ugly or mentally deficient child which the
fairies were supposed to leave in place of a normal child which they stole.
This sense occurs in *The Sad Shepherd*, II. ii. 10 (Jonson, VII, 28). It
could also refer, however, to the normal, stolen child, as in *MND.*, II. i. 23,
and *The Sad Shepherd*, II. viii. 53–4 (Jonson, VII, 41). From these specific
meanings was derived the use of the word simply as an equivalent for
'idiot', as in the play, where Antonio is 'The Changeling', though he is
never referred to by this name in the actual text of the play. Several other
meanings became attached to the word—an inferior substitute, a waverer
or unreliable person, and an inconstant woman, as in *The Widow's Tears*,
II. i. 82 (Chapman, *Comedies*, 382)—and various critics have suggested
that other characters in the play, such as Beatrice, Diaphanta, and De
Flores, could be considered as 'The Changeling'. There is some plausibility in this, though it does not seem very likely.
   1–12.] This speech condenses Reynolds's lengthy account of the first
meeting of Alsemero and Beatrice in the church.
   4. *or*] Possibly a misprint for 'of'; cf. I. i. 111.
   5. *place . . . holy*] 'Holy place' is used as a synonym for temple several
times in Leviticus (e.g. vi. 27 and 30). Alsemero refers back to this line at
v. iii. 72–6.
   6. *the holy purpose*] Marriage.

With man's first creation, the place blest,
And is his right home back, if he achieve it.
The church hath first begun our interview,   10
And that's the place must join us into one,
So there's beginning and perfection too.

Enter JASPERINO.

Jas. Oh sir, are you here? Come, the wind's fair with you,
Y'are like to have a swift and pleasant passage.

Als. Sure y'are deceived, friend, 'tis contrary   15
In my best judgment.

Jas.   What, for Malta?
If you could buy a gale amongst the witches,
They could not serve you such a lucky pennyworth
As comes a' God's name.

Als.   Even now I observ'd
The temple's vane to turn full in my face,   20
I know 'tis against me.

Jas.   Against you?
Then you know not where you are.

---

8. *the place blest*] Paradise, the Garden of Eden. 'The meaning of
Alsemero is, that a happy marriage is the most proper means for man to
recover that paradise which Adam lost' (Dilke). Cf. *The Duchess of Malfi*,
I. i. 437–8:

> Begin with that first good deed began i'th'world,
> After mans creation, the Sacrament of marriage.
>   (Webster, II, 48).

15. *contrary*] In Reynolds there is none of this atmosphere of uncertainty: Alsemero is delayed by a contrary wind.
16. *Malta*] Cf. Reynolds, p. 108: '. . . so taking order for his lands and
affaires, hee resolues to see *Malta* that inexpugnable Rampier of *Mars*, the
glorie of Christendome, and the terrour of Turkie, to see if he could gaine
any place of command and honour either in that Iland, or in their
Gallies'.
17. *buy . . . witches*] Cf. Webster and Rowley's *A Cure for a Cuckold*,
IV. ii. 97: 'The winds which Lapland Witches sell to men—' (Webster,
III, 76) and *Mac.*, I. iii. II. R. R. Cawley, *The Voyagers and Elizabethan
Drama* (1938), pp. 250–2, gives several other references.
19. *a' God's name*] Free, for nothing. Cf. *The Shoemaker's Holiday*, I. ii.
59–60: 'ile take any thing that comes a Gods name' (Dekker, I, 18).

Als.   Not well indeed.

Jas. Are you not well, sir?

Als.   Yes, Jasperino.
  —Unless there be some hidden malady
  Within me, that I understand not.

Jas.   And that   25
  I begin to doubt, sir; I never knew
  Your inclinations to travels at a pause
  With any cause to hinder it, till now.
  Ashore you were wont to call your servants up,
  And help to trap your horses for the speed;   30
  At sea I have seen you weigh the anchor with 'em,
  Hoist sails for fear to lose the foremost breath,
  Be in continual prayers for fair winds,
  And have you chang'd your orisons?

Als.   No, friend,
  I keep the same church, same devotion.   35

Jas. Lover I'm sure y'are none, the stoic was
  Found in you long ago; your mother nor
  Best friends, who have set snares of beauty (ay,
  And choice ones, too), could never trap you that
      way.
  What might be the cause?

Als.   Lord, how violent   40
  Thou art! I was but meditating of
  Somewhat I heard within the temple.

Jas. Is this violence? 'Tis but idleness
  Compar'd with your haste yesterday.

Als. I'm all this while a-going, man.   45

---

27. inclinations to travels] *Q, Neilson;* inclination to travel *Dilke, Dyce.*

22–3.] For other examples of this play on words, which D. M. Robb,
M.L.R. XLV (April 1950), 133, calls 'cue-catching', see Introduction, p. xl.
  30. *for the speed*] In order to hasten matters.
  36–9.] Cf. Reynolds, p. 108: 'for he spurnes at the pleasures of the
Court, and refuseth to haunt and frequent the companies of Ladies'.
  38. *snares of beauty*] Cf. Reynolds, p. 128: '. . . hee is so caught and
intangled in the snares of her beautie . . .'

Enter Servants.

Jas. Backwards, I think, sir. Look, your servants.

1 Ser. The seamen call; shall we board your trunks?

Als. No, not to-day.

Jas. 'Tis the critical day, it seems, and the sign in Aquarius.

2 Ser. [*aside.*] We must not to sea to-day; this smoke will bring   50
forth fire.

Als. Keep all on shore; I do not know the end
(Which needs I must do) of an affair in hand
Ere I can go to sea.

1 Ser. Well, your pleasure.   55

2 Ser. [*aside.*] Let him e'en take his leisure too, we are safer on
land.   *Exeunt Servants.*

Enter BEATRICE, DIAPHANTA, *and Servants.* [ALSEMERO *greets*
BEATRICE *and kisses her.*]

Jas. [*aside.*] How now! The laws of the Medes are chang'd
sure, salute a woman? He kisses too: wonderful! Where
learnt he this? And does it perfectly too; in my conscience   60
he ne'er rehears'd it before. Nay, go on, this will be
stranger and better news at Valencia than if he had ran-
som'd half Greece from the Turk.

Bea. You are a scholar, sir?

Als.   A weak one, lady.

50. aside.] *This ed.*   56. aside.] *This ed.*   57.1. Enter . . . Servants.]
Dilke, Dyce; Enter . . . Servants, Joanna. Q.   57.1–2. Alsemero . . . her.]
Dyce.   58. aside.] Dyce.   62. Valencia] *All eds.; Valentia Q (and
throughout the play).*

_____

49. *critical*] See G.

sign in Aquarius] Not, as Brooke suggests, indicating 'watery vacilla-
tion', but rather that the time is propitious for travel by water.

57.1. *Beatrice*] Q adds '*Joanna*' after '*Servants*'; the text from which
the transcriber was copying probably had 'Beatrice Joanna'; he omitted
'Joanna' and then, uncertain whether 'Beatrice Joanna' was one character
or two (it is her first entry), replaced 'Joanna' at the end of the line.

60. *in my conscience*] A stock phrase; 'on my word', 'truly'.

63. *Greece . . . Turk*] As Sampson points out, Greece at this time, and
for long afterwards, was part of the Turkish Empire.

Bea. Which of the sciences is this love you speak of?   65
Als. From your tongue I take it to be music.
Bea. You are skilful in't, can sing at first sight.
Als. And I have show'd you all my skill at once.
    I want more words to express me further,
    And must be forc'd to repetition: 70
    I love you dearly.
Bea.   Be better advis'd, sir:
    Our eyes are sentinels unto our judgments,
    And should give certain judgment what they see;
    But they are rash sometimes, and tell us wonders
    Of common things, which when our judgments find,   75
    They can then check the eyes, and call them blind.
Als. But I am further, lady; yesterday
    Was mine eyes' employment, and hither now
    They brought my judgment, where are both agreed.
    Both houses then consenting, 'tis agreed;   80
    Only there wants the confirmation
    By the hand royal, that's your part, lady.
Bea. Oh, there's one above me, sir. [*Aside.*] For five days past
    To be recall'd! Sure, mine eyes were mistaken,
    This was the man was meant me; that he should come   85
    So near his time, and miss it!
Jas. [*aside.*] We might have come by the carriers from Valencia,

83. *Aside.*] *Dilke.*   87. *aside.*] *Dilke.*

---

67. *sing at first sight*] He can sight-read this music immediately. Cf.
A Cure for a Cuckold, II. iii. 87–8 (Webster, III, 49), and *Troil.*, v. ii. 9:
'She will sing any man at first sight.'

80–2.] The bill having been approved by both houses of Parliament
('eyes' and 'judgment'), only the king's signature is needed for it to become law.

83. *one above me*] Her father, according to Spencer; but she may be
thinking of God, to whom even kings are responsible.

five days past] Presumably Beatrice was betrothed to Alonzo five days
ago, though there is nothing as definite as this in Reynolds.

85. *the man was meant me*] Cf. Reynolds, p. 116: '. . . although shee were
not yet acquainted with *Alsemero*, yet shee made it the thirteenth article of
her Creede, that the supreme power had ordained her another husband,
and not *Piracquo* . . .'

I see, and sav'd all our sea-provision: we are at farthest
sure. Methinks I should do something too;
I meant to be a venturer in this voyage.   90
Yonder's another vessel, I'll board her,
If she be lawful prize, down goes her top-sail.

> [*Greets* DIAPHANTA.]

Enter DE FLORES.

De F. Lady, your father—
Bea.   Is in health, I hope.
De F. Your eye shall instantly instruct you, lady.
He's coming hitherward.
Bea.   What needed then   95
Your duteous preface? I had rather
He had come unexpected; you must stall
A good presence with unnecessary blabbing:
And how welcome for your part you are,
I'm sure you know.
De F. [*aside.*]   Will't never mend this scorn   100
One side nor other? Must I be enjoin'd
To follow still whilst she flies from me? Well,
Fates do your worst, I'll please myself with sight
Of her, at all opportunities,
If but to spite her anger; I know she had   105

92.1. *Greets Diaphanta.*] *Dyce.*   97. stall] *Q, Neilson;* stale *Dilke,*
Dyce.   100. *aside.*] *Dilke.*   100. Will't] *Dilke, Dyce;* Wilt *Q.*

91–2.] 'She' is obviously Diaphanta. For the nautical metaphor cf.
Oth., I. ii. 50–1, and Day's *Humour out of Breath*, II. i:
Boy. . . . Board her.
Asp. But how? the meanes?
Boy. Make but a shotte of flattery at hir broad side, and sheele strike
saile presently.
(*Works*, ed. Bullen, 1881, III, 25). The lowered sail indicates surrender.
97. *stall*] Several editors emend to 'stale'—'make flat, deprive of zest'
(Bullen). But 'stall' could be, as Dilke suggests, a contraction of 'forestall', or it could mean 'satiate, surfeit with' (*O.E.D.* vb. 12). 'Forestall'
seems the more likely meaning.
98. *A good presence*] That of her father, whose dignity is lessened for her
by De Flores' 'blabbing'.

Rather see me dead than living, and yet
She knows no cause for't, but a peevish will.

Als. You seem'd displeas'd, lady, on the sudden.

Bea. Your pardon, sir, 'tis my infirmity,
Nor can I other reason render you,   110
Than his or hers, of some particular thing
They must abandon as a deadly poison,
Which to a thousand other tastes were wholesome;
Such to mine eyes is that same fellow there,
The same that report speaks of the basilisk.   115

Als. This is a frequent frailty in our nature;
There's scarce a man amongst a thousand sound,
But hath his imperfection: one distastes
The scent of roses, which to infinites
Most pleasing is, and odoriferous;   120
One oil, the enemy of poison;
Another wine, the cheerer of the heart,
And lively refresher of the countenance.
Indeed this fault (if so it be) is general,
There's scarce a thing but is both lov'd and loath'd: 125
Myself (I must confess) have the same frailty.

Bea. And what may be your poison, sir? I am bold with you.

Als. What might be your desire, perhaps, a cherry.

Bea. I am no enemy to any creature

111. of] *All eds.;* or *Q.*   117. sound] *Q;* found *All eds.*   128. What . . .
cherry.] *Dilke, Dyce;* And what . . . cherry. *Q;* And what might be your
desire? perhaps, a cherry. *Brooke.*

109ff.] Cf. *Mer. V.*, IV. i. 40–62.

115. *basilisk*] A fabulous beast that could kill by a glance, discussed by
Sir Thomas Browne, *Vulgar Errors*, Bk. III, Ch. vii (*Works*, ed. Keynes,
1928, II, 199ff).

117. *sound*] All editors read 'found', even though the long 's' of Q is quite
distinct and makes perfect sense: 'there's hardly a man in a thousand sound
people who has not some imperfection'.

119. *infinites*] See G. Rowley uses the word twice in *All's Lost by Lust*,
I. ii. 13, 18 (ed. Stork, 1910, pp. 87–8).

128.] Dilke's version of the line seems better than Brooke's; Alsemero
would hardly answer a question from Beatrice with another question.
Presumably 'And what' is an accidental repetition of the beginning of l. 127.

My memory has, but yon gentleman.   130

Als. He does ill to tempt your sight, if he knew it.

Bea. He cannot be ignorant of that, sir,
    I have not spar'd to tell him so; and I want
    To help myself, since he's a gentleman
    In good respect with my father, and follows him.   135

Als. He's out of his place then now.   [*They talk apart.*]

Jas. I am a mad wag, wench.

Dia. So methinks; but for your comfort I can tell you, we
    have a doctor in the city that undertakes the cure of such.

Jas. Tush, I know what physic is best for the state of mine   140
    own body.

Dia. 'Tis scarce a well-govern'd state, I believe.

Jas. I could show thee such a thing with an ingredient that
    we two would compound together, and if it did not tame
    the maddest blood i' th' town for two hours after, I'll   145
    ne'er profess physic again.

Dia. A little poppy, sir, were good to cause you sleep.

Jas. Poppy! I'll give thee a pop i' th' lips for that first, and
    begin there: [*kisses her*] poppy is one simple indeed, and
    cuckoo (what you call't) another: I'll discover no more   150
    now, another time I'll show thee all.

Bea. My father, sir.

136. *They . . . apart.*] Dilke.   149. *kisses her*] *This ed.*   151.] *Q; Exit
Jasperino. Dyce.*

133–5. *I want . . . him.*] i.e. I am unable to do anything about it because
my father likes and employs him.

139. *a doctor*] Alibius.

150. *cuckoo (what you call't)*] This obscure phrase is perhaps explained by
Rowley's *All's Lost by Lust*, III. iii. 103–8:
    . . . what sallet do you thinke she long'd for tother day ?
Ant. I know not:
Iaq. For a what doe call'um ? those long upright things that grow a yard
    above the ground; oh Cuckow pintle roots, but I got her belly full
    at last.
(ed. Stork, 126). Cuckoo pintle-root is the wild or common arum, *Arum
maculatum*, or wake-robin. There is another reference to the plant in
Lyly's *Love's Metamorphosis*, I. ii. 18–19 (*Works*, ed. Bond, 1902, III, 303).

151.] Dyce's exit for Jasperino is surely unnecessary; he breaks off because of the approach of Vermandero, but remains on the stage.

Enter VERMANDERO *and Servants.*

Ver. Oh, Joanna, I came to meet thee,
  Your devotion's ended?

Bea.   For this time, sir.
  [*Aside.*] I shall change my saint, I fear me, I find   155
  A giddy turning in me; [*to Ver.*] sir, this while
  I am beholding to this gentleman,
  Who left his own way to keep me company,
  And in discourse I find him much desirous
  To see your castle: he hath deserv'd it, sir,   160
  If ye please to grant it.

Ver.   With all my heart, sir.
  Yet there's an article between, I must know
  Your country; we use not to give survey
  Of our chief strengths to strangers; our citadels
  Are plac'd conspicuous to outward view,   165
  On promonts' tops; but within are secrets.

Als. A Valencian, sir.

Ver.   A Valencian?
  That's native, sir; of what name, I beseech you?

Als. Alsemero, sir.

Ver.   Alsemero; not the son
  Of John de Alsemero?

Als.   The same, sir.   170

Ver. My best love bids you welcome.

Bea. [*aside.*]   He was wont
  To call me so, and then he speaks a most
  Unfeigned truth.

Ver.   Oh, sir, I knew your father;

155. *Aside.*] Dilke. 171. *aside.*] Brooke.

---

162. *an article between*] A term or condition that must first be satisfied.
 167.] The biographical details from here to l. 186 are all derived from
Reynolds, except that in Reynolds there is no suggestion that Vermandero
knew Alsemero's father.
 171-3.] i.e. Vermandero used to refer to his daughter Beatrice as 'my
best love', and if, in using the phrase now, he means that Beatrice bids
Alsemero welcome, he is certainly speaking the truth.

We two were in acquaintance long ago,
Before our chins were worth Iulan down,   175
And so continued till the stamp of time
Had coin'd us into silver: well, he's gone,
A good soldier went with him.

Als. You went together in that, sir.

Ver. No, by Saint Jacques, I came behind him.   180
Yet I have done somewhat too; an unhappy day
Swallowed him at last at Gibraltar
In fight with those rebellious Hollanders,
Was it not so?

Als.   Whose death I had reveng'd,
Or followed him in fate, had not the late league   185
Prevented me.

175. Iulan] *Dyce, Bullen;* Julan *Q;* the Julan *Dilke.*

---

175. *Iulan down*] i.e. Before our beards began to grow. 'Iulan' is tri-syllabic and its use here with this meaning appears to be unique. Dilke sees in the word a reference to the emperor Julian the Apostate, whose apostasy 'gave such offence to the people of Antioch, that during the Saturnalia his manners, religion, and even *beard*, were the universal subjects of lampoons and satirical ballads'. This, however, is rather far-fetched; it is more likely that Rowley knew of the young hero Iulus Ascanius in the *Aeneid* (I, 267), as Sampson suggests, and had read in a commentary (e.g. Servius) that his first name was possibly derived from the Greek ἴουλος, 'the first growth of the beard'. Rowley may, of course, have coined the word straight from the Greek, though this is not very probable. There is a similar allusion in Swift's *On Poetry: A Rhapsody*, ll. 429–32:

> Our eldest Hope, divine *Iulus*,
> (Late, very late, O, may he rule us.)
> What early Manhood has he shown,
> Before his downy Beard was grown!
>   (*Poems*, ed. Williams, 1937, II, 655).

180. *Saint Jacques*] St James the Greater, the Patron Saint of Spain. His shrine is at Compostella.

181–4.] Cf. Reynolds, p. 106: '. . . whose father, *Don Iuan de Alsemero*, beeing slayne by the Hollanders in the Sea-fight at *Gibralter*, he resolued to addict himselfe to Nauall & sea actions, thereby to make himselfe capeable to reuenge his fathers death . . .' The battle of Gibraltar, in which the Dutch fleet gained a decisive victory over a larger Spanish fleet, took place on 25 April 1607.

185. *the late league*] The treaty of the Hague was signed on 9 April 1609, and provided, among other things, for a truce of hostilities between Spain and the Netherlands lasting twelve years.

Ver.   Ay, ay, 'twas time to breathe:
            Oh, Joanna, I should ha' told thee news,
            I saw Piracquo lately.
Bea. [*aside.*]   That's ill news.
Ver. He's hot preparing for this day of triumph,
            Thou must be a bride within this sevennight.
Als. [*aside.*]   Ha!   190
Bea. Nay, good sir, be not so violent, with speed
            I cannot render satisfaction
            Unto the dear companion of my soul,
            Virginity, whom I thus long have liv'd with,
            And part with it so rude and suddenly;   195
            Can such friends divide, never to meet again,
            Without a solemn farewell?
Ver.   Tush, tush, there's a toy.
Als. [*aside.*] I must now part, and never meet again
            With any joy on earth; [*to Ver.*] sir, your pardon,
            My affairs call on me.
Ver.   How, sir? By no means;   200
            Not chang'd so soon, I hope? You must see my castle,
            And her best entertainment, ere we part,
            I shall think myself unkindly us'd else.
            Come, come, let's on, I had good hope your stay
            Had been a while with us in Alicant;   205
            I might have bid you to my daughter's wedding
Als. [*aside.*] He means to feast me, and poisons me
                beforehand;
            [*To Ver.*] I should be dearly glad to be there, sir,
            Did my occasions suit as I could wish.
Bea. I shall be sorry if you be not there   210
            When it is done, sir; —but not so suddenly.
Ver. I tell you, sir, the gentleman's complete,
            A courtier and a gallant, enrich'd
            With many fair and noble ornaments;

188. *aside.*] *Dilke.*   189. this] *Q, Dilke, Dyce;* his *Schelling* (*conj.*
Dyce).   190. *aside.*] *Dyce.*   198. *aside.*] *Dyce.*   205. Alicant] *Dilke;*
Alligant *Q.*   207. *aside.*] *Dilke.*

I would not change him for a son-in-law   215
For any he in Spain, the proudest he,
And we have great ones, that you know.
Als.   He's much
Bound to you, sir.
Ver.   He shall be bound to me,
As fast as this tie can hold him; I'll want
My will else.
Bea. [*aside.*]   I shall want mine if you do it.   220
Ver. But come, by the way I'll tell you more of him.
Als. [*aside.*] How shall I dare to venture in his castle,
When he discharges murderers at the gate?
But I must on, for back I cannot go.   224
Bea. [*aside.*] Not this serpent gone yet?   [*Drops a glove.*]
Ver.   Look, girl, thy glove's fall'n;
Stay, stay,—De Flores, help a little.
        [*Exeunt* VERMANDERO, ALSEMERO, JASPERINO, *and Servants.*]
De F.   Here, lady. [*Offers the glove.*]
Bea. Mischief on your officious forwardness!
Who bade you stoop? They touch my hand no more:
There, for t'other's sake I part with this,
                [*Takes off the other glove and throws it down.*]
Take 'em and draw thine own skin off with 'em.   230
                        Exeunt [BEATRICE *and* DIAPHANTA.]
De F. Here's a favour come, with a mischief! Now I know

---

220. *aside.*] Dilke.   222. *aside.*] Dyce.   225. *aside.*] Dyce.   225.
Drops...glove.] Dyce.   226.1. *Exeunt...Servants.*] Dyce.   226. *Offers
...glove.*] Dyce.   229.1. *Takes...down.*] Dyce.   230.1. *Beatrice
...Diaphanta.*] Brooke.

---

223. *murderers*] See G. A striking example of dramatic irony.

224.] Cf. the ill-fated Frank Thorney in *The Witch of Edmonton*, I. ii:
'But on I must: / Fate leads me: I will follow' (Dekker, IV, 364).

225.] The audience is probably intended to regard the dropping of the
glove as an accident, though Beatrice may have dropped it deliberately for
Alsemero to pick up and return to her. There is nothing to correspond to
this striking incident in Reynolds.

231. *Now I know*] i.e. Although, even though I know. It is not an adverb
of time; De Flores has known it for a long time.

She had rather wear my pelt tann'd in a pair
Of dancing pumps, than I should thrust my fingers
Into her sockets here, I know she hates me,
Yet cannot choose but love her: 235
No matter, if but to vex her, I'll haunt her still;
Though I get nothing else, I'll have my will.   *Exit.*

[I. ii]

Enter ALIBIUS *and* LOLLIO.

Alib. Lollio, I must trust thee with a secret,
       But thou must keep it.
Lol. I was ever close to a secret, sir.
Alib. The diligence that I have found in thee,
       The care and industry already past,   5
       Assures me of thy good continuance.
       Lollio, I have a wife.
Lol. Fie, sir, 'tis too late to keep her secret, she's known to be
       married all the town and country over.
Alib. Thou goest too fast, my Lollio, that knowledge   10
       I allow no man can be barr'd it;
       But there is a knowledge which is nearer,
       Deeper and sweeter, Lollio.
Lol. Well, sir, let us handle that between you and I.
Alib. 'Tis that I go about, man; Lollio,   15
       My wife is young.
Lol. So much the worse to be kept secret, sir.
Alib. Why, now thou meet'st the substance of the point:
       I am old, Lollio.
Lol. No, sir, 'tis I am old Lollio.   20
Alib. Yet why may not this concord and sympathise?
       Old trees and young plants often grow together,
       Well enough agreeing.
Lol. Ay, sir, but the old trees raise themselves higher and
       broader than the young plants.   25

I. ii. 6. Assures] *Q, Dilke, Bullen;* Assure *Dyce.*   21. this] *Q, Neilson;*
these *Dilke, Dyce.*

Alib. Shrewd application! There's the fear, man;
    I would wear my ring on my own finger;
    Whilst it is borrowed it is none of mine,
    But his that useth it.

Lol. You must keep it on still then; if it but lie by, one or other   30
    will be thrusting into't.

Alib. Thou conceiv'st me, Lollio; here thy watchful eye
    Must have employment, I cannot always be
    At home.

Lol. I dare swear you cannot.   35

Alib. I must look out.

Lol. I know't, you must look out, 'tis every man's case.

Alib. Here I do say must thy employment be,
    To watch her treadings, and in my absence
    Supply my place.   40

Lol. I'll do my best, sir, yet surely I cannot see who you should
    have cause to be jealous of.

Alib. Thy reason for that, Lollio? 'Tis a comfortable question.

Lol. We have but two sorts of people in the house, and both
    under the whip, that's fools and madmen; the one has not   45
    wit enough to be knaves, and the other not knavery
    enough to be fools.

Alib. Ay, those are all my patients, Lollio.
    I do profess the cure of either sort:
    My trade, my living 'tis, I thrive by it;   50
    But here's the care that mixes with my thrift:
    The daily visitants, that come to see

---

26. *Shrewd application*] 'The "shrewd application" meant is, I conceive, to that perpetual jest of the age, the cuckold's horns; which Lollio
supposes might raise Alibius's head above his wife's' (Dilke).

27. *wear my ring*] Cf. Middleton's *The Family of Love*, v. iii. 418–21:
'. . . be it proclaimed to all that are jealous, to wear their wife's ring still
on their fingers, as best for their security, and the only charm against
cuckoldry' (Bullen, III, 118). The point of the phrase is made very clear in
an anecdote, 'Of the iolous man', xviii of *Mery Tales and Quicke Answers* (in
Shakespeare Jest-Books, ed. W. C. Hazlitt, 1864, I, 28), and see also the
story of Hans Carvel's ring in Rabelais' *Pantagruel, Le Tiers Livre*, Ch.
XXVIII (ed. Marty-Laveaux, Paris, 1870, II, 141–2).

52. *daily visitants*] Bethlehem Hospital (the 'Bedlam' of the 17th cen-

        My brainsick patients, I would not have
        To see my wife: gallants I do observe
        Of quick enticing eyes, rich in habits,   55
        Of stature and proportion very comely:
        These are most shrewd temptations, Lollio.

Lol. They may be easily answered, sir; if they come to see the
        fools and madmen, you and I may serve the turn, and let
        my mistress alone, she's of neither sort.   60

Alib. 'Tis a good ward; indeed, come they to see
        Our madmen or our fools, let 'em see no more
        Than what they come for; by that consequent
        They must not see her, I'm sure she's no fool.

Lol. And I'm sure she's no madman.   65

Alib. Hold that buckler fast, Lollio; my trust
        Is on thee, and I account it firm and strong.
        What hour is't, Lollio?

Lol. Towards belly-hour, sir.

Alib. Dinner time? Thou mean'st twelve o'clock.   70

61. indeed,] *Dyce;* indeed *Q, Dilke.*

---

tury) was regarded as a place of entertainment by the citizens of London,
who went to it to be amused by the antics of the inmates. The usual attitude
is clearly shown in *Northward Ho*, IV. iii. 27–36:

  Bel. . . . what place is this?
  May. Bedlam ist not?
  Bell. Where the mad-men are, I neuer was amongst them, as you loue
    me Gentlemen, lets see what Greekes are within.
  Green. Wee shall stay too long.
  Bell. Not a whit, *Ware* will stay for our comming I warrant you: come
    a spurt and away, lets bee mad once in our dayes: this is the doore.
                Enter Full-moone.
  May. Saue you sir, may we see some a your mad-folkes, doe you keepe
    em?

(Dekker, III, 56–7). They are then shown a selection of the inmates.

  69–70. *belly-hour . . . twelve o'clock.*] Cf. Rowley's *A Shoemaker a Gentle-man*, I. ii. 182–5:

  Shoo. Whats a clocke Barnaby?
  Bar. The chimes of my belly has gone, it should be past twelve.
  Shoo. Provide dinner Sis.

(ed. Stork, 1910, p. 183). This parallel suggests Rowley's presence, though
the phrase is fairly common; cf. Heywood's *The English Traveller*, I. i:
'I know not how the day goes with you, but my stomacke hath strucke

Lol. Yes, sir, for every part has his hour: we wake at six and
  look about us, that's eye-hour; at seven we should pray,
  that's knee-hour; at eight walk, that's leg-hour; at nine
  gather flowers and pluck a rose, that's nose-hour; at ten
  we drink, that's mouth-hour; at eleven lay about us for   75
  victuals, that's hand-hour; at twelve go to dinner, that's
  belly-hour.

Alib. Profoundly, Lollio! It will be long
  Ere all thy scholars learn this lesson, and
  I did look to have a new one entered; —stay,   80
  I think my expectation is come home.

             Enter PEDRO, *and* ANTONIO *like an idiot.*

Ped. Save you, sir; my business speaks itself,
  This sight takes off the labour of my tongue.

Alib. Ay, ay, sir;
  'Tis plain enough, you mean him for my patient.   85

Ped. And if your pains prove but commodious, to give but
  some little strength to his sick and weak part of nature in
  him, these are [*gives money*] but patterns to show you of
  the whole pieces that will follow to you, beside the charge
  of diet, washing, and other necessaries fully defrayed.   90

Alib. Believe it, sir, there shall no care be wanting.

Lol. Sir, an officer in this place may deserve something; the
  trouble will pass through my hands.

Ped. 'Tis fit something should come to your hands then, sir.
                                         [*Gives him money.*]

87. his] *Q, Neilson;* the *Dilke, Dyce.*   88. *gives money*] *Dilke.*   94.1.
Gives . . . money.] *Dilke.*

---

twelue' (*Dramatic Works*, 1874, IV, 13) and *Appius and Virginia*, IV. ii. 11–
12 (Webster, III, 208).

  74. *pluck a rose*] Pass water. Cf. *The Knight of the Burning Pestle*, II. iv. 8
(Fletcher, VI, 184).

  81.1.] For a description of what may have been Antonio's costume, see
Introduction, p. xxx.

  89. *charge*] For proof that it was normal to pay money on behalf of new
inmates of Bethlehem Hospital, see the quotation from Stow's *A Survey of
London* in the Introduction, p. xxxvii, n. 1.

Lol. Yes, sir, 'tis I must keep him sweet, and read to him; what   95
    is his name?

Ped. His name is Antonio; marry, we use but half to him, only
    Tony.

Lol. Tony, Tony, 'tis enough, and a very good name for a
    fool; what's your name, Tony?   100

Ant. He, he, he! well, I thank you, cousin; he, he, he!

Lol. Good boy! Hold up your head: he can laugh, I perceive
    by that he is no beast.

Ped. Well, sir,
    If you can raise him but to any height,   105
    Any degree of wit, might he attain
    (As I might say) to creep but on all four
    Towards the chair of wit, or walk on crutches,
    'Twould add an honour to your worthy pains,
    And a great family might pray for you,   110
    To which he should be heir, had he discretion
    To claim and guide his own; assure you, sir,
    He is a gentleman.

---

98. *Tony*] In the later 17th century 'Tony' was sometimes used to mean
'fool', as in Dryden's *All For Love*, Prologue, 15 (*Works*, ed. Scott-Saints-
bury, 1883, v, 340) and Wycherley, *The Plain Dealer*, III. i (*Works*. ed.
Summers, 1924, II, 148), and *O.E.D.* suggests that this usage derives from
Antonio in *The Changeling*. Edmund Gayton uses the word in his *Pleasant
Notes Upon Don Quixot* (1654), pp. 140–1: 'Many have by representation of
strong passions been so transported, that they have gone weeping, some
from Tragedies, some from Comedies; so merry, lightsome and free, that
they have not been sober in a week after, and have so courted the Players to
re-act the same matters in the Tavernes, that they came home, as able
Actors as themselves; so that their Friends and VVives have took them
for Tonies or Mad-men'. Possibly Gayton has *The Changeling* definitely in mind; cf. his comment on the play quoted in the Introduction,
p. xxviii.

    102–3. *laugh . . . no beast.*] Cf. Addison, *The Spectator*, No. 494, 26 Sep-
tember 1712: 'If we may believe our logicians, man is distinguished from all
other creatures by the faculty of laughter' (*Works*, 1721, III, 611). The doctrine appears to go back to Aristotle, *De Partibus Animalium*, III, 10 (ed.
Ogle, 1882, p. 84).

    113. *a gentleman*] Cf. *Northward Ho*, IV. iii. 143–4: 'hee's a Gentleman of
a very good house, you shall bee paid well if you conuert him' (Dekker,
III, 61).

Lol. Nay, there's nobody doubted that; at first sight I knew
    him for a gentleman, he looks no other yet.   115

Ped. Let him have good attendance and sweet lodging.

Lol. As good as my mistress lies in, sir; and as you allow us
    time and means, we can raise him to the higher degree of
    discretion.

Ped. Nay, there shall no cost want, sir.   120

Lol. He will hardly be stretch'd up to the wit of a magnifico.

Ped. Oh no, that's not to be expected, far shorter will be
    enough.

Lol. I'll warrant you I make him fit to bear office in five
    weeks; I'll undertake to wind him up to the wit of   125
    constable.

Ped. If it be lower than that it might serve turn.

Lol. No, fie, to level him with a headborough, beadle, or
    watchman were but little better than he is; constable I'll
    able him: if he do come to be a justice afterwards, let him   130
    thank the keeper. Or I'll go further with you; say I do
    bring him up to my own pitch, say I make him as wise as
    myself.

Ped. Why, there I would have it.

Lol. Well, go to, either I'll be as arrant a fool as he, or he shall   135
    be as wise as I, and then I think 'twill serve his turn.

Ped. Nay, I do like thy wit passing well.

Lol. Yes, you may, yet if I had not been a fool, I had had more

124. you I] *This ed.;* you *Q, Dilke;* you I'll *Dyce.*

114-15.] Does this mean that Lollio sees through Antonio's disguise at
the very beginning?

125-6. *wit of constable*] As Dogberry shows, the constable was a figure of
fun on the Elizabethan stage, and was notorious for his stupidity. Cf.
Middleton's *A Mad World, My Masters,* v. ii. 86-7: 'This is some new
player now; they put all their fools to the constable's part still' (Bullen, III,
349) and *Every Man out of his Humour,* I. ii. 15-17 (Jonson, III, 444). The
title of Glapthorne's play, *Wit in a Constable,* is meant to be a kind of
paradox.

130. *justice*] Justices Silence and Shallow prove that the reputation of the
justice was little higher than that of the constable. All these references by
Lollio are intended ironically.

wit than I have too; remember what state you find me in.

Ped. I will, and so leave you: your best cares, I beseech you.   140

Alib. Take you none with you, leave 'em all with us.   *Exit* PEDRO.

Ant. Oh, my cousin's gone, cousin, cousin, oh!

Lol. Peace, peace, Tony, you must not cry, child, you must be
whipt if you do; your cousin is here still, I am your
cousin, Tony.   145

Ant. He, he, then I'll not cry, if thou be'st my cousin, he, he,
he.

Lol. I were best try his wit a little, that I may know what form
to place him in.

Alib. Ay, do, Lollio, do.   150

Lol. I must ask him easy questions at first; Tony, how many
true fingers has a tailor on his right hand?

Ant. As many as on his left, cousin.

Lol. Good; and how many on both?

Ant. Two less than a deuce, cousin.   155

Lol. Very well answered; I come to you again, cousin Tony:
how many fools goes to a wise man?

Ant. Forty in a day sometimes, cousin.

Lol. Forty in a day? How prove you that?

---

141. *Exit Pedro.*] *Dyce; after l. 140 in Q, Dilke.*

---

139. *state*] 'i.e. As a keeper of fools and madmen' (Dilke).

148. *try his wit*] In *Northward Ho*, IV. iii. 177–9, Full-moon tests the
intelligence of a suspected madman by setting him problems: 'Ile trie that,
answer me to this question: loose his armes a little, looke you sir, three
Geese nine pence; euery Goose three pence, whats that a Goose, roundly,
roundly, one with another' (Dekker, III, 62). Both dramatists are obviously
making fun of the practice.

152. *true*] See G. Tailors had a proverbial reputation for dishonesty; cf.
Chapman's *May-Day*, II. i. 569–73:

    Inn. How make you this in Latin, boy, 'My father is an honest tail-
        or'?

    Boy. That will hardly be done in true Latin, sir.

    Inn. No? Why so, sir?

    Boy. Because it is false English, sir.   (Chapman, *Comedies*, 190).

155.] i.e. None at all.

157. *goes to*] A Rowley pun: (i) make up, constitute; (ii) visit. Lollio
intends the word in the first sense, Antonio takes it in the second.

Ant. All that fall out amongst themselves, and go to a lawyer   160
    to be made friends.

Lol. A parlous fool! He must sit in the fourth form at least, I
    perceive that; I come again, Tony: how many knaves
    make an honest man?

Ant. I know not that, cousin.   165

Lol. No, the question is too hard for you: I'll tell you, cousin,
    there's three knaves may make an honest man, a sergeant,
    a jailor, and a beadle; the sergeant catches him, the jailor
    holds him, and the beadle lashes him; and if he be not
    honest then, the hangman must cure him.   170

Ant. Ha, ha, ha, that's fine sport, cousin!

Alib. This was too deep a question for the fool, Lollio.

Lol. Yes, this might have serv'd yourself, though I say't;
    once more, and you shall go play, Tony.

Ant. Ay, play at push-pin, cousin, ha, he!   175

Lol. So thou shalt; say how many fools are here—

Ant. Two, cousin, thou and I.

Lol. Nay, y'are too forward there, Tony; mark my ques-
    tion: how many fools and knaves are here? A fool before
    a knave, a fool behind a knave, between every two fools   180
    a knave; how many fools, how many knaves?

Ant. I never learnt so far, cousin.

Alib. Thou putt'st too hard questions to him, Lollio.

Lol. I'll make him understand it easily; cousin, stand there.

Ant. Ay, cousin.   185

Lol. Master, stand you next the fool.

Alib. Well, Lollio?

---

169. *the beadle lashes him*] There is an example of the beadle lashing a
man to make him honest in *2 H 6*, II. i. 135–53.

175. *push-pin*] 'Push-pin is a very silly sport, being nothing more than
simply pushing one pin across another', J. Strutt, *The Sports and Pastimes
of the People of England*, ed. J. C. Cox (1903), p. 311. The references to
push-pin in such plays as *Women Pleased*, II. iv (Fletcher, VII, 252), suggest however that the game Antonio wishes to play is not quite so innocent.

184ff.] Antonio, Alibius, and Lollio stand in a row, Alibius being the
knave between two fools. The others, of course, are really the knaves who
are trying to make a fool of Alibius.

Lol. Here's my place: mark now, Tony, there a fool before
　　a knave.

Ant. That's I, cousin.　　　　　　　　　　　　　　　190

Lol. Here's a fool behind a knave, that's I, and between us
　　two fools there is a knave, that's my master; 'tis but we
　　three, that's all.

Ant. We three, we three, cousin!　　　　*Madmen within.*

1 Within. Put's head i' th' pillory, the bread's too little.　　195

2 Within. Fly, fly, and he catches the swallow.

3 Within. Give her more onion, or the devil put the rope
　　about her crag.

Lol. You may hear what time of day it is, the chimes of Bed-
　　lam goes.　　　　　　　　　　　　　　　　　200

Alib. Peace, peace, or the wire comes!

3 Within. Cat-whore, cat-whore, her permasant, her perma-
　　sant!

Alib. Peace, I say; their hour's come, they must be fed,
　　Lollio.　　　　　　　　　　　　　　　　　205

Lol. There's no hope of recovery of that Welsh madman, was

188. there] *Q, Baskervill;* there's *Dilke, Dyce.*

192–4. *we three*] 'Alluding to the humorous picture of the two boobies,
with the inscription "We three, Loggerheads be", the spectator being of
course the third—or to games or jests of a similar nature', R. B. McKerrow,
note to Nashe's *Have with You to Saffron Walden* (*Works,* ed. McKerrow,
1904–10, IV, 359). Cf. *Tw. N.,* II. iii. 16–17.

195–8.] These lines probably meant more to a Jacobean audience than
they do to a 20th-century reader, though it hardly seems necessary to dis-
cuss them at length. The 'rope' of l. 197 is both a hangman's rope and a
rope of onions.

198. *crag*] See G.

199–200. *chimes of Bedlam*] The cries of the inmates for food; see above,
note on ll. 69–70.

202. *Cat-whore*] Apparently the Welsh madman is reviling his cat for
failing to protect his Parmesan cheese.

her] Sampson points out that 'her' is stage-Welsh for 'my'; cf. Nashe's
Summer's Last Will and Testament, ll. 342–6 (*Works,* ed. McKerrow,
III, 244).

206–8.] The fondness of the Welsh for cheese was proverbial in Elizabethan England; cf. *The Devil's Law Case,* v. iv. 20–7 (Webster, II, 311)
where 'Parma cheese' is mentioned, and the Welsh madman in *The Pilgrim,*
IV. iii: 'He run mad because a Rat eat up's Cheese' (Fletcher, v, 211).

undone by a mouse, that spoil'd him a permasant; lost
his wits for't.

Alib. Go to your charge, Lollio, I'll to mine.

Lol. Go you to your madmen's ward, let me alone with your   210
fools.

Alib. And remember my last charge, Lollio.   *Exit.*

Lol. Of which your patients do you think I am ? Come, Tony,
you must amongst your school-fellows now; there's
pretty scholars amongst 'em, I can tell you, there's some   215
of 'em at *stultus, stulta, stultum.*

Ant. I would see the madmen, cousin, if they would not bite
me.

Lol. No, they shall not bite thee, Tony.

Ant. They bite when they are at dinner, do they not, coz ?   220

Lol. They bite at dinner indeed, Tony. Well, I hope to get
credit by thee, I like thee the best of all the scholars that
ever I brought up, and thou shalt prove a wise man, or
I'll prove a fool myself.   *Exeunt.*

212.] Alibius is reminding Lollio to keep watch on Isabella (see ll. 32–40
above).

215–16.] i.e. They are able to decline the Latin word for 'foolish'.

Act II

Enter BEATRICE *and* JASPERINO *severally.*

Bea. Oh sir, I'm ready now for that fair service,
 Which makes the name of friend sit glorious on you.
 Good angels and this conduct be your guide, [*Gives a paper.*]
 Fitness of time and place is there set down, sir.
Jas. The joy I shall return rewards my service.   *Exit.* 5
Bea. How wise is Alsemero in his friend!
 It is a sign he makes his choice with judgment.
 Then I appear in nothing more approv'd,
 Than making choice of him;
 For 'tis a principle, he that can choose   10
 That bosom well, who of his thoughts partakes,
 Proves most discreet in every choice he makes.
 Methinks I love now with the eyes of judgment,
 And see the way to merit, clearly see it.
 A true deserver like a diamond sparkles,   15

Act II] *Dilke, Dyce;* ACTUS SECUNDUS. *Q.* 3. *Gives a paper.*] *Dilke.*

1–4.] In Reynolds (p. 122), Beatrice summons Alsemero by means of a
letter. The rest of the scene owes little to Reynolds.
 13. *eyes of judgment*] 'Eyes of judgment' is something of a stock phrase;
cf. Middleton's *The Triumphs of Honour and Virtue*:
   You that have eyes of judgment, and discern
   Things that the best of man and life concern.
(Bullen, VII, 358) and *The Spanish Curate*, III. iii: '. . . and then with eyes of
Judgement / (Hood-wink'd with Lust before) . . .' (Fletcher, II, 101).
 15.] A favourite metaphor of Middleton's; cf. *Women Beware Women*,
v. i. 48–9:
   A goodness set in greatness; how it sparkles
   Afar off, like pure diamonds set in gold!
(Bullen, VI, 361) and *The Sun in Aries*:

In darkness you may see him, that's in absence,
Which is the greatest darkness falls on love;
Yet is he best discern'd then
With intellectual eyesight; what's Piracquo
My father spends his breath for? And his blessing   20
Is only mine, as I regard his name,
Else it goes from me, and turns head against me,
Transform'd into a curse: some speedy way
Must be remembered; he's so forward too,
So urgent that way, scarce allows me breath   25
To speak to my new comforts.

Enter DE FLORES.

De F. [*aside.*]   Yonder's she.
Whatever ails me, now a-late especially,
I can as well be hang'd as refrain seeing her;
Some twenty times a day, nay, not so little,
Do I force errands, frame ways and excuses   30

26. *aside.*] *Dyce.*

Diamonds will shine though set in lead; true worth
Stands always in least need of setting forth.
(Bullen, VII, 349).

16.] Diamonds were supposed to be luminous; cf. III. ii. 20–3 and *Tit.*,
II. iii. 226–30.

20. *his blessing*] Her father's: he will not bless her unless she marries well
and maintains the family reputation ('his name'). For the thought of
ll. 20–3 cf. Middleton's *A Game at Chess*, II. i. 106–9:
                    . . . yet presume not
          To make that curteous care a priuiledge
          For willfull disobedience, it turnes then
          Into the blacknes of a Curse uppon you.
(ed. Bald, 1929, p. 66) and Middleton and Rowley's *A Fair Quarrel*, III. ii.
52–6:
          Defend and keep me from a father's rage,
          Whose love yet infinite, not knowing this,
          Might, knowing, turn a hate as infinite;
          Sure, he would throw me ever from his blessings,
          And cast his curses on me!
(Bullen, IV, 217). As the second of these quotations is from what is generally
agreed to be Rowley's share of *A Fair Quarrel*, the similarity of the three
passages gives little guide to their authorship.

To come into her sight, and I have small reason for't,
And less encouragement; for she baits me still
Every time worse than other, does profess herself
The cruellest enemy to my face in town,
At no hand can abide the sight of me,   35
As if danger or ill luck hung in my looks.
I must confess my face is bad enough,
But I know far worse has better fortune,
And not endur'd alone, but doted on:
And yet such pick-hair'd faces, chins like witches',   40
Here and there five hairs, whispering in a corner,
As if they grew in fear one of another,
Wrinkles like troughs, where swine-deformity swills
The tears of perjury that lie there like wash
Fallen from the slimy and dishonest eye,—   45
Yet such a one pluck'd sweets without restraint,
And has the grace of beauty to his sweet.
Though my hard fate has thrust me out to servitude,
I tumbled into th'world a gentleman.
She turns her blessed eye upon me now,   50
And I'll endure all storms before I part with't.
Bea. [*aside.*] Again!
          —This ominous ill-fac'd fellow more disturbs me
          Than all my other passions.
De F. [*aside.*]   Now't begins again;
          I'll stand this storm of hail though the stones pelt me.   55
Bea. Thy business? What's thy business?
De F. [*aside.*]   Soft and fair,
          I cannot part so soon now.
Bea. [*aside.*]   The villain's fix'd—

46. pluck'd] *Q;* plucks *All eds.*   52. *aside.*] *Dyce.*   54. *aside.*] *Dyce.*
56. *aside.*] *Dilke.*   57. *aside.*] *Dyce.*

---

35. *At no hand*] By no means, on no account; cf. IV. ii. 53.
35-6.] Cf. II. i. 89-90 and v. iii. 154-7.
47. *to his sweet*] 'In his sweetheart's eyes' (Spencer).
56. *Soft and fair*] A common phrase (cf. *Ado,* v. iv. 72), linked to the proverb, 'Soft and fair goes far'.

    [*To De F.*] Thou standing toad-pool!
De F. [*aside.*]   The shower falls amain now.
Bea. Who sent thee ? What's thy errand ? Leave my sight.
De F. My lord your father charg'd me to deliver   60
    A message to you.
Bea.   What, another since ?
    Do't and be hang'd then, let me be rid of thee.
De F. True service merits mercy.
Bea.   What's thy message ?
De F. Let beauty settle but in patience,
    You shall hear all.
Bea.   A dallying, trifling torment!   65
De F. Signor Alonzo de Piracquo, lady,
    Sole brother to Tomazo de Piracquo—
Bea. Slave, when wilt make an end ?
De F. [*aside.*]   Too soon I shall.
Bea. What all this while of him ?
De F.   The said Alonzo,
    With the foresaid Tomazo—
Bea.   Yet again ?   70
De F. Is new alighted.
Bea.   Vengeance strike the news!
    Thou thing most loath'd, what cause was there in this

---

58. *aside.*] *Dilke.*   68. wilt] *All eds.;* wil't *Q.*   68. *aside.*] *This ed.*

---

   58. *standing toad-pool*] This extremely violent insult refers to the repulsive appearance of De Flores, who suffers presumably from some form of skin disease. Cf. *Bussy D'Ambois*, III. ii. 450–2:
                           . . . thy gall
      Turns all thy blood to poison, which is cause
      Of that toad-pool that stands in thy complexion.
(Chapman, *Tragedies*, 44) and Glapthorne's *The Hollander*, I. i:
            . . . a standing poole,
      On whose salt wombe the too lascivious sun
      Begets of Frogs and Toads a numerous off-spring,
      Compar'd with you is empty of corruption.
(*Plays*, 1874, I, 81).
   60–76.] De Flores tries to prolong the interview by using elaborately formal language, but succeeds only in exasperating Beatrice.
   61. *another since*] i.e. Yet another; cf. I. i. 93ff.

  To bring thee to my sight?

De F.   My lord your father

  Charg'd me to seek you out.

Bea.   Is there no other

  To send his errand by?

De F.   It seems 'tis my luck   75

  To be i' th'way still.

Bea.   Get thee from me.

De F. [*aside.*]   So;

  Why, am not I an ass to devise ways

  Thus to be rail'd at? I must see her still!

  I shall have a mad qualm within this hour again,

  I know't, and like a common Garden-bull,   80

  I do but take breath to be lugg'd again.

  What this may bode I know not; I'll despair the less,

  Because there's daily precedents of bad faces

  Belov'd beyond all reason; these foul chops

  May come into favour one day 'mongst his fellows: 85

  Wrangling has prov'd the mistress of good pastime;

  As children cry themselves asleep, I ha' seen

  Women have chid themselves abed to men. *Exit* DE FLORES.

Bea. I never see this fellow, but I think

  Of some harm towards me, danger's in my mind still;   90

  I scarce leave trembling of an hour after.

  The next good mood I find my father in,

  I'll get him quite discarded: oh, I was

  Lost in this small disturbance, and forgot

  Affliction's fiercer torrent that now comes   95

  To bear down all my comforts.

    Enter VERMANDERO, ALONZO, TOMAZO.

Ver.   Y'are both welcome,

---

76. *aside.*] *Dyce.*   85. his] *Q, Schelling;* their *Dilke, Dyce.*

---

 80. *common Garden-bull*] 'The allusion is to Paris Garden in Southwark where both bulls and bears were baited' (Dyce).

 91. *of*] i.e. For.

But an especial one belongs to you, sir,
To whose most noble name our love presents
The addition of a son, our son Alonzo.

Alon. The treasury of honour cannot bring forth   100
A title I should more rejoice in, sir.

Ver. You have improv'd it well; daughter, prepare,
The day will steal upon thee suddenly.

Bea. [*aside.*] Howe'er, I will be sure to keep the night,
If it should come so near me.

                  [BEATRICE *and* VERMANDERO *talk apart.*]

Tom.   Alonzo.

Alon.   Brother?   105

Tom. In troth I see small welcome in her eye.

Alon. Fie, you are too severe a censurer
Of love in all points, there's no bringing on you;
If lovers should mark everything a fault,
Affection would be like an ill-set book,   110
Whose faults might prove as big as half the volume.

Bea. That's all I do entreat.

Ver.   It is but reasonable;
I'll see what my son says to't: son Alonzo,
Here's a motion made but to reprieve
A maidenhead three days longer; the request   115
Is not far out of reason, for indeed
The former time is pinching.

Alon.   Though my joys
Be set back so much time as I could wish

---

104. *aside.*] *Dilke.*   105. *Beatrice . . . apart.*] *Dilke.*   108. you;] *Dilke;*
you *Q.*

---

104. *keep the night*] Schelling interprets this phrase simply as 'watch';
perhaps the implication is that Beatrice will not allow Alonzo to consum-
mate the marriage.

105ff.] In Reynolds, p. 126, Tomazo warns his brother of Beatrice's real
attitude by means of a letter.

108. *there's . . . you*] The most likely meaning seems to be, 'I cannot bring
you to a more reasonable point of view'; Sampson, however, interprets it as
'there's no making you concede anything'. We might also follow Q in link-
ing it with the next line: 'I cannot make you realize that if . . .'

They had been forward, yet since she desires it,
The time is set as pleasing as before,   120
I find no gladness wanting.

Ver. May I ever meet it in that point still:
Y'are nobly welcome, sirs.

Exeunt VERMANDERO *and* BEATRICE.

Tom. So; did you mark the dulness of her parting now?

Alon. What dulness? Thou art so exceptious still!   125

Tom. Why, let it go then, I am but a fool
To mark your harms so heedfully.

Alon.   Where's the oversight?

Tom. Come, your faith's cozened in her, strongly cozened;
Unsettle your affection with all speed
Wisdom can bring it to, your peace is ruin'd else.   130
Think what a torment 'tis to marry one
Whose heart is leap'd into another's bosom:
If ever pleasure she receive from thee,
It comes not in thy name, or of thy gift;
She lies but with another in thine arms,   135
He the half-father unto all thy children
In the conception; if he get 'em not,
She helps to get 'em for him, and how dangerous

---

138. him, and] *Dilke, Dyce;* him, in his passions, and *Q, Baskervill.*

---

133. *pleasure*] See G.

138.] It is not easy to explain Q's 'in his passions', which most editors
omit. Baskervill follows Q, with a footnote that 'his' are 'the husband's',
though this hardly accounts for the phrase, and it would be extremely difficult for the audience to understand it, as the 'he' and 'him' of ll. 136–8
plainly refer to the lover. Sampson has suggested that a stage-direction
telling Alonzo to become angry (cf. ll. 150–2) has crept into the text by
mistake, though Alonzo's manner seems to be complacent and assured
rather than angry. Sampson also suggests, less plausibly, that 'passions' is a
misprint for 'absence'. What we have here, however, may be a sign of
omission rather than of addition.

> She helps to get 'em for him, in his passions,
> . . . and how dangerous,
> And shameful her restraint may go in time to . . .

There may have been a phrase at the beginning of the second line which
gave point to 'in his passions' in the line before, but it is difficult to explain
how it came to be omitted, especially if we assume that the transcriber was

And shameful her restraint may go in time to,
It is not to be thought on without sufferings.   140
Alon. You speak as if she lov'd some other, then.
Tom. Do you apprehend so slowly ?
Alon.   Nay, and that
Be your fear only, I am safe enough.
Preserve your friendship and your counsel, brother,
For times of more distress; I should depart   145
An enemy, a dangerous, deadly one
To any but thyself, that should but think
She knew the meaning of inconstancy,
Much less the use and practice; yet w'are friends.
Pray let no more be urg'd; I can endure   150
Much, till I meet an injury to her,
Then I am not myself. Farewell, sweet brother,
How much w'are bound to heaven to depart lovingly.   *Exit.*
Tom. Why, here is love's tame madness; thus a man
Quickly steals into his vexation.   *Exit.*   155

[II. ii]

Enter DIAPHANTA *and* ALSEMERO.

Dia. The place is my charge, you have kept your hour,
And the reward of a just meeting bless you.
I hear my lady coming; complete gentleman,

149. w'are] *Q (corrected), Dyce, Bullen;* we are *Q (uncorrected), Dilke.*

---

working from prompt-copy. Possibly the words were marked in some
way (underlined, perhaps, or placed in brackets), so that the transcriber
wrongly assumed that they were intended to be omitted. The page of Q on
which this occurs, D1ʳ, must have been proof-read, for it exists in an uncorrected state with seven minor misprints, among them 'bis' for 'his' in the
phrase in question.

138–40. *how dangerous ... sufferings*] It is painful to think how dangerously and shamefully she may behave if too much restraint is imposed on her.

153.] i.e. How grateful we should be to heaven that we have parted
without a quarrel.

II. ii. 1ff.] This scene should be contrasted with the much more leisurely
and diffuse narrative of Reynolds, pp. 123ff.

    I dare not be too busy with my praises,
    Th'are dangerous things to deal with.   *Exit.*

Als.   This goes well;   5
    These women are the ladies' cabinets,
    Things of most precious trust are lock'd into 'em.

                  Enter BEATRICE.

Bea. I have within mine eye all my desires;
    Requests that holy prayers ascend heaven for,
    And brings 'em down to furnish our defects,   10
    Come not more sweet to our necessities
    Than thou unto my wishes.

Als.   W'are so like
    In our expressions, lady, that unless I borrow
    The same words, I shall never find their equals.   [*Kisses her.*]

Bea. How happy were this meeting, this embrace,   15
    If it were free from envy! This poor kiss,
    It has an enemy, a hateful one,
    That wishes poison to't: how well were I now
    If there were none such name known as Piracquo,
    Nor no such tie as the command of parents!   20
    I should be but too much blessed.

7. lock'd] *All eds.;* lock *Q.*   10. brings] *Q, Bullen;* bring *Dilke, Dyce.*
14. *Kisses her.*] *This ed.*

   4–5.] Beatrice may become suspicious if she overhears Diaphanta prais-
ing Alsemero too enthusiastically.

   6–7.] Cf. Middleton's *Women Beware Women*, I. i. 54–6:
        View but her face, you may see all her dowry,
        Save that which lies lock'd up in hidden virtues,
        Like jewels kept in cabinets.   (Bullen, VI, 239).

   9–10.] The general meaning of these lines is clear enough, though the
details are a little obscure. Presumably ' 'em' are the requests; 'brings'
could refer to 'heaven', though it is more likely to be an example of a
singular verb with a plural subject, the prayers, which ascend to heaven
with requests and then bring them back to us.

   10. *furnish our defects*] i.e. Supply those things which we lack.

   16–18.] Sampson takes this to mean, 'the kiss she must give Alonzo
wishes itself poisoned'; but the meaning is surely, 'the kiss she has just
given Alsemero ("this embrace") has an enemy (Alonzo) who would like to
put poison into it'.

Als.   One good service
Would strike off both your fears, and I'll go near it too,
Since you are so distress'd; remove the cause,
The command ceases, so there's two fears blown out
With one and the same blast.

Bea.   Pray let me find you, sir.   25
What might that service be so strangely happy?

Als. The honourablest piece 'bout man, valour.
I'll send a challenge to Piracquo instantly.

Bea. How? Call you that extinguishing of fear,
When 'tis the only way to keep it flaming?   30
Are not you ventured in the action,
That's all my joys and comforts? Pray, no more, sir.
Say you prevail'd, y'are danger's and not mine then;
The law would claim you from me, or obscurity
Be made the grave to bury you alive.   35
I'm glad these thoughts come forth; oh keep not one
Of this condition, sir; here was a course
Found to bring sorrow on her way to death:
The tears would ne'er ha' dried, till dust had chok'd 'em.
Blood-guiltiness becomes a fouler visage,   40
[*Aside.*]—And now I think on one: I was to blame,
I ha' marr'd so good a market with my scorn;

27. piece] *Dyce, Bullen;* peece *Q;* peace *Dilke.*   33. y'are] *Dyce,
Bullen;* your *Q, Dilke.*   41. *Aside.*] *Dilke.*

---

22. *strike off*] i.e. As fetters are struck off.
23–4. *remove . . . ceases*] i.e. If you get rid of Alonzo, your father can no
longer order you to marry him. Adapted from the scholastic tag, 'remove
the cause and the effect ceases'; cf. Greene's *Friar Bacon and Friar Bungay*,
III. i. 997–8:

> I haue learnd at *Oxford*, there, this point of schooles,
> *Ablata causa, tollitur effectus.*

(*Plays*, ed. Collins, 1905, II, 45).
24–5.] Alsemero's metaphor, as Sampson points out, is of blowing out
two lights with one breath.
40. *Blood-guiltiness*] Possibly an echo of Psalm li. 14: 'Deliver me from
bloodguiltiness, O God . . .'
42.] i.e. For having been so scornful to someone (De Flores) I could use
greatly to my own advantage. 'Mar the market' is a proverbial phrase; cf.

'T had been done questionless; the ugliest creature
Creation fram'd for some use, yet to see
I could not mark so much where it should be!   45
Als. Lady—
Bea. [*aside.*] Why, men of art make much of poison,
  Keep one to expel another; where was my art?
Als. Lady, you hear not me.
Bea.   I do especially, sir;
  The present times are not so sure of our side
  As those hereafter may be; we must use 'em then   50
  As thrifty folks their wealth, sparingly now,
  Till the time opens.
Als.   You teach wisdom, lady.
Bea. Within there; Diaphanta!

Enter DIAPHANTA.

Dia.   Do you call, madam?
Bea. Perfect your service, and conduct this gentleman
  The private way you brought him.

46. *aside.*] Dilke.

The Meeting of Gallants at an Ordinary: 'Well, I haue almost mard their
market . . .' (Dekker, *Plague Pamphlets*, ed. Wilson, 1925, p. 115) and
Middleton's *No Wit, No Help like a Woman's*, I. i. 266–8: '*The ninth day,
the market is marred,*—that's 'long of the hucksters, I warrant you' (Bullen,
IV, 295).
    44. *for some use*] Cf. Middleton's *Women Beware Women*, I. ii. 182–3:
            That providence, that has made every poison
            Good for some use . . .
(Bullen, VI, 252). The doctrine that everything in nature has some use or
purpose is referred to twice by Marston, in *Antonio and Mellida*, III. i
(*Plays*, ed. Wood, 1934–9, I, 32) and in *Sophonisba*, II. i (*ibid.*, II, 20). In
Marston, and possibly in Middleton also, the doctrine derives from Mon-
taigne's *Essais*, Bk. III, Ch. I, 'De L'Utile et de L'Honneste' (*Œuvres*, Paris,
1927, V, 3–4).
    46–7.] Cf. *The White Devil*, III. iii. 59–60:
            Phisitians, that cure poisons, still doe worke
            With counterpoisons.
(Webster, I, 147). Howell gives it as a proverb: 'One poison expells another'
(*Proverbs*, 1659, p. 34).
    52. *opens*] Becomes more favourable.

Dia.   I shall, madam.   55
Als. My love's as firm as love e'er built upon.

           Exeunt DIAPHANTA *and* ALSEMERO.

           Enter DE FLORES.

De F. [*aside.*] I have watch'd this meeting, and do wonder much
    What shall become of t'other; I'm sure both
    Cannot be serv'd unless she transgress; happily
    Then I'll put in for one: for if a woman   60
    Fly from one point, from him she makes a husband,
    She spreads and mounts then like arithmetic,
    One, ten, a hundred, a thousand, ten thousand,
    Proves in time sutler to an army royal.
    Now do I look to be most richly rail'd at,   65
    Yet I must see her.
Bea. [*aside.*]   Why, put case I loath'd him
    As much as youth and beauty hates a sepulchre,
    Must I needs show it? Cannot I keep that secret,
    And serve my turn upon him?—See, he's here.
    [*To him.*] De Flores.

57. *aside.*] *Dyce.*   66. *aside.*] *Dilke.*

57ff.] The following interview between Beatrice and De Flores owes
virtually nothing to Reynolds.
    58. *t'other*] Alonzo.
    60. *put in for one*] Apply for a share; cf. IV. iii. 36.
    60–4.] Cf. Middleton's *Hengist, King of Kent*, IV. ii. 274–77:
        For as at a small Breach in towne or Castle
        When one has entrance, a whole Army followes,
        In woman, so abusiuely once knowne,
        Thousandes of sins has passadge made with one.
(ed. Bald, 1938, pp. 68–9). But similar metaphors can be found elsewhere;
cf. *The Revenger's Tragedy*, IV. iv. 87–9:
        . . . shee first begins with one,
        Who afterward to thousand prooues a whore:
        Breake Ice in one place, it will crack in more.
            (Tourneur, *Works*, ed. Nicoll, 1930, p. 141).
    66–7.] Cf. Middleton's *Women Beware Women*, II. i. 84–5:
        I loathe him more than beauty can hate death,
        Or age her spiteful neighbour. (Bullen, VI, 264).
    69. *serve my turn*] i.e. Make use of him for my own purposes. Cf. *Oth.*,
I. i. 42: 'I follow him to serve my turn upon him'.

De F. [*aside.*]   Ha, I shall run mad with joy;   70
    She call'd me fairly by my name De Flores,
    And neither rogue nor rascal!
Bea.   What ha' you done
    To your face a-late? Y'have met with some good physician;
    Y'have prun'd yourself, methinks, you were not wont
    To look so amorously.
De F. [*aside.*]   Not I;   75
    'Tis the same physnomy, to a hair and pimple,
    Which she call'd scurvy scarce an hour ago:
    How is this?
Bea.   Come hither; nearer, man!
De F. [*aside.*] I'm up to the chin in heaven.
Bea.   Turn, let me see;
    Faugh, 'tis but the heat of the liver, I perceiv't.   80
    I thought it had been worse.
De F. [*aside.*]   Her fingers touch'd me!
    She smells all amber.
Bea. I'll make a water for you shall cleanse this
    Within a fortnight.
De F.   With your own hands, lady?
Bea. Yes, mine own, sir; in a work of cure   85
    I'll trust no other.
De F. [*aside.*]   'Tis half an act of pleasure
    To hear her talk thus to me.
Bea.   When w'are us'd
    To a hard face, 'tis not so unpleasing;
    It mends still in opinion, hourly mends,
    I see it by experience.
De F. [*aside.*]   I was blest   90
    To light upon this minute; I'll make use on't.
Bea. Hardness becomes the visage of a man well,
    It argues service, resolution, manhood,
    If cause were of employment.

---

70. *aside.*] *Dilke.*   75. *aside.*] *Dilke.*   79. *aside.*] *Dilke.*   80. Faugh]
Dyce, Bullen; vauh *Q.*   81. *aside.*] *Dilke.*   86. *aside.*] *Dyce.*
90. *aside.*] *Dyce.*

De F.   'Twould be soon seen,
If e'er your ladyship had cause to use it.   95
I would but wish the honour of a service
So happy as that mounts to.
Bea.   We shall try you—
Oh my De Flores!
De F. [*aside.*]   How's that?
She calls me hers already, *my* De Flores!
[*To Bea.*] —You were about to sigh out somewhat,
    madam.   100
Bea. No, was I? I forgot, —Oh!
De F.   There 'tis again,
The very fellow on't.
Bea.   You are too quick, sir.
De F. There's no excuse for't now, I heard it twice, madam;
That sigh would fain have utterance, take pity on't,
And lend it a free word; 'las, how it labours   105
For liberty! I hear the murmur yet
Beat at your bosom.
Bea.   Would creation—
De F. Ay, well said, that's it.
Bea.   Had form'd me man.
De F. Nay, that's not it.
Bea.   Oh, 'tis the soul of freedom!
I should not then be forc'd to marry one   110
I hate beyond all depths, I should have power
Then to oppose my loathings, nay, remove 'em
For ever from my sight.
De F.   Oh blest occasion!—
Without change to your sex, you have your wishes.
Claim so much man in me.
Bea.   In thee, De Flores?   115
There's small cause for that.
De F.   Put it not from me,
It's a service that I kneel for to you.   [*Kneels.*]
Bea. You are too violent to mean faithfully;

98. *aside.*] Dyce.   99. *my*] Dilke, Dyce; my *Q*.   117. *Kneels.*] Dilke.

> There's horror in my service, blood and danger,
> Can those be things to sue for ?

De F.   If you knew   120
> How sweet it were to me to be employed
> In any act of yours, you would say then
> I fail'd, and us'd not reverence enough
> When I receive the charge on't.

Bea. [*aside.*]   This is much, methinks;
> Belike his wants are greedy, and to such   125
> Gold tastes like angels' food. [*To De F.*] —Rise.

De F. I'll have the work first.

Bea. [*aside.*]   Possible his need
> Is strong upon him; [*gives him money*]—there's to encourage
>   thee:
> As thou art forward and thy service dangerous,
> Thy reward shall be precious.

De F.   That I have thought on;   130
> I have assur'd myself of that beforehand,
> And know it will be precious, the thought ravishes.

Bea. Then take him to thy fury.

De F.   I thirst for him.

Bea. Alonzo de Piracquo.

De F.   His end's upon him;
> He shall be seen no more.   [*Rises.*]

Bea.   How lovely now   135
> Dost thou appear to me! Never was man
> Dearlier rewarded.

---

124. receive] *Q, Schelling;* receiv'd *Dilke, Dyce.*   124. aside.] *Dilke.*
127. aside.] *Dilke.*   128. gives . . . money] *Dilke.*   131. myself of that] *Q*
(*corrected*), all eds.; myselfe that *Q* (*uncorrected*).   135. Rises.] *Dyce.*

---

126. *angels' food*] In its biblical uses the phrase means nothing more than
'manna', the food which fell from heaven (Psalm lxxviii. 25 and Wisdom of
Solomon, xvi. 20). In *The Wisdom of Solomon Paraphrased* (a metrical paraphrase of the latter) Middleton has: 'They angels were, and fed with
angels' food' (Bullen, VIII, 269). The phrase is used again by Middleton in
A Game at Chess, I. i. 141 (ed. Bald, 1929, p. 57), though here it seems to
mean divinity, the word of God.

129. *As thou art*] In proportion as, according as.

De F.   I do think of that.
Bea. Be wondrous careful in the execution.
De F. Why, are not both our lives upon the cast?
Bea. Then I throw all my fears upon thy service.   140
De F. They ne'er shall rise to hurt you.
Bea.   When the deed's done,
    I'll furnish thee with all things for thy flight;
    Thou may'st live bravely in another country.
De F. Ay, ay, we'll talk of that hereafter.
Bea. [*aside.*]   I shall rid myself
    Of two inveterate loathings at one time,   145
    Piracquo, and his dog-face.   *Exit.*
De F.   Oh my blood!
    Methinks I feel her in mine arms already,
    Her wanton fingers combing out this beard,
    And being pleased, praising this bad face.
    Hunger and pleasure, they'll commend sometimes   150
    Slovenly dishes, and feed heartily on 'em,
    Nay, which is stranger, refuse daintier for 'em.
    Some women are odd feeders.—I'm too loud.
    Here comes the man goes supperless to bed,
    Yet shall not rise to-morrow to his dinner.   155

                        Enter ALONZO.

Alon. De Flores.
De F.   My kind, honourable lord?
Alon. I am glad I ha' met with thee.
De F.   Sir.
Alon.   Thou canst show me
    The full strength of the castle?
De F.   That I can, sir.
Alon. I much desire it.
De F.   And if the ways and straits

144. *aside.*] *Dilke.*

___

146. *his dog-face*] An ironical title for De Flores.
    blood] See G., and Introduction, p. xlvi, n. 1.
    156ff.] The remainder of the scene is taken from Reynolds, p. 128.

  Of some of the passages be not too tedious for you,   160
  I will assure you, worth your time and sight, my lord.
Alon. Push, that shall be no hindrance.
De F.   I'm your servant, then:
  'Tis now near dinner-time, 'gainst your lordship's rising
  I'll have the keys about me.
Alon.   Thanks, kind De Flores.
De F. [*aside.*] He's safely thrust upon me beyond hopes. 165
                 Exeunt.

---

162. Push] *This ed.;* Puh *Q, Dilke;* Pooh *Dyce.* 165. *aside.*] *Dilke.*

---

 161. *worth*] i.e. It will be worth.
 163. *'gainst . . . rising*] i.e. Before your lordship rises from dinner.

Act III

[III. i]

Enter ALONZO *and* DE FLORES.
(*In the act-time* DE FLORES *hides a naked rapier.*)

De F. Yes, here are all the keys; I was afraid, my lord,
  I'd wanted for the postern, this is it.
  I've all, I've all, my lord: this for the sconce.
Alon. 'Tis a most spacious and impregnable fort.
De F. You'll tell me more, my lord: this descent   5
  Is somewhat narrow, we shall never pass
  Well with our weapons, they'll but trouble us.
Alon. Thou say'st true.
De F.   Pray let me help your lordship.
Alon. 'Tis done. Thanks, kind De Flores.
De F.   Here are hooks, my lord,
  To hang such things on purpose.   [*He hangs up the swords.*]
Alon.   Lead, I'll follow thee.   10
                  Exeunt at one door and enter at the other.

Act III] *Dilke, Dyce;* Actus Tertius. *Q.*   10. *He . . . swords.*] *Dyce.*

0.2. *In the act-time*] In the interval between Acts II and III. The two
scenes that follow should be compared to the two paragraphs in Reynolds
beginning 'Whiles *Piracquo* is at dinner . . .' (pp. 128–9).

8–9.] Alonzo takes off his sword-belt, assisted by De Flores.

10.1.] This stage-direction is quite common; cf. *The Spanish Gipsy*,
1653, 13ʳ. The exit and re-entrance indicated to the audience that a change
of scene had taken place; we are now to imagine that Alonzo and De Flores
are somewhere in the underground parts of the castle.

[III. ii]

De F. All this is nothing; you shall see anon
    A place you little dream on.

Alon.   I am glad
    I have this leisure: all your master's house
    Imagine I ha' taken a gondola.

De F. All but myself, sir, —[*aside*] which makes up my safety.   5
    [*To Alon.*] My lord, I'll place you at a casement here
    Will show you the full strength of all the castle.
    Look, spend your eye awhile upon that object.

Alon. Here's rich variety, De Flores.

De F.   Yes, sir.

Alon. Goodly munition.

De F.   Ay, there's ordnance, sir,   10
    No bastard metal, will ring you a peal like bells
    At great men's funerals; keep your eye straight, my lord,
    Take special notice of that sconce before you,
    There you may dwell awhile.   [*Takes up the rapier.*]

Alon.   I am upon't.

III. ii. 5. aside] *Dyce.*   14. *Takes . . . rapier.*] *Dyce.*

III. ii. 1–2.] For a very similar irony cf. Middleton's *Women Beware Women*, II. ii. 461–3:
    Faith, I've seen that I little thought to see
    I' the morning when I rose.
    Moth. Nay, so I told you
    Before you saw't, it would prove worth your sight.
(Bullen, VI, 291). The last line might be compared to II. ii. 161 of *The Changeling*. The two situations are similar: Bianca in *Women Beware Women* is shown round Livia's house and then suddenly betrayed to the Duke just as Alonzo is shown the castle by De Flores, and then treacherously murdered.

2–4.] In Reynolds, p. 130, De Flores is ordered by Beatrice, after she has heard of Alonzo's death, to spread false rumours 'that *Piracquo* was seene gone foorth the Castle gate; then, that in the City hee was seene to take boate, and went (as it was thought) to take the ayre of the sea'.

6ff.] Presumably De Flores leads Alonzo to one side of the stage, to a small window which looks on to the underground armoury of the castle (invisible, of course, to the audience). While Alonzo's back is turned, De Flores picks up the hidden rapier and stabs him.

14. *dwell*] This seems to be a sadistic pun: (i) pause, linger; (ii) inhabit (because that is where De Flores intends to put his corpse).

De F. And so am I. [*Stabs him.*]

Alon.   De Flores! Oh, De Flores,   15
     Whose malice hast thou put on?

De F.   Do you question
     A work of secrecy? I must silence you.   [*Stabs him.*]

Alon. Oh, oh, oh.

De F.   I must silence you.   [*Stabs him.*]
     So, here's an undertaking well accomplish'd.
     This vault serves to good use now.—Ha! what's that   20
     Threw sparkles in my eye? Oh, 'tis a diamond
     He wears upon his finger: it was well found,
     This will approve the work. What, so fast on?
     Not part in death? I'll take a speedy course then,   24
     Finger and all shall off.[*Cuts off the finger.*] So, now I'll clear
     The passages from all suspect or fear.   *Exit with body.*

[III. iii]

        Enter ISABELLA *and* LOLLIO.

Isa. Why, sirrah? Whence have you commission
     To fetter the doors against me?
     If you keep me in a cage, pray whistle to me,
     Let me be doing something.

Lol. You shall be doing, if it please you; I'll whistle to you if   5
     you'll pipe after.

Isa. Is it your master's pleasure, or your own,
     To keep me in this pinfold?

15. *Stabs him.*] Dilke.   17. *Stabs him.*] Dilke.   18. *Stabs him.*] Dyce.
25. *Cuts . . . finger.*] Dyce.

20–2.] Cf. II. i. 15–16. In a modern production the scene should perhaps be played in semi-darkness.
23–5.] This brutal touch is not in Reynolds.

III. iii. 5–6. *whistle . . . after*] This seems to be a variant on the common tag, of biblical origin, 'to dance after someone's pipe', as in *The Puritan*, I. v. 32–3: 'I feare mee I shall daunce after their pipe for't' (ed. Brooke, *Shakespeare Apocrypha*, 1908, p. 226).

Lol. 'Tis for my master's pleasure, lest being taken in another
    man's corn, you might be pounded in another place.   10

Isa. 'Tis very well, and he'll prove very wise.

Lol. He says you have company enough in the house, if you
    please to be sociable, of all sorts of people.

Isa. Of all sorts? Why, here's none but fools and madmen.

Lol. Very well: and where will you find any other, if you   15
    should go abroad? There's my master and I to boot too.

Isa. Of either sort one, a madman and a fool.

Lol. I would ev'n participate of both then, if I were as you; I
    know y'are half mad already, be half foolish too.

Isa. Y'are a brave saucy rascal! Come on, sir,   20
    Afford me then the pleasure of your bedlam;
    You were commending once to-day to me
    Your last come lunatic, what a proper
    Body there was without brains to guide it,
    And what a pitiful delight appear'd   25
    In that defect, as if your wisdom had found
    A mirth in madness; pray, sir, let me partake,
    If there be such a pleasure.

Lol. If I do not show you the handsomest, discreetest mad-
    man, one that I may call the understanding madman,   30
    then say I am a fool.

Isa. Well, a match, I will say so.

Lol. When you have a taste of the madman, you shall (if you

33. have] *Q, Baskervill;* have had *Dilke, Dyce.*

9–10.] Lollio takes over Isabella's metaphor, and gives it a double
meaning which should be obvious enough. This kind of metaphor, with a
similar implication, is fairly common; cf. *The Humorous Lieutenant,* II. ii:
'. . . they are all i' th' pound sir, / They'l never ride o're other mens corn
again, I take it' (Fletcher, II, 299).

21. *bedlam*] 'Bedlam' is of course a corruption of 'Bethlehem' Hospital
(see Introduction, p. xxxvi). The term came to mean a mad-house of any
kind, and this reference does not necessarily mean that Rowley has
Bethlehem Hospital in mind.

26–7]. Evidently Isabella does not find madness amusing; cf. ll.
43–4.

please) see Fools' College, o' th' side; I seldom lock there,
'tis but shooting a bolt or two, and you are amongst 'em.   35
Exit. Enter presently. —Come on, sir, let me see how
handsomely you'll behave yourself now.

Enter FRANCISCUS.

Fran. How sweetly she looks! Oh, but there's a wrinkle in her
brow as deep as philosophy; Anacreon, drink to my mistress' health, I'll pledge it: stay, stay, there's a spider in   40
the cup! No, 'tis but a grape-stone, swallow it, fear nothing, poet; so, so, lift higher.

Isa. Alack, alack, 'tis too full of pity
To be laugh'd at; how fell he mad? Canst thou tell?

Lol. For love, mistress: he was a pretty poet too, and that set   45
him forwards first; the muses then forsook him, he ran

---

34. th' side] *Q, Dilke;* th'other side *Dyce, Bullen.*   37.1. *Enter Franciscus.] Neilson; Enter Loll: Franciscus. Q.*

---

34. *o' th' side*] Dyce's emendation does not seem essential. Possibly
Lollio is supposed to make his meaning clear by a nod of the head or by
pointing.

35. *shooting a bolt*] A punning reference to the proverbial 'A fool's bolt is
soon shot.' Cf. Armin, *A Nest of Ninnies*: '. . . you know a fooles boult is
soone shot' (ed. 1842, p. 15), and *The Praise of The Red Herring*: '. . . and,
to shoote my fooles bolt amongst you . . .' (Nashe, *Works,* ed. McKerrow,
III, 193).

36-7.] Possibly some, or even the whole, of this passage is spoken off-
stage by Lollio as he begins to lead Franciscus in.

39-41. *Anacreon . . . grape-stone*] The story, recorded in Valerius Maxi-
mus, Lib. IX, Cap. xii, Ext. 8 (ed. London, 1823, II, 887) and Pliny, vii, 7
(translated Holland, 1601, I, 159), that Anacreon choked to death on a
grape-stone while drinking a cup of wine, was familiar to the dramatists'
contemporaries; Overbury, in his character of 'A Roaring Boy', says that
'He commonly dyes like *Anacreon*, with a Grape in's throate' (ed. Paylor,
1936, p. 59).

40-1. *spider in the cup*] Spiders were considered to be poisonous. Cf.
Middleton's *No Wit, No Help like a Woman's,* II. i. 390-4:

> Have I so happily found
> What many a widow has with sorrow tasted,
> Even when my lip touch'd the contracting cup,
> Even then to see the spider? 'twas miraculous!
> Crawl with thy poisons hence . . .

(Bullen, IV, 336-7) and also *Wint.,* II. i. 39-45.

mad for a chambermaid, yet she was but a dwarf neither.

Fran. Hail, bright Titania!

Why stand'st thou idle on these flow'ry banks ?

Oberon is dancing with his Dryades;   50

I'll gather daisies, primrose, violets,

And bind them in a verse of poesie.

Lol. Not too near; you see your danger.   [*Shows the whip.*]

Fran. Oh hold thy hand, great Diomed,

Thou feed'st thy horses well, they shall obey thee;   55

Get up, Bucephalus kneels.   [*Kneels.*]

Lol. You see how I awe my flock; a shepherd has not his dog at

more obedience.

Isa. His conscience is unquiet, sure that was

The cause of this. A proper gentleman.   60

Fran. Come hither, Esculapius; hide the poison.   [*Rises.*]

53. *Shows . . . whip.*] *Dyce.*   56. *Kneels.*] *Dilke.*   61. *Rises.*] *This ed.*

---

47. *dwarf*] Cf. *Northward Ho*, iv. iii. 45–6:
    Bell. A Musition, how fell he mad for Gods sake ?
    Ful. For loue of an Italian Dwarfe.   (Dekker, iii, 57).

48ff.] 'Oberon' and 'Titania' are derived presumably from *MND.*, though 'Oberon' is the traditional name for the king of the fairies. The speech can be interpreted as an invitation to Isabella; Franciscus insinuates that Oberon (i.e. Alibius) is out enjoying himself with other women ('dancing with his Dryades'), and suggests that Titania (i.e. Isabella) should solace herself with him.

53. *your danger*] Lollio shows the whip to Franciscus as a warning to him not to misbehave.

54. *Diomed*] Not the Greek hero of the Trojan War, but Diomedes, a son of Ares, and king of the Bistonians in Thrace, who fed his horses with human flesh. The eighth labour of Hercules was to kill him and feed his body to his horses, whereupon they grew tame. Lyly refers to him in *Campaspe*, The Epilogue at Court (*Works*, ed. Bond, 1902, ii, 360) and in *Midas*, iii. i. 20 (*ibid.*, iii, 130).

56. *Bucephalus*] The monstrous horse of Alexander the Great, which only he could ride. Rowley mentions him in *A Search for Money*: 'Nay, (saies hee) hee is a very Alexander, for none but himselfe dares mount his Bucephalus' (ed. 1840, p. 16). The story is found in Plutarch, *Morals* (translated Holland, 1603, pp. 963–4). Evidently Franciscus kneels down on all fours so that Lollio can 'ride' him.

61. *Esculapius*] The Greek god of healing and medicine. These 'mock-heroic' descriptions of Lollio are of course intended to be sarcastic.
    the poison] The whip; cf. l. 86.

Lol. Well, 'tis hid.

Fran. Didst thou never hear of one Tiresias,
    A famous poet?

Lol. Yes, that kept tame wild-geese.   65

Fran. That's he; I am the man.

Lol. No!

Fran. Yes; but make no words on't, I was a man
    Seven years ago.

Lol. A stripling I think you might.   70

Fran. Now I'm a woman, all feminine.

Lol. I would I might see that.

Fran. Juno struck me blind.

Lol. I'll ne'er believe that; for a woman, they say, has an eye
    more than a man.   75

Fran. I say she struck me blind.

Lol. And Luna made you mad; you have two trades to beg
    with.

Fran. Luna is now big-bellied, and there's room
    For both of us to ride with Hecate;   80

64. poet] *Q, Dilke, Ellis;* prophet *Dyce, Bullen.*

---

63. *Tiresias*] The famous Theban soothsayer and prophet, who changed into a woman, and then seven years later back into a man. In Ovid's version of the legend (*Metamorphoses*, Bk. III) he was struck blind by Juno for having revealed that love gave more pleasure to women than to men.

64. *poet*] Dyce's emendation is perhaps a little pedantic; Franciscus is after all a madman.

65. *tame wild-geese*] This phrase appears to have had some meaning which is now lost; cf. *All Fools*, v. ii. 330–1:
        . . . now take your several wives,
    And spread like wild-geese, though you now grow tame.
                (Chapman, *Comedies*, 162).

70.] Possibly a word such as 'say' or 'be' has dropped out from the end of the line.

77. *Luna*] The moon.

two trades] Madness and blindness.

79. *big-bellied*] At the full; cf. *The Meeting of Gallants at an Ordinary*: '. . . the Moone hath had aboue sixe great Bellies since wee walkt here last together . . .' (*ed. cit.*, p. 115).

80. *Hecate*] The Greek goddess of witchcraft and magic. The word is often used, however, to mean simply 'the moon'. Cf. Milton's *Comus*, 134–5:

I'll drag thee up into her silver sphere,
And there we'll kick the dog, and beat the bush,
That barks against the witches of the night:
The swift lycanthropi that walks the round,
We'll tear their wolvish skins, and save the sheep.   85

> [*Tries to seize* LOLLIO.]

Lol. Is't come to this? Nay, then my poison comes forth
again; mad slave, indeed, abuse your keeper!

Isa. I prithee hence with him, now he grows dangerous.

Fran. Sings.

> *Sweet love, pity me,*
> *Give me leave to lie with thee.*   90

Lol. No, I'll see you wiser first: to your own kennel.

Fran. No noise, she sleeps, draw all the curtains round;
Let no soft sound molest the pretty soul
But love, and love creeps in at a mouse-hole.

Lol. I would you would get into your hole. *Exit* FRANCISCUS.   95
Now, mistress, I will bring you another sort, you shall be
fool'd another while; Tony, come hither, Tony; look
who's yonder, Tony.

> *Enter* ANTONIO.

---

82. kick . . . bush] *Q, Bullen;* beat the bush, and kick the dog *Dilke, Dyce.*
85.1. *Tries . . . Lollio.*] *Dilke.*   89. *Sings.*] *Dilke; Sing. Q (at end of l. 88).*

> Stay thy cloudy Ebon chair,
> Wherin thou rid'st with *Hecat* . . .

82-3.] The confusion in these lines seems to be deliberate, and there is
no real need for emendation. The dog and the bush belong, as Tatlock
points out, to the man in the moon; cf. *MND.*, v. i. 136-7 and *Tp.*, II. ii.
141-4. For the barking dogs, cf. *The Sad Shepherd*, II. iii. 42-4:

> . . . when our Dame *Hecat*
> Made it her gaing-night, over the Kirk-yard,
> With all the barkeand parish tykes set at her.

> (Jonson, VII, 31).

84. *lycanthropi*] Persons suffering from lycanthropia or wolf-madness, a
derangement in which they imagine themselves to be wolves, and behave
accordingly. The effects are described by Burton, *The Anatomy of Melancholy*, Pt. I, Sec. I, Memb. I, Subsec. 4 (ed. Shilleto, 1893, I, 161-2), and by
the doctor in *The Duchess of Malfi*, v. ii. 6-22 (Webster, II, 106-7).

Ant. Cousin, is it not my aunt?

Lol. Yes, 'tis one of 'em, Tony.   100

Ant. He, he, how do you, uncle?

Lol. Fear him not, mistress, 'tis a gentle nigget; you may play
    with him, as safely with him as with his bauble.

Isa. How long hast thou been a fool?

Ant. Ever since I came hither, cousin.   105

Isa. Cousin? I'm none of thy cousins, fool.

Lol. Oh mistress, fools have always so much wit as to claim
    their kindred.

Madman within. Bounce, bounce, he falls, he falls!

Isa. Hark you, your scholars in the upper room   110
    Are out of order.

Lol. Must I come amongst you there? Keep you the fool,
    mistress; I'll go up and play left-handed Orlando
    amongst the madmen.   *Exit.*

Isa. Well, sir.   115

Ant. 'Tis opportuneful now, sweet lady! Nay,
    Cast no amazing eye upon this change.

Isa. Ha!

99. aunt] *All eds.;* Ant *Q.*

---

99. *aunt*] See G.

103.] The repetition of 'with him' may be a printer's error.

105. *cousin*] It is common in Elizabethan drama for an unfaithful woman
and her lover to gain access to each other by pretending to be cousins. Cf.
Love's Cure, or the Martial Maid, III. ii:

           Is my Cuz stirring yet?

    Alg. Your Cuz (good cousin?)

           A Whore is like a fool, a kin to all
           The gallants in the Town: Your Cuz, good Signior,
           Is gone abroad; Sir, with her other Cosin,
           My Lord *Vitelli*: since when there hath been
           Some dozen Cosins here to enquire for her.

(Fletcher, VII, 196). This may help to account for Isabella's indignant
repudiation of the relationship (l. 106).

113. *left-handed Orlando*] The reference is presumably to the hero of
Ariosto's *Orlando Furioso,* but the point of the adjective is not clear. Cf.
Rowley's *A New Wonder, A Woman Never Vexed,* II. i: 'How now, my fine
trundletails; my wooden cosmographers; my bowling-alley in an uproar?
Is Orlando up in arms?' (ed. Dilke, *Old English Plays,* 1815, V, 259).

Ant. This shape of folly shrouds your dearest love,
    The truest servant to your powerful beauties,   120
    Whose magic had this force thus to transform me.
Isa. You are a fine fool indeed.
Ant.   Oh, 'tis not strange:
    Love has an intellect that runs through all
    The scrutinous sciences, and like
    A cunning poet, catches a quantity   125
    Of every knowledge, yet brings all home
    Into one mystery, into one secret
    That he proceeds in.
Isa.   Y'are a parlous fool.
Ant. No danger in me: I bring nought but love,
    And his soft-wounding shafts to strike you with: 130
    Try but one arrow; if it hurt you,
    I'll stand you twenty back in recompense.   [*Kisses her.*]
Isa. A forward fool too!
Ant.   This was love's teaching:
    A thousand ways he fashion'd out my way,
    And this I found the safest and the nearest   135
    To tread the Galaxia to my star.
Isa. Profound, withal! Certain, you dream'd of this;
    Love never taught it waking.
Ant.   Take no acquaintance
    Of these outward follies; there is within
    A gentleman that loves you.
Isa.   When I see him,   140
    I'll speak with him; so in the meantime keep

---

132. *Kisses her.*] *Neilson.*   134. he] *Dyce, Bullen;* she *Q, Dilke.*
135. the nearest] *Dilke, Dyce,* nearest *Q.*   137. withal! Certain,] *All
eds.;* withall certain: *Q.*

119–21.] Cf. Middleton and Rowley's *The Spanish Gipsy,* v. iii. 3–5:
                Beauty in youth, and wit
      To set it forth, I see, transforms the best
      Into what shape love fancies.   (Bullen, VI, 224).
134. he] Love is personified as masculine in ll. 128 and 130.
136. *Galaxia*] The Milky-Way.

Your habit, it becomes you well enough.
As you are a gentleman, I'll not discover you;
That's all the favour that you must expect:
When you are weary, you may leave the school,   145
For all this while you have but play'd the fool.

Enter LOLLIO.

Ant. And must again. —He, he, I thank you, cousin;
   I'll be your valentine to-morrow morning.
Lol. How do you like the fool, mistress?
Isa. Passing well, sir.   150
Lol. Is he not witty, pretty well for a fool?
Isa. If he hold on as he begins, he is like
   To come to something.
Lol. Ay, thank a good tutor: you may put him to't; he begins
   to answer pretty hard questions. Tony, how many is five   155
   times six?
Ant. Five times six, is six times five.
Lol. What arithmetician could have answer'd better? How
   many is one hundred and seven?
Ant. One hundred and seven, is seven hundred and one,   160
   cousin.
Lol. This is no wit to speak on; will you be rid of the fool
   now?
Isa. By no means, let him stay a little.
Madman within. Catch there, catch the last couple in hell!   165

148.] Possibly a faint echo of Ophelia's song, *Ham.*, IV. v. 48–51.

165.] An allusion to 'barley-brake', which R. W. Bond describes as 'a
game . . . in which two players, occupying a marked space called "Hell" in
the centre of the ground, tried to catch the others as they ran through it from
the two opposite ends, those caught being obliged to replace or reinforce
them in the centre' (Lyly, *Works*, ed. Bond, 1902, III, 536). The game was
played by pairs of men and women, who held hands and were not usually
allowed to separate, and went on until each pair had taken its turn at
occupying 'Hell'. The fullest description of a game is in a poem by Sidney
(*Works*, ed. Feuillerat, 1922, II, 219–24), but there are countless references
to it in the poets and dramatists of the period. Cf. *The Virgin Martyr*, v. i:
'Hee's at Barli-break, and the last couple are now in hell' (Dekker, IV, 80)

Lol. Again? Must I come amongst you? Would my master
    were come home! I am not able to govern both these
    wards together.   *Exit.*
Ant. Why should a minute of love's hour be lost?
Isa. Fie, out again! I had rather you kept   170
    Your other posture: you become not your tongue,
    When you speak from your clothes.
Ant.   How can he freeze,
    Lives near so sweet a warmth? Shall I alone
    Walk through the orchard of the Hesperides,
    And cowardly not dare to pull an apple?   175
    This with the red cheeks I must venture for. [*Tries to kiss her.*]

Enter LOLLIO *above.*

Isa. Take heed, there's giants keep 'em.
Lol. [*aside.*] How now, fool, are you good at that? Have you
    read Lipsius? He's past *Ars Amandi*; I believe I must

176. *Tries . . . her.*] *Dilke.*   178. *aside.*] *Dyce.*

---

and *Match Me in London*, IV. iv: 'How now at Barle-brake, who are in
Hell?' (*ibid.*, IV, 203).

    167–8. *both . . . wards*] The fools' and the madmen's wards.

    171–2. *you . . . clothes*] i.e. The clothes you are wearing do not suit you
when you speak seriously.

    173–5.] A favourite metaphor of Rowley's: cf. *All's Lost by Lust*, I. i.
135–6:
                If Words will serve, if not, by rapines force;
                Wee'le plucke this apple from th' Hesperides.
(ed. Stork, p. 85), *The Maid in the Mill*, IV. i:
                Shall I walk by the tree? desire the fruit,
                Yet be so nice to pull till I ask leave
                Of the churlish Gard'ner, that will deny me?
(Fletcher, VII, 50) and *A Cure for a Cuckold*, IV. i. 166–8 (Webster, III, 71).
But it is a common metaphor; cf. Ford and Dekker's *The Sun's Darling*, III:
                    . . . I doat upon thee.
                Unlock my garden of th' Hesperides,
                By draggons kept (the Apples beeing pure gold)
                Take all that fruit, 'tis thine.   (Dekker, IV, 323).
    179. *Lipsius*] Justus Lipsius (1547–1606), the famous scholar and jurist.
'Is it necessary to notice that the name of this great scholar is introduced
merely for the sake of its first syllable?' (Dyce).

    Ars Amandi] According to Sampson, 'He's gone beyond such simple

    put harder questions to him, I perceive that—   180
Isa. You are bold without fear too.
Ant.   What should I fear,
    Having all joys about me ? Do you smile,
    And love shall play the wanton on your lip,
    Meet and retire, retire and meet again :
    Look you but cheerfully, and in your eyes   185
    I shall behold mine own deformity,
    And dress myself up fairer; I know this shape
    Becomes me not, but in those bright mirrors
    I shall array me handsomely.
Lol. Cuckoo, cuckoo!   *Exit.* 190

       [*Enter*] *Madmen above, some as birds, others as beasts.*

Ant. What are these ?
Isa.   Of fear enough to part us;
    Yet are they but our schools of lunatics,
    That act their fantasies in any shapes
    Suiting their present thoughts; if sad, they cry;
    If mirth be their conceit, they laugh again;   195
    Sometimes they imitate the beasts and birds,
    Singing, or howling, braying, barking; all
    As their wild fancies prompt 'em.   [*Exeunt madmen above.*]

190.1. *Enter . . . beasts.*] *This ed.; Mad-men . . . beasts. Q; Cries of Madmen
are heard within, like those of birds and beasts. Dyce, Bullen.*   198. *Exeunt
. . . above.*] *This ed.*

---

writers as Ovid'. But the main implication is surely, 'He's no novice in the
art of making love'. The *Ars Amandi* as a lover's handbook is mentioned in
Day's *Humour out of Breath*, II. ii :
    Hip. Hast any skill in loue ?
    Oct. I am one of Cupids agents; haue *Ovids Ars Amandi ad ungues*;
        know *causam*, and can apply *remedium*, and minister *effectum* to a
        haire.
(*Works*, 1881, III, 27). Its lurid reputation is shown also in the Prelude to
The Isle of Gulls (*ibid.*, II, 5–6).
    182. *Do you smile*] An old form of the imperative; cf. l. 185, and IV. i. 78.
    190. *Cuckoo, cuckoo!*] Implying that Alibius is about to be cuckolded.
    190.1.] Dyce's emendation seems quite unjustified. Madmen appear
on the upper stage and imitate birds and beasts, Antonio asks what they are,
and Isabella explains it to him.

Enter LOLLIO.

Ant.   These are no fears.

Isa. But here's a large one, my man.

Ant. Ha, he, that's fine sport indeed, cousin.   200

Lol. I would my master were come home, 'tis too much for
    one shepherd to govern two of these flocks; nor can I
    believe that one churchman can instruct two benefices at
    once; there will be some incurable mad of the one side,
    and very fools on the other. Come, Tony.   205

Ant. Prithee, cousin, let me stay here still.

Lol. No, you must to your book now you have play'd suffi-
    ciently.

Isa. Your fool is grown wondrous witty.

Lol. Well, I'll say nothing; but I do not think but he will put   210
    you down one of these days.   *Exeunt* LOLLIO *and* ANTONIO.

Isa. Here the restrained current might make breach,
    Spite of the watchful bankers; would a woman stray,
    She need not gad abroad to seek her sin,
    It would be brought home one ways or other: 215
    The needle's point will to the fixed north;
    Such drawing arctics women's beauties are.

Enter LOLLIO.

Lol. How dost thou, sweet rogue?

Isa. How now?

Lol. Come, there are degrees, one fool may be better than   220
    another.

Isa. What's the matter?

Lol. Nay, if thou giv'st thy mind to fool's-flesh, have at thee!

                    [*Tries to kiss her.*]

Isa. You bold slave, you!

Lol. I could follow now as t'other fool did: 225

215. ways] *Q, Schelling;* way *Dilke, Dyce.*   223.1. *Tries . . . her.*] *Schelling.*

216.] Cf. Congreve, *The Old Bachelor*, III. ii. 19–20: 'There stands my
North, and thither my Needle points—' (*Comedies*, ed. Dobrée, 1925,
p. 54).

'What should I fear,
Having all joys about me ? Do you but smile,
And love shall play the wanton on your lip,
Meet and retire, retire and meet again:
Look you but cheerfully, and in your eyes   230
I shall behold my own deformity,
And dress myself up fairer; I know this shape
Becomes me not—' And so as it follows; but is not this
the more foolish way ? Come, sweet rogue; kiss me, my
little Lacedemonian. Let me feel how thy pulses beat;   235
thou hast a thing about thee would do a man pleasure,
I'll lay my hand on't.

Isa. Sirrah, no more! I see you have discovered
This love's knight-errant, who hath made adventure
For purchase of my love; be silent, mute,   240
Mute as a statue, or his injunction
For me enjoying, shall be to cut thy throat:
I'll do it, though for no other purpose,
And be sure he'll not refuse it.

Lol. My share, that's all; I'll have my fool's part with you.   245
Isa. No more! Your master.

Enter ALIBIUS.

Alib.   Sweet, how dost thou ?
Isa. Your bounden servant, sir.

---

235. *Lacedemonian*] Sampson glosses this as 'light woman, with perhaps
a hint of *laced-mutton*', the latter being a cant term for 'prostitute', as in
Blurt, Master Constable, I. ii. 7 (Bullen, I, 15). But it may mean nothing
more than 'someone who speaks briefly and to the point'; cf. *The Honest
Whore, Part I*, III. i. 6–10:

> What Coz! sweet Coz! how dost ifayth, since last night after candle-
> light ? we had good sport ifayth, had we not ? and when shals laugh
> agen ?

Wife. When you will, Cozen.
Fust. Spoke like a kind Lacedemonian.
(Dekker, II, 39–40), and Congreve, *The Way of the World*, IV. ix. 9 (*ed. cit.*,
p. 411).

247–8.] Isabella evidently resents the restraints laid upon her by Alibius.

Alib.   Fie, fie, sweetheart,
    No more of that.
Isa.   You were best lock me up.
Alib. In my arms and bosom, my sweet Isabella,
    I'll lock thee up most nearly. Lollio,   250
    We have employment, we have task in hand;
    At noble Vermandero's, our castle-captain,
    There is a nuptial to be solemnis'd
    (Beatrice-Joanna, his fair daughter, bride),
    For which the gentleman hath bespoke our pains: 255
    A mixture of our madmen and our fools,
    To finish, as it were, and make the fag
    Of all the revels, the third night from the first;
    Only an unexpected passage over,
    To make a frightful pleasure, that is all,   260
    But not the all I aim at; could we so act it,
    To teach it in a wild distracted measure,
    Though out of form and figure, breaking time's head,
    It were no matter, 'twould be heal'd again
    In one age or other, if not in this: 265
    This, this, Lollio, there's a good reward begun,
    And will beget a bounty, be it known.
Lol. This is easy, sir, I'll warrant you: you have about you
    fools and madmen that can dance very well; and 'tis no
    wonder, your best dancers are not the wisest men; the   270
    reason is, with often jumping they jolt their brains down
    into their feet, that their wits lie more in their heels than
    in their heads.
Alib. Honest Lollio, thou giv'st me a good reason,
    And a comfort in it.
Isa.   Y'have a fine trade on't,   275
    Madmen and fools are a staple commodity.
Alib. Oh wife, we must eat, wear clothes, and live;

259ff.] The wedding-entertainment to be given at Vermandero's is less
ambitious than a formal masque; the madmen are to rush in suddenly 'To
make a frightful pleasure, that is all'. The rest of the passage is rather
clumsily expressed, though no emendation seems necessary.

Just at the lawyer's haven we arrive,
By madmen and by fools we both do thrive.   *Exeunt.*

[III. iv]

Enter VERMANDERO, ALSEMERO, JASPERINO, *and* BEATRICE.

Ver. Valencia speaks so nobly of you, sir,
    I wish I had a daughter now for you.
Als. The fellow of this creature were a partner
    For a king's love.
Ver.   I had her fellow once, sir,
    But heaven has married her to joys eternal;   5
    'Twere sin to wish her in this vale again.
    Come, sir, your friend and you shall see the pleasures
    Which my health chiefly joys in.
Als. I hear the beauty of this seat largely.
Ver. It falls much short of that.   *Exeunt. Manet* BEATRICE.
Bea.   So, here's one step   10
    Into my father's favour; time will fix him.
    I have got him now the liberty of the house:
    So wisdom by degrees works out her freedom;
    And if that eye be darkened that offends me
    (I wait but that eclipse), this gentleman   15
    Shall soon shine glorious in my father's liking,
    Through the refulgent virtue of my love.

Enter DE FLORES.

III. iv. 9. I . . . largely.] *Q, Dilke;* I hear / The . . . largely commended.
Dyce, Bullen.

278–9.] Cf. No. 70 of *Conceits, Clinches, Flashes, and Whimzies*: 'A rich
Lawyer, that had got a great estate by the Law, upon his death bed was
desirous to give twenty pound per annum to the house of Bedlam. Being
demanded why he would give it to that house rather then another, he
answered that he had got it of madmen, and to them he would give it
againe' (*Shakespeare Jest-Books*, ed. Hazlitt, 1864, III, 21).

III. iv. 9.] Q's text seems to make satisfactory sense.
14.] Possibly an echo of the New Testament: 'And if thine eye offend
thee . . .' (Matthew, xviii. 9, Mark, ix. 47). She is, of course, thinking of
Alonzo.

De F. [*aside.*] My thoughts are at a banquet for the deed;
     I feel no weight in't, 'tis but light and cheap
     For the sweet recompense that I set down for't.   20

Bea. De Flores.

De F.   Lady?

Bea.   Thy looks promise cheerfully.

De F. All things are answerable, time, circumstance,
     Your wishes, and my service.

Bea.   Is it done then?

De F. Piracquo is no more.

Bea. My joys start at mine eyes; our sweet'st delights   25
     Are evermore born weeping.

De F.   I've a token for you.

Bea. For me?

De F.   But it was sent somewhat unwillingly,
     I could not get the ring without the finger.

                                        [*Shows her the finger.*]

Bea. Bless me! What hast thou done?

De F.   Why, is that more
     Than killing the whole man? I cut his heart-strings.   30
     A greedy hand thrust in a dish at court,

18. *aside.*] *Dyce.*   18. banquet . . . deed;] *Dilke;* banquet . . . deed, *Q;*
banquet; . . . deed, *Dyce, Bullen.*   28.1. *Shows . . . finger.*] *Dyce.*

18.] Most editors link 'for the deed' with l. 19. But Q seems to make good
sense, with 'for' meaning 'because of', as in l. 20.

25–6.] Weeping as a sign of joy is frequent in Middleton's plays; cf. *The
Phoenix*, v. i. 56 (Bullen, I, 198), *A Fair Quarrel*, I. i. 29–30 (Bullen, IV, 162),
The Old Law, IV. ii. 35–6 (Bullen, II, 204) and also some lines in *The
Triumphs of Truth*, 'The Speech of London' (Bullen, VII, 237). It is here,
however, as Bullen observes (I, Introduction, lxiii) that the image is given
its final and fullest expression, and is used with an ironic power lacking in
the other plays. Other dramatists, of course, use the same idea; cf. *Tp.*, III.
i. 73–4: 'I am a fool / To weep at what I am glad of.'

31–2.] 'As much as this' appears to be equivalent to 'lost a finger': the
hand has been pushed into the dish to take food, and has had a finger cut off
by someone else's knife. Cf. *Westward Ho*, III. ii. 29–32:

     . . . when wilt come to Court and dine with me?

Whirl. One of these daies *Franke*, but Ile get mee two Gaunlets for feare
     I lose my fingers in the dishes.   (Dekker, II, 316).

We might also compare Wycherley, *The Country Wife*, v. iv:

In a mistake hath had as much as this.

Bea. 'Tis the first token my father made me send him.

De F. And I made him send it back again
    For his last token; I was loath to leave it,   35
    And I'm sure dead men have no use of jewels.
    He was as loath to part with't, for it stuck
    As if the flesh and it were both one substance.

Bea. At the stag's fall the keeper has his fees:
    'Tis soon apply'd, all dead men's fees are yours, sir;   40
    I pray, bury the finger, but the stone
    You may make use on shortly; the true value,
    Take't of my truth, is near three hundred ducats.

De F. 'Twill hardly buy a capcase for one's conscience, though,
    To keep it from the worm, as fine as 'tis.
    Well, being my fees I'll take it;   45
    Great men have taught me that, or else my merit
    Would scorn the way on't.

Bea.   It might justly, sir:
    Why, thou mistak'st, De Flores, 'tis not given
    In state of recompense.

De F.   No, I hope so, lady,   50
    You should soon witness my contempt to't then!

Bea. Prithee, thou look'st as if thou wert offended.

De F. That were strange, lady; 'tis not possible
    My service should draw such a cause from you.
    Offended? Could you think so? That were much   55
    For one of my performance, and so warm
    Yet in my service.

Bea. 'Twere misery in me to give you cause, sir.

De F. I know so much, it were so, misery
    In her most sharp condition.

---

34. made] *Q, Schelling;* have made *Dyce, Bullen.*

    People always eat with the best stomach at an ordinary, where every
    man is snatching for the best bit.
    L. Fid. Though he get a cut over the fingers. (*Works,* 1924, II, 80).
    39.] This line has the ring of a proverb, though nothing comparable to it
is to be found in collections of proverbs.

Bea.　　　　　　　　　　　　'Tis resolv'd then;　　　60
　　Look you, sir, here's three thousand golden florins:
　　I have not meanly thought upon thy merit.
De F. What, salary? Now you move me.
Bea.　　　　　　　　　　How, De Flores?
De F. Do you place me in the rank of verminous fellows,
　　To destroy things for wages? Offer gold?　　　65
　　The life blood of man! Is anything
　　Valued too precious for my recompense?
Bea. I understand thee not.
De F.　　　　　　　I could ha' hir'd
　　A journeyman in murder at this rate,
　　And mine own conscience might have slept at ease,　　70
　　And have had the work brought home.
Bea. [*aside.*]　　　　　　　I'm in a labyrinth;
　　What will content him? I would fain be rid of him.
　　[*To De F.*] I'll double the sum, sir.
De F.　　　　　　　　　You take a course
　　To double my vexation, that's the good you do.
Bea. [*aside.*] Bless me! I am now in worse plight than I
　　was;　　　　　　　　　　　75
　　I know not what will please him. [*To De F.*] —For my fear's
　　sake,
　　I prithee make away with all speed possible.
　　And if thou be'st so modest not to name
　　The sum that will content thee, paper blushes not;
　　Send thy demand in writing, it shall follow thee,　　80
　　But prithee take thy flight.

---

66. The] *Q, Baskervill;* For the *Dilke, Dyce.*　　70. slept at ease] *Dilke;*
not in *Q.*　　71. aside.] *Dilke.*　　75. aside.] *Dilke.*

---

61. *florins*] See G. The exact value of such a sum is hard to determine. It
is possible, as Dyce suggests, that Beatrice offers De Flores a promissory
note; the amount in coins would be extremely heavy.
　　65–6.] Most editors accept Dilke's emendation. But it may be that De
Flores becomes slightly incoherent in his anger and disappointment.
　　68–9.] i.e. For this amount of money I could have hired a professional
murderer.
　　70.] All editors accept Dilke's addition. The line is obviously incomplete.

De F.   You must fly too then.

Bea. I?

De F.   I'll not stir a foot else.

Bea.   What's your meaning?

De F. Why, are not you as guilty, in (I'm sure)
        As deep as I? And we should stick together.
        Come, your fears counsel you but ill, my absence   85
        Would draw suspect upon you instantly;
        There were no rescue for you.

Bea. [*aside.*]   He speaks home.

De F. Nor is it fit we two, engag'd so jointly,
        Should part and live asunder.   [*Tries to kiss her.*]

Bea.   How now, sir?
        This shows not well.

De F.   What makes your lip so strange?   90
        This must not be betwixt us.

Bea. [*aside.*]   The man talks wildly.

De F. Come, kiss me with a zeal now.

Bea. [*aside.*]   Heaven, I doubt him!

De F. I will not stand so long to beg 'em shortly.

Bea. Take heed, De Flores, of forgetfulness,
        'Twill soon betray us.

De F.   Take you heed first;   95
        Faith, y'are grown much forgetful, y'are to blame in't.

Bea. [*aside.*] He's bold, and I am blam'd for't!

De F.   I have eas'd you
        Of your trouble, think on't, I'm in pain,
        And must be eas'd of you; 'tis a charity,

87. aside.] *Dilke.*   89. *Tries . . . her.*] *This ed.*   91. betwixt] *Q, Dilke,*
Dyce; 'twixt *Neilson.*   91. aside.] *Oliphant.*   92. aside.] *Dilke.*
97. aside.] *Dilke.*

83-4.] Cf. *R 3*, I. iv. 220: 'For in this sin he is as deep as I.'
90.] Cf. Middleton's *Women Beware Women*, III. i. 157-8:
                Speak, what's the humour, sweet,
                You make your lip so strange?   (Bullen, VI, 300).
94. *forgetfulness*] A word of which Middleton is noticeably fond; cf.
Michaelmas Term, I. i. 163 (Bullen, I, 225), *The Witch*, I. i. 34 (*ibid.*, V, 358)
and *Women Beware Women*, I. ii. 205 and V. i. 187 (*ibid.*, VI, 253 and 368).

Justice invites your blood to understand me.   100
Bea. I dare not.
De F.   Quickly!
Bea.   Oh, I never shall!
Speak it yet further off that I may lose
What has been spoken, and no sound remain on't.
I would not hear so much offence again
For such another deed.
De F.   Soft, lady, soft;   105
The last is not yet paid for! Oh, this act
Has put me into spirit; I was as greedy on't
As the parch'd earth of moisture, when the clouds weep.
Did you not mark, I wrought myself into't,
Nay, sued and kneel'd for't: why was all that pains took? 110
You see I have thrown contempt upon your gold,
Not that I want it not, for I do piteously:
In order I will come unto't, and make use on't,
But 'twas not held so precious to begin with;
For I place wealth after the heels of pleasure,   115
And were I not resolv'd in my belief
That thy virginity were perfect in thee,
I should but take my recompense with grudging,
As if I had but half my hopes I agreed for.
Bea. Why, 'tis impossible thou canst be so wicked,   120
Or shelter such a cunning cruelty,

112. it not] *Dilke, Dyce;* it *Q, Baskervill.*

112.] Possibly there was a confusion of negatives on the part of Middleton himself.
113. *In order*] In due time.
115.] Cf. Middleton's *The Widow*, II. i. 81: 'I count wealth but a fiddle to make us merry' (Bullen, V, 151).
121. *cunning cruelty*] Cf. *Women Beware Women*, IV. ii. 149–50:
            That I may practise the like cruel cunning
            Upon her life as she has on mine honour.
(Bullen, VI, 351). Both phrases may echo *Oth.*, V. ii. 332–5:
                        For this slave,
            If there be any cunning cruelty
            That can torment him much and hold him long,
            It shall be his.

To make his death the murderer of my honour!
Thy language is so bold and vicious,
I cannot see which way I can forgive it
With any modesty.

De F.   Push, you forget yourself!   125
A woman dipp'd in blood, and talk of modesty?

Bea. Oh misery of sin! Would I had been bound
Perpetually unto my living hate
In that Piracquo, than to hear these words.
Think but upon the distance that creation   130
Set 'twixt thy blood and mine, and keep thee there.

De F. Look but into your conscience, read me there,
'Tis a true book, you'll find me there your equal:
Push, fly not to your birth, but settle you
In what the act has made you, y'are no more now;   135
You must forget your parentage to me:
Y'are the deed's creature; by that name
You lost your first condition, and I challenge you,
As peace and innocency has turn'd you out,
And made you one with me.

Bea.   With thee, foul villain?   140

De F. Yes, my fair murd'ress; do you urge me?
Though thou writ'st maid, thou whore in thy affection!
'Twas chang'd from thy first love, and that's a kind
Of whoredom in thy heart; and he's chang'd now,
To bring thy second on, thy Alsemero,   145
Whom (by all sweets that ever darkness tasted)
If I enjoy thee not, thou ne'er enjoy'st;
I'll blast the hopes and joys of marriage,
I'll confess all; my life I rate at nothing.

Bea. De Flores!   150

De F. I shall rest from all lovers' plagues then;

144. thy] *Q, Neilson;* the *Dilke, Dyce.*   151. lovers' plagues] *Q, Dilke;*
love's plagues *Dyce, Bullen;* plagues *Ellis (conj. Dyce).*

136.] Brooke glosses 'to' as 'in your relation with'; 'in favour of' is also
possible.
144. *he's chang'd*] i.e. He (Alonzo) is dead.

I live in pain now: that shooting eye
Will burn my heart to cinders.

Bea.   Oh sir, hear me.

De F. She that in life and love refuses me,
In death and shame my partner she shall be.   155

Bea. Stay, hear me once for all; [*kneels*] I make thee master
Of all the wealth I have in gold and jewels:
Let me go poor unto my bed with honour,
And I am rich in all things.

De F.   Let this silence thee:
The wealth of all Valencia shall not buy   160
My pleasure from me;
Can you weep fate from its determin'd purpose?
So soon may you weep me.

Bea.   Vengeance begins;
Murder I see is followed by more sins.
Was my creation in the womb so curs'd,   165
It must engender with a viper first?

De F. Come, rise, and shroud your blushes in my bosom;

                                        [*Raises her.*]

Silence is one of pleasure's best receipts:

152. shooting] *Q, Dilke, Dyce;* love-shooting *Ellis (conj. Dyce).*   156.
kneels] *Dyce.*   163. you] *Dyce; not in Q.*   167.1. *Raises her.*] *Dyce.*

162.] Contrast this line with Dekker's expression of the same idea in *Old Fortunatus*, I. i. 196: 'No teares can melt the heart of destinie' (Dekker, I, 93).

165–6.] The editors who comment on these lines see in them a reference to contemporary lore about vipers, as expressed by Sir Thomas Browne, *Vulgar Errors*, Bk. III, Ch. xvi: 'That the young Vipers force their way through the bowels of their Dam, or that the Female Viper in the act of generation bites off the head of the male, in revenge whereof the young ones eat through the womb and belly of the female, is a very ancient tradition' (*Works*, ed. Keynes, 1928, II, 237). But it is difficult to see exactly how this explains the lines. Possibly no reference is intended, and the couplet might be paraphrased, 'when I was created in my mother's womb, was a curse laid upon me that I must engender with an unnatural being, a viper, before I could do so with a normal man?'

167. *shroud*] See G. The line is possibly a reminiscence of *The Duchess of Malfi*, I. i. 574: 'Oh, let me shrowd my blushes in your bosome' (Webster, II, 51).

Thy peace is wrought for ever in this yielding.
'Las, how the turtle pants! Thou'lt love anon   170
What thou so fear'st and faint'st to venture on.   *Exeunt.*

170.] Middleton is particularly fond of this metaphor; cf. *Women Beware Women*, II. ii. 326–7:

> I feel thy breast shake like a turtle panting
> Under a loving hand that makes much on't.

(Bullen, VI, 285) and *A Game at Chess*, III. iii. 4–7:

> A Suddayne feare inuades mee, a faynt trembling
> Under this omen
> As is oft felt the panting of a Turtle
> Under a Stroaking hand.   (ed. Bald, p. 92).

Act IV

[Dumb Show.]

Enter Gentlemen, VERMANDERO *meeting them with action of wonderment at the flight of* PIRACQUO. *Enter* ALSEMERO, *with* JASPERINO, *and Gallants;* VERMANDERO *points to him, the Gentlemen seeming to applaud the choice; [Exeunt in procession]* ALSEMERO, JASPERINO, *and Gentlemen;* BEATRICE *the bride following in great state, accompanied with* DIAPHANTA, ISABELLA *and other Gentlewomen:* DE FLORES *after all, smiling at the accident;* ALONZO's *ghost appears to* DE FLORES *in the midst of his smile, startles him, showing him the hand whose finger he had cut off. They pass over in great solemnity.*

Enter BEATRICE.

Bea. This fellow has undone me endlessly,
  Never was bride so fearfully distress'd;
  The more I think upon th'ensuing night,
  And whom I am to cope with in embraces,
  One that's ennobled both in blood and mind,   5
  So clear in understanding (that's my plague now),
  Before whose judgment will my fault appear
  Like malefactors' crimes before tribunals—
  There is no hiding on't, the more I dive
  Into my own distress; how a wise man   10

Act IV] *Dilke, Dyce;* ACTUS QUARTUS. *Q.* Dumb Show.] *Dilke.*
0.4. *Exeunt in procession*] *This ed.* 5. that's] *This ed.;* both *Q;* who's
Dilke, Dyce.

Dumb Show.] B. R. Pearn, 'The Dumb-Show in Elizabethan Drama',
R.E.S. XI (October 1935), 396, has shown that dumb-shows of this type,
forming an intrinsic part of the plot, are fairly common in drama up to the
end of the Jacobean period.

Stands for a great calamity! There's no venturing
Into his bed, what course soe'er I light upon,
Without my shame, which may grow up to danger;
He cannot but in justice strangle me
As I lie by him, as a cheater use me;   15
'Tis a precious craft to play with a false die
Before a cunning gamester. Here's his closet,
The key left in't, and he abroad i' th' park:
Sure 'twas forgot; I'll be so bold as look in't.   [*Opens closet.*]
Bless me! A right physician's closet 'tis,   20
Set round with vials, every one her mark too.
Sure he does practise physic for his own use,
Which may be safely call'd your great man's wisdom.
What manuscript lies here? 'The Book of Experiment,
Call'd Secrets in Nature'; so 'tis, 'tis so;   25

19. *Opens closet.*] Dyce.

---

11. *Stands for*] Most editors gloss this as 'stands open to'; but there is no
reason why a wise man should be more liable to suffer a great calamity than
anyone else. Perhaps 'represents' would be a better equivalent; in times of
difficulty a wise man is less easily deceived than others, and to encounter
him is a calamity for the would-be plotter.

23.] 'Since it safeguards him against poison' (Spencer).

25. *Secrets in Nature*] *De Arcanis Naturae* is the title of a book by
Antonius Mizaldus (1520–78), a French scholar and compiler of various
works of science and pseudo-science, but, as Dyce points out, there are no
passages in it resembling those quoted by Beatrice. Sampson has shown,
however, that in the same author's *Centuriae IX. Memorabilium* (1566) there
are virginity and pregnancy tests, such as Centuriae VI, 54, 'Experiri an
mulier sit grauida' (ed. Frankfurt, 1613, p. 127), Centuriae VII, 12 and 64,
'Mulierem corruptam ab incorrupta discernere' (*ibid.*, pp. 141–2, 154), and
also in the 'Appendix Secretorum Experimentorum Antidotorumque
contra varios morbos', p. 253, 'Noscendi ratio an mulier sit virgo integra &
intacta an non'. Two of these tests prescribe liquids for the woman to
drink, though in none of them are her reactions those described in ll.
48–50 below. Beatrice's use of the formula 'the author Antonius Mizaldus'
makes it plain that she is quoting from a manuscript compilation, presumably by Alsemero himself, into which some of Mizaldus' experiments have
been copied out. But this kind of test is very common; the second and third
of Mizaldus' tests are attributed by him to Baptista Porta, and probably
derive ultimately from Pliny's *Natural History*, xxxvi. 19 (translated by
Holland, 1601, II, 589). Burton scornfully dismisses all such tests: 'To what
end are all those Astrological questions, *an sit virgo, an sit casta, an sit*

'How to know whether a woman be with child or no.'
I hope I am not yet; if he should try though!
Let me see, folio forty-five. Here 'tis;
The leaf tuck'd down upon't, the place suspicious.
'If you would know whether a woman be with child or   30
not, give her two spoonfuls of the white water in glass
C—'
Where's that glass C? Oh yonder, I see't now—
'and if she be with child, she sleeps full twelve hours
after, if not, not.'   35
None of that water comes into my belly.
I'll know you from a hundred; I could break you now,
Or turn you into milk, and so beguile
The master of the mystery, but I'll look to you.
Ha! That which is next is ten times worse.   40
'How to know whether a woman be a maid or not';
If that should be apply'd, what would become of me?
Belike he has a strong faith of my purity,
That never yet made proof; but this he calls
'A merry sleight, but true experiment, the author An-   45

---

45. sleight] *Baskervill;* slight *Q, Dilke, Dyce.*

---

mulier? and such strange absurd trials in *Albertus Magnus, Bap. Porta, Mag. lib.* 2, *cap.* 21, in *Wecker, lib.* 5. *de secret.,* by stones, perfumes, to make them piss, and confess I know not what in their sleep; some jealous brain was the first founder of them' (*Anatomy of Melancholy,* Pt. III, Sec. 3, Memb. 2; ed. Shilleto, III, 327). There is some similarity between the pregnancy test (30–5) and a test contained in Thomas Lupton's *A Thousand Notable Things of Sundry Sorts,* The Fifth Book, No. 56: 'If you would know whether a Woman be conceived with Child or not, give her two spoonfuls of Water and one spoonful of Clarified Honey, mingled together, to drink when she goeth to sleep; and if she feels Gripings and Pains in the Belly in the night, she is with child; if she feel none, she is not' (1579; reprint of 1814, p. 43). The fantastic nature of the virginity test makes it seem very probable that Middleton devised it himself and then fathered it upon Mizaldus; his interest in such matters is shown in *Hengist, King of Kent,* II. iii. 248–89 (ed. Bald, 1938, pp. 35–6), where the virginity test is based on the belief that the touch of a virgin can cure an epileptic fit. It is interesting to note that, as in *The Changeling,* the heroine fakes the result in order to conceal her loss of virginity.

45. *sleight*] This is almost certainly the intended meaning of Q's 'slight'. Both forms of the word are common.

tonius Mizaldus. Give the party you suspect the quan-
tity of a spoonful of the water in the glass M, which upon
her that is a maid makes three several effects: 'twill make
her incontinently gape, then fall into a sudden sneezing,
last into a violent laughing; else dull, heavy, and lumpish.'   50
Where had I been?
I fear it, yet 'tis seven hours to bedtime.

Enter DIAPHANTA.

Dia. Cuds, madam, are you here?
Bea. [*aside.*]   Seeing that wench now,
A trick comes in my mind; 'tis a nice piece
Gold cannot purchase. [*To Dia.*] I come hither, wench,   55
To look my lord.
Dia. [*aside.*] Would I had such a cause to look him too!
[*To Bea.*] Why, he's i' th' park, madam.
Bea. There let him be.
Dia.   Ay, madam, let him compass
Whole parks and forests, as great rangers do;   60
At roosting time a little lodge can hold 'em.
Earth-conquering Alexander, that thought the world
Too narrow for him, in the end had but his pit-hole.
Bea. I fear thou art not modest, Diaphanta.
Dia. Your thoughts are so unwilling to be known, madam;   65

53. *aside.*] *Dilke.*   57. *aside.*] *Dilke.*

---

51. *Where . . . been?*] Probably meaning, 'where should I have been if I
had not discovered this?'

54–5. *'tis . . . purchase*] i.e. It's a scrupulous girl that cannot be bribed
with gold.

63. *pit-hole*] See G. Lines 62–3 might be compared to *Ham.*, v. i. 224–6:
'Why may not imagination trace the noble dust of Alexander, till he find it
stopping a bung-hole?' But there can be no doubt that a double meaning is
intended, as is shown by the use of 'pit-hole' in such contexts as Middleton's *A Mad World, My Masters*, I. ii. 138–40 (Bullen, III, 267), and *May-
Day*, III. i. 206–8 (Chapman, *Comedies*, 199). Cf. also *Women Beware
Women*, I. i. 26–7:

But beauty, able to content a conqueror
Whom earth could scarce content, keeps me in compass.
(Bullen, VI, 238).

'Tis ever the bride's fashion towards bed-time,
To set light by her joys, as if she ow'd 'em not.

Bea. Her joys ? Her fears, thou would'st say.

Dia.   Fear of what ?

Bea. Art thou a maid, and talk'st so to a maid ?
You leave a blushing business behind,   70
Beshrew your heart for't!

Dia.   Do you mean good sooth, madam ?

Bea. Well, if I'd thought upon the fear at first,
Man should have been unknown.

Dia.   Is't possible ?

Bea. I will give a thousand ducats to that woman
Would try what my fear were, and tell me true   75
To-morrow, when she gets from't: as she likes
I might perhaps be drawn to't.

Dia.   Are you in earnest ?

Bea. Do you get the woman, then challenge me,
And see if I'll fly from't; but I must tell you
This by the way, she must be a true maid,   80
Else there's no trial, my fears are not hers else.

Dia. Nay, she that I would put into your hands, madam,
Shall be a maid.

Bea.   You know I should be sham'd else,
Because she lies for me.

Dia.   'Tis a strange humour:
But are you serious still ? Would you resign   85
Your first night's pleasure, and give money too ?

Bea. As willingly as live; [*aside*] —alas, the gold
Is but a by-bet to wedge in the honour.

74. I will] *Q, Dilke;* I'd *Dyce, Bullen.*   87. *aside*] *Dyce.*

---

80. *maid*] i.e. Virgin.

88. *by-bet*] This phrase is recorded in *O.E.D.*, but without any precise
explanation. It is also found in Rowley and Webster's *A Cure for a Cuckold*,
III. ii. 110–11:

> I will spend more then a whole childe in getting,
> Some win by play, and others by— by-betting.

(Webster, III, 63). Lucas notes the use of the phrase in *The Changeling*, and

Dia. I do not know how the world goes abroad
    For faith or honesty, there's both requir'd in this.   90
    Madam, what say you to me, and stray no further?
    I've a good mind, in troth, to earn your money.
Bea. Y'are too quick, I fear, to be a maid.
Dia. How? Not a maid? Nay, then you urge me, madam;
    Your honourable self is not a truer   95
    With all your fears upon you—
Bea. [*aside.*]   Bad enough then.
Dia. Than I with all my lightsome joys about me.
Bea. I'm glad to hear't then; you dare put your honesty
    Upon an easy trial?
Dia.   Easy? Anything.
Bea. I'll come to you straight.   [*Goes to the closet.*]
Dia. [*aside.*]   She will not search me, will she,
    Like the forewoman of a female jury?   101
Bea. Glass M: ay, this is it; look, Diaphanta,
    You take no worse than I do.   [*Drinks.*]
Dia.   And in so doing,

96. *aside.*] *Dilke.*   100. *Goes . . . closet.*] *Dyce.*   100. *aside.*] *This ed.*
103. *Drinks.*] *Dyce.*

---

comments, 'Can it mean "betting on another's performance"? There
Beatrice is staking her honour on her woman's passing, in her place, the test
of chastity; so here Compass wants to win the child another has begotten'
(*ibid.*, p. 106). But the context of *The Changeling* makes a different explanation seem more probable. 'By' is perhaps from dicing phraseology (cf. her
metaphor in ll. 16–17 above), where the 'main chance' is opposed to the
'buy' or 'by', as in Lyly's *Euphues and His England*: 'alwayes haue an eye to
the mayne, what soeuer thou art chaunced at the buy' (*Works*, ed. Bond, II,
188). Diaphanta expresses surprise that Beatrice should not only be willing
to give up her wedding night to another woman, but should even pay her
for it. Beatrice, in an aside, makes it clear that the money is only a subsidiary
issue, a side-bet, the vital point being whether or not she can successfully
deceive her husband and thus preserve her 'honour'.

    89–90. *I . . . honesty*] i.e. I do not know how much faith or honesty can be
found in the world nowadays.

    101.] Bullen sees in this line an allusion to the notorious divorce trial
of the Countess of Essex in 1613. The Countess sued for divorce on the
grounds of non-consummation of the marriage, and during the trial was
examined by a group of matrons and noblewomen. See *State Trials*, ed.
Howell (1816), II, 802–3.

I will not question what 'tis, but take it.   [*Drinks.*]

Bea. [*aside.*] Now if the experiment be true, 'twill praise itself,
And give me noble ease: —begins already;   106

[DIAPHANTA *gapes.*]

There's the first symptom; and what haste it makes
To fall into the second, there by this time!

[DIAPHANTA *sneezes.*]

Most admirable secret! On the contrary,
It stirs not me a whit, which most concerns it.   110

Dia. Ha, ha, ha!

Bea. [*aside.*]   Just in all things and in order
As if 'twere circumscrib'd; one accident
Gives way unto another.

Dia.   Ha, ha, ha!

Bea.   How now, wench?

Dia. Ha, ha, ha! I am so, so light at heart— ha, ha, ha!—
so pleasurable!
But one swig more, sweet madam.

Bea.   Ay, to-morrow;   115
We shall have time to sit by't.

Dia.   Now I'm sad again.

Bea. [*aside.*] It lays itself so gently, too! [*To Dia.*] Come,
wench,
Most honest Diaphanta I dare call thee now.

Dia. Pray tell me, madam, what trick call you this?

Bea. I'll tell thee all hereafter; we must study   120
The carriage of this business.

Dia.   I shall carry't well,
Because I love the burthen.

Bea.   About midnight

104. *Drinks.*] Dyce.   105. *aside.*] Dilke.   106.1. *Diaphanta gapes.*]
Dilke.   108.1. *Diaphanta sneezes.*] *Dilke.*   111. *aside.*] *Dyce.*
117. *aside.*] *Dilke.*

110. *which . . . it*] i.e. Who am the person whose reaction to the test is of
most importance.

121–2.] Diaphanta is evidently a connoisseur of double meanings. She
is very different from the Julia of Digges's *Gerardo* (see Appendix A).

You must not fail to steal forth gently,
That I may use the place.

Dia.   Oh, fear not, madam,
I shall be cool by that time; —the bride's place,   125
And with a thousand ducats! I'm for a justice now,
I bring a portion with me; I scorn small fools.   *Exeunt.*

[IV. ii]

Enter VERMANDERO *and Servant.*

Ver. I tell thee, knave, mine honour is in question,
A thing till now free from suspicion,
Nor ever was there cause; who of my gentlemen
Are absent? Tell me and truly how many and who.

Ser. Antonio, sir, and Franciscus.   5

Ver. When did they leave the castle?

Ser. Some ten days since, sir, the one intending to Briamata,
th'other for Valencia.

Ver. The time accuses 'em; a charge of murder
Is brought within my castle gate, Piracquo's murder;   10
I dare not answer faithfully their absence:
A strict command of apprehension
Shall pursue 'em suddenly, and either wipe
The stain off clear, or openly discover it.
Provide me winged warrants for the purpose. *Exit Servant.* 15
See, I am set on again.

Enter TOMAZO.

Tom. I claim a brother of you.

IV. ii. 15. *Exit Servant.*] Dyce; *after l. 16, Q, Dilke.*

126–7.] 'i.e. I'm for a big fool, a justice' (Spencer). Cf. I. ii. 130.

IV. ii. 7. *Briamata*] Cf. Reynolds, p. 117: '. . . *Briamata*: a fayre house of
his, tenne leagues from *Alicant*'.
    11. *answer faithfully*] Explain confidently, in good faith.
    16. *set on*] Presumably in the sense of 'attacked, assaulted'; he has noticed
the entrance of Tomazo.

Ver.   Y'are too hot,
    Seek him not here.
Tom.   Yes, 'mongst your dearest bloods,
    If my peace find no fairer satisfaction;
    This is the place must yield account for him,   20
    For here I left him, and the hasty tie
    Of this snatch'd marriage, gives strong testimony
    Of his most certain ruin.
Ver.   Certain falsehood!
    This is the place indeed; his breach of faith
    Has too much marr'd both my abused love,   25
    The honourable love I reserv'd for him,
    And mock'd my daughter's joy; the prepar'd morning
    Blush'd at his infidelity; he left
    Contempt and scorn to throw upon those friends
    Whose belief hurt 'em: oh, 'twas most ignoble   30
    To take his flight so unexpectedly,
    And throw such public wrongs on those that lov'd him.
Tom. Then this is all your answer?
Ver.   'Tis too fair
    For one of his alliance; and I warn you
    That this place no more see you.   *Exit.*

Enter DE FLORES.

Tom.   The best is,   35
    There is more ground to meet a man's revenge on.
    Honest De Flores!
De F.   That's my name indeed!
    Saw you the bride? Good sweet sir, which way took she?
Tom. I have blest mine eyes from seeing such a false one.

23ff.] It might be argued as an inconsistency that Vermandero has just
ordered Antonio and Franciscus to be arrested on suspicion of murder, but
is now accusing Alonzo of having stayed away from his own wedding. It
may be that Vermandero, an honourable man whose reputation is now in
question, is determined to do all he can (in private) to bring the truth to
light; but he is also proud, and Tomazo's blunt accusations rouse him to a
counter-attack. At this point, of course, nobody except Beatrice and De
Flores knows exactly what has happened to Alonzo.

De F. [*aside.*] I'd fain get off, this man's not for my company,   40
    I smell his brother's blood when I come near him.

Tom. Come hither, kind and true one; I remember
    My brother lov'd thee well.

De F.   Oh purely, dear sir!
    [*Aside.*] —Methinks I am now again a-killing on him,
    He brings it so fresh to me.

Tom.   Thou canst guess, sirrah,   45
    (One honest friend has an instinct of jealousy)
    At some foul guilty person?

De F. 'Las, sir, I am so charitable, I think none
    Worse than myself. —You did not see the bride then?

Tom. I prithee name her not. Is she not wicked?   50

De F. No, no, a pretty, easy, round-pack'd sinner,
    As your most ladies are, else you might think
    I flatter'd her; but, sir, at no hand wicked,
    Till th'are so old their chins and noses meet,
    And they salute witches. I am call'd, I think, sir: 55
    [*Aside.*] —His company ev'n o'erlays my conscience.   *Exit.*

Tom. That De Flores has a wondrous honest heart;
    He'll bring it out in time, I'm assur'd on't.
    Oh, here's the glorious master of the day's joy.

---

40. aside.] *Dilke.*   44. *Aside.*] *Dilke.*   46. One] *Q, Dilke;* An *Dyce,*
Bullen.   51. pack'd] *Q, all eds.;* pac'd *conj. Dyce.*   54. chins and
noses] *Ellis (conj. Dyce);* sins and vices *Q, Dilke, Dyce.*   56. *Aside.*]
Dilke.

---

51. *round-pack'd*] The meaning of the phrase is uncertain. Most editors
gloss it as 'plump', though Schelling suggests 'thoroughly dishonest'.
Dyce's emendation would mean 'brisk, lively'.

54. *chins and noses*] Dyce's emendation is accepted by all later editors.
Presumably the prompt-copy read 'Chins and Noses'; either the compositor or the transcriber of the MS. copy for Q, with 'sinner' and 'wicked'
in his mind from the preceding lines, misread 'Chins' as 'Sins', which
could easily be done in the English or secretary hand if the 'h' curved back
under the line (cf. the misreading of 'Phosphorus' as 'Bosphorus' at v. i. 25).
Possibly 'Noses' was badly written (in any case 'N' and 'V' in the secretary
hand are very easily confused), and the compositor or transcriber searched
about for a word to fit the context without considering that his first assumption might be mistaken. At some stage the upper-case letters of the original
phrase were changed to lower-case.

    'Twill not be long till he and I do reckon.   60

Enter ALSEMERO.

  Sir!

Als.   You are most welcome.

Tom.   You may call that word back;
    I do not think I am, nor wish to be.

Als. 'Tis strange you found the way to this house then.

Tom. Would I'd ne'er known the cause! I'm none of those, sir,
    That come to give you joy, and swill your wine;   65
    'Tis a more precious liquor that must lay
    The fiery thirst I bring.

Als.   Your words and you
    Appear to me great strangers.

Tom.   Time and our swords
    May make us more acquainted; this the business:
    I should have a brother in your place;   70
    How treachery and malice have dispos'd of him,
    I'm bound to enquire of him which holds his right,
    Which never could come fairly.

Als.   You must look
    To answer for that word, sir.

Tom.   Fear you not,
    I'll have it ready drawn at our next meeting.   75
    Keep your day solemn. Farewell, I disturb it not;
    I'll bear the smart with patience for a time.   *Exit.*

Als. 'Tis somewhat ominous this: a quarrel enter'd
    Upon this day; my innocence relieves me,

Enter JASPERINO.

    I should be wondrous sad else. —Jasperino,   80
    I have news to tell thee, strange news.

Jas.   I ha' some too,

60. 'Twill] *Dilke, Dyce;* I will *Q, Spencer.*   60–1. reckon. | *Enter Alsemero.* | Sir!] *Dyce;* reckon sir. | *Enter Alsemero. Q.*   70. have] *Q, Schelling;* have had *Dilke, Dyce.*

---

    75. *it*] His answer: a sword.

   I think as strange as yours; would I might keep
   Mine, so my faith and friendship might be kept in't!
   Faith, sir, dispense a little with my zeal,
   And let it cool in this.
Als.   This puts me on,   85
   And blames thee for thy slowness.
Jas.   All may prove nothing;
   Only a friendly fear that leapt from me, sir.
Als. No question it may prove nothing; let's partake it, though.
Jas. 'Twas Diaphanta's chance (for to that wench
   I pretend honest love, and she deserves it)   90
   To leave me in a back part of the house,
   A place we chose for private conference;
   She was no sooner gone, but instantly
   I heard your bride's voice in the next room to me;
   And lending more attention, found De Flores   95
   Louder than she.
Als.   De Flores? Thou art out now.
Jas. You'll tell me more anon.
Als.   Still I'll prevent thee;
   The very sight of him is poison to her.
Jas. That made me stagger too, but Diaphanta
   At her return confirm'd it.
Als.   Diaphanta!   100
Jas. Then fell we both to listen, and words pass'd
   Like those that challenge interest in a woman.
Als. Peace, quench thy zeal; 'tis dangerous to thy bosom.
Jas. Then truth is full of peril.
Als.   Such truths are.

---

88. though] *All eds.;* thou *Q.*

 84–5. *dispense . . . this*] i.e. Allow me not to be so zealous in your service as I usually am, so that I may keep back this news.

 87. *friendly fear*] Cf. Middleton and Rowley's *A Fair Quarrel*, II. i. 77: 'Now, what's the friendly fear that fights within me . . .' (Bullen, IV, 186).

 89ff.] Jasperino's description would seem to fit III. iv; he overheard De Flores claiming his reward from Beatrice (see below, ll. 101–2).

 97. *prevent*] See G.

    —Oh, were she the sole glory of the earth,   105
    Had eyes that could shoot fire into kings' breasts,
    And touch'd, she sleeps not here! Yet I have time,
    Though night be near, to be resolv'd hereof;
    And prithee do not weigh me by my passions.

Jas. I never weigh'd friend so.

Als.   Done charitably.   110
    That key will lead thee to a pretty secret,   *[Gives key.]*
    By a Chaldean taught me, and I've made
    My study upon some; bring from my closet
    A glass inscrib'd there with the letter *M*,
    And question not my purpose.

Jas.   It shall be done, sir. *Exit.* 115

Als. How can this hang together? Not an hour since,
    Her woman came pleading her lady's fears,
    Deliver'd her for the most timorous virgin
    That ever shrunk at man's name, and so modest,
    She charg'd her weep out her request to me,   120
    That she might come obscurely to my bosom.

Enter BEATRICE.

Bea. [*aside.*] All things go well; my woman's preparing yonder
    For her sweet voyage, which grieves me to lose;
    Necessity compels it; I lose all else.

Als. [*aside.*] Push, modesty's shrine is set in yonder forehead. 125
    I cannot be too sure though. [*To her.*] —My Joanna!

Bea. Sir, I was bold to weep a message to you,
    Pardon my modest fears.

Als. [*aside.*]   The dove's not meeker,
    She's abus'd, questionless.

111. *Gives key.*] *Dilke.*   112. I've made] *This ed.;* I've *Q, Dilke;* I have
Dyce, Bullen.   116. since,] *This ed.;* since? *Q;* since *Dyce.*   122.
aside.] *Dilke.*   125. *aside.*] *Dilke.*   128. *aside.*] *Dilke.*

  107. *touch'd*] See G.
  121. *she*] Beatrice.
  obscurely] In darkness; Beatrice is preparing for the substitution of
Diaphanta for herself.

Enter JASPERINO [*with glass*].

                    —Oh, are you come, sir ?

Bea. [*aside.*] The glass, upon my life! I see the letter.   130
Jas. Sir, this is M.
Als.   'Tis it.
Bea. [*aside.*]   I am suspected.
Als. How fitly our bride comes to partake with us!
Bea. What is't, my lord ?
Als.   No hurt.
Bea.   Sir, pardon me,
    I seldom taste of any composition.
Als. But this upon my warrant you shall venture on.   135
Bea. I fear 'twill make me ill.
Als.   Heaven forbid that.
Bea. [*aside.*] I'm put now to my cunning; th'effects I know,
    If I can now but feign 'em handsomely.   [*Drinks.*]
Als. [*to Jas.*] It has that secret virtue, it ne'er miss'd, sir,
    Upon a virgin.
Jas.   Treble qualitied ?   140
                [BEATRICE *gapes, then sneezes.*]
Als. By all that's virtuous it takes there, proceeds!
Jas. This is the strangest trick to know a maid by.
Bea. Ha, ha, ha!
    You have given me joy of heart to drink, my lord.
Als. No, thou hast given me such joy of heart,   145
    That never can be blasted.
Bea.   What's the matter, sir ?
Als. [*to Jas.*] See, now 'tis settled in a melancholy,
    Keeps both the time and method; [*to her*] my Joanna!
    Chaste as the breath of heaven, or morning's womb,

129. *with glass*] *Dyce.*   130. *aside.*] *Dilke.*   131. *aside.*] *Dilke.*
137. *aside.*] *Dilke.*   138. *Drinks.*] *Dilke.*   139. *to Jas.*] *This ed.*
140.1. *Beatrice . . . sneezes.*] *Dilke.*   147. *to Jas.*] *Dilke.*   148. Keeps]
Dyce, Bullen; Keep *Q, Dilke.*

148.] Dyce's emendation seems justified, though a case could be made
for Q's reading, with 'Keep' as an imperative addressed to Beatrice.
149–50.] Cf. Middleton's *The Triumphs of Truth*: 'Before the day sprang

That brings the day forth; thus my love encloses thee.   150
                              [*Embraces her.*] *Exeunt.*

[IV. iii]

            Enter ISABELLA *and* LOLLIO.

Isa. Oh heaven! Is this the waiting moon?
      Does love turn fool, run mad, and all at once?
      Sirrah, here's a madman, akin to the fool too,
      A lunatic lover.
Lol. No, no, not he I brought the letter from?   5
Isa. Compare his inside with his out, and tell me.

                              [*Gives him the letter.*]

Lol. The out's mad, I'm sure of that; I had a taste on't.
      [*Reads.*] 'To the bright Andromeda, chief chambermaid

150.1. *Embraces her.*] *This ed.*

IV. iii. 1. waiting] *Q, Dilke;* new or waning *conj. Dilke;* waning *Dyce,*
Bullen.   6.1. *Gives . . . letter.*] *This ed.*   8. *Reads.*] *Neilson.*
8–11. 'To the . . . post.'] *Q, Dilke; Isa.* 'To the . . . post.' *Dyce, Bullen.*

from the morning's womb . . .' (Bullen, VII, 258), and the anonymous *The
Second Maiden's Tragedy,* V. ii:
            wellcome to myne eyes
            as is the daye-springe from the morninges woombe.
                              (*M.S.R.*, 1909, p. 75).

   IV. iii. 1. *waiting*] The text appears to be corrupt, unless 'waiting moon'
had some special meaning which is now lost. But an emendation to 'waning'
hardly seems justified; a waning moon would surely imply the return of
sanity.
   6. *Compare . . . out*] i.e. Compare the contents of the letter with what is
written on the cover of it.
   8–11.] It is very probable that a Jacobean audience would find meanings
in this gibberish that are hidden from modern readers. Isabella is addressed
as Andromeda presumably because Franciscus is the Perseus who is to
rescue her from the dragon Alibius. In his character of 'A Chamber-
Mayde' (whom he describes as being extremely lascivious), Overbury says
of her that 'Shee reads *Greenes* workes over and over, but is so carried
away with the *Myrrour of Knighthood,* she is many times resolv'd to run out
of her selfe, and become a Ladie Errant' (ed. Paylor, 1936, p. 43). The
Knight of the Sun is one of the heroes of the work Overbury mentions,
The Mirrour of Princely deedes and Knighthood, 'Wherein is shewed the

to the Knight of the Sun, at the sign of Scorpio, in the
middle region, sent by the bellows mender of Aeolus. Pay   10
the post.' This is stark madness.

Isa. Now mark the inside. [*Takes the letter and reads.*] 'Sweet
lady, having now cast off this counterfeit cover of a madman, I appear to your best judgment a true and faithful
lover of your beauty.'   15

Lol. He is mad still.

Isa. 'If any fault you find, chide those perfections in you,
which have made me imperfect; 'tis the same sun that
causeth to grow, and enforceth to wither—'

Lol. Oh rogue!   20

Isa. '—Shapes and transshapes, destroys and builds again; I
come in winter to you dismantled of my proper orna-
ments: by the sweet splendour of your cheerful smiles, I
spring and live a lover.'

Lol. Mad rascal still!   25

Isa. 'Tread him not under foot, that shall appear an honour to
your bounties. I remain—mad till I speak with you, from
whom I expect my cure. Yours all, or one beside himself,
FRANCISCUS.'

Lol. You are like to have a fine time on't; my master and I may   30
give over our professions, I do not think but you can cure
fools and madmen faster than we, with little pains too.

Isa. Very likely.

Lol. One thing I must tell you, mistress: you perceive that I

---

12. *Takes . . . reads.*] *Neilson.*

---

worthinesse of the Knight of the Sunne, and his brother Rosicleer, sonnes
to the great Emperour Trebetio', a romance translated from the Spanish of
Diego Ortunez de Calahorra, and published in nine parts from 1578 to
1601. References to it, somewhat contemptuous in tone, occur fairly often
in the dramatists of the period, especially Ben Jonson. Scorpio was the sign
governing the privy parts of the body, and this turns 'middle region', an
astronomical term, into an obvious pun (cf. Middleton's *A Mad World, My
Masters*, IV. iii. 33, Bullen, III, 323). The remaining references appear to be
simple jokes. There seems to be no reason why we should not follow Q in
making Lollio read these lines; that he can read is plain from ll. 160ff.
below.

    am privy to your skill; if I find you minister once and set   35
    up the trade, I put in for my thirds, I shall be mad or fool
    else.

Isa. The first place is thine, believe it, Lollio;
    If I do fall—

Lol. I fall upon you.   40

Isa. So.

Lol. Well, I stand to my venture.

Isa. But thy counsel now, how shall I deal with 'em?

Lol. Why, do you mean to deal with 'em?

Isa. Nay, the fair understanding, how to use 'em.   45

Lol. Abuse 'em! That's the way to mad the fool, and make a
    fool of the madman, and then you use 'em kindly.

Isa. 'Tis easy, I'll practise; do thou observe it;
    The key of thy wardrobe.

Lol. There; fit yourself for 'em, and I'll fit 'em both for you.   50
                                    [*Gives her the key.*]

Isa. Take thou no further notice than the outside.   *Exit.*

Lol. Not an inch; I'll put you to the inside.

Enter ALIBIUS.

Alib. Lollio, art there? Will all be perfect, think'st thou?
    To-morrow night, as if to close up the solemnity,
    Vermandero expects us.   55

Lol. I mistrust the madmen most; the fools will do well
    enough; I have taken pains with them.

Alib. Tush, they cannot miss; the more absurdity,
    The more commends it, —so no rough behaviours
    Affright the ladies; they are nice things, thou know'st.   60

Lol. You need not fear, sir; so long as we are there with our
    commanding pizzles, they'll be as tame as the ladies them-
    selves.

44. Why,] *All eds.;* We *Q.*   50.1. *Gives . . . key.*] *Dilke.*

36. *thirds*] See G. In this case the other two-thirds would go to Alibius
and to whichever lover Isabella chooses.

45. *the fair understanding*] 'i.e. Nay, understand my speeches in the fair
and modest sense in which they are uttered' (Dilke).

Alib. I will see them once more rehearse before they go.

Lol. I was about it, sir; look you to the madmen's morris, and 65
    let me alone with the other; there is one or two that I mis-
    trust their fooling; I'll instruct them, and then they shall
    rehearse the whole measure.

Alib. Do so; I'll see the music prepar'd: but Lollio,
    By the way, how does my wife brook her restraint? 70
    Does she not grudge at it?

Lol. So, so; she takes some pleasure in the house, she would
    abroad else; you must allow her a little more length, she's
    kept too short.

Alib. She shall along to Vermandero's with us; 75
    That will serve her for a month's liberty.

Lol. What's that on your face, sir?

Alib. Where, Lollio? I see nothing.

Lol. Cry you mercy, sir, 'tis your nose; it show'd like the trunk
    of a young elephant. 80

Alib. Away, rascal! I'll prepare the music, Lollio.

                             Exit ALIBIUS.

Lol. Do, sir, and I'll dance the whilst; Tony, where art thou,
    Tony?

                 Enter ANTONIO.

Ant. Here, cousin; where art thou?

Lol. Come, Tony, the footmanship I taught you. 85

Ant. I had rather ride, cousin.

Lol. Ay, a whip take you; but I'll keep you out. Vault in; look
    you, Tony: fa, la la, la la.   [*Dances.*]

Ant. Fa, la la, la la.   [*Dances.*]

67. fooling] *Q, Dilke, Dyce;* footing *Bullen.*   88. *Dances.*] *Dilke.*
89. *Dances.*] *Dilke.*

---

    67. *fooling*] Bullen's emendation is not necessary; Lollio is probably
thinking of Antonio and Franciscus, who will 'fool about' in the wrong way
if they are not watched.

    79–80.] The long nose may be an equivalent of the cuckold's horns, or it
may mean, as Spencer suggests, that Alibius is being led by the nose.

    86. *ride*] Cf. l. 151 below, and also Middleton's *The Family of Love*,
I. ii. 106 (Bullen, III, 18).

Lol. There, an honour.   90

Ant. Is this an honour, coz?   [*Bows.*]

Lol. Yes, and it please your worship.

Ant. Does honour bend in the hams, coz?

Lol. Marry does it; as low as worship, squireship, nay, yeo-
    manry itself sometimes, from whence it first stiffened;   95
    there rise, a caper.

Ant. Caper after an honour, coz?

Lol. Very proper; for honour is but a caper, rises as fast and
    high, has a knee or two, and falls to th'ground again. You
    can remember your figure, Tony?   *Exit.*

Ant. Yes, cousin; when I see thy figure, I can remember mine. 101

       Enter ISABELLA [*like a madwoman*].

Isa. Hey, how he treads the air! Shough, shough, t'other way!
    He burns his wings else; here's wax enough below, Icarus,
    more than will be cancelled these eighteen moons;
    He's down, he's down, what a terrible fall he had!   105
    Stand up, thou son of Cretan Dedalus,
    And let us tread the lower labyrinth;
    I'll bring thee to the clue.

Ant. Prithee, coz, let me alone.

Isa. Art thou not drown'd?   110
    About thy head I saw a heap of clouds,
    Wrapp'd like a Turkish turban; on thy back
    A crook'd chamelion-colour'd rainbow hung
    Like a tiara down unto thy hams.

---

91. *Bows.*] *This ed.*   98. rises] *All eds.;* rise *Q.*   101.1. *like a madwoman*] *Dilke.*   102. he] *All eds.;* she *Q.*

100–1. *figure*] Another Rowley pun: (i) dance-figure, pattern of steps;
(ii) face, appearance.

103. *wax*] Obviously alluding to the wax with which Icarus assembled his
wings; but the next line shows that Isabella is thinking of it in terms of the
wax used for seals on legal deeds.

107–8.] A reference to the thread Ariadne gave to Theseus so that he
could find his way out of the labyrinth. (Presumably Alibius is the Mino-
taur.) Cf. Webster and Rowley's *A Cure for a Cuckold*, v. i. 348–9: '. . . come
Ile be the clew / To lead you forth this Labyrinth . . .' (Webster, III, 92).

  Let me suck out those billows in thy belly;   115
  Hark how they roar and rumble in the straits!
  Bless thee from the pirates.
Ant. Pox upon you, let me alone!
Isa. Why shouldst thou mount so high as Mercury,
  Unless thou hadst reversion of his place?   120
  Stay in the moon with me, Endymion,
  And we will rule these wild rebellious waves,
  That would have drown'd my love.
Ant. I'll kick thee if again thou touch me,
  Thou wild unshapen antic; I am no fool,   125
  You bedlam!
Isa.   But you are, as sure as I am, mad.
  Have I put on this habit of a frantic,
  With love as full of fury to beguile
  The nimble eye of watchful jealousy,
  And am I thus rewarded?   *[Reveals herself.]* 130
Ant. Ha! Dearest beauty!
Isa.   No, I have no beauty now,
  Nor never had, but what was in my garments.
  You a quick-sighted lover? Come not near me!
  Keep your caparisons, y'are aptly clad;
  I came a feigner to return stark mad.   *Exit.* 135

Enter LOLLIO.

Ant. Stay, or I shall change condition,
  And become as you are.
Lol. Why, Tony, whither now? Why, fool?
Ant. Whose fool, usher of idiots? You coxcomb!
  I have fool'd too much.   140

---

116. straits] *Dyce, Bullen;* streets *Q, Dilke.* 130. *Reveals herself.]*
This ed.

---

 116. *straits*] Presumably the sea between Crete and Greece, if Isabella is
still thinking in terms of the Icarus legend.
 121. *Endymion*] A beautiful youth with whom Luna (the moon) fell in
love. Isabella is borrowing the imagery that Franciscus had used, III. iii.
79ff.

Lol. You were best be mad another while then.

Ant. So I am, stark mad, I have cause enough;
　　And I could throw the full effects on thee,
　　And beat thee like a fury!

Lol. Do not, do not; I shall not forbear the gentleman under　145
　　the fool, if you do; alas, I saw through your fox-skin
　　before now: come, I can give you comfort; my mistress
　　loves you, and there is as arrant a madman i' th' house as
　　you are a fool, your rival, whom she loves not; if after the
　　masque we can rid her of him, you earn her love, she　150
　　says, and the fool shall ride her.

Ant. May I believe thee?

Lol. Yes, or you may choose whether you will or no.

Ant. She's eas'd of him; I have a good quarrel on't.

Lol. Well, keep your old station yet, and be quiet.　155

Ant. Tell her I will deserve her love.　　　　　　[*Exit.*]

Lol. And you are like to have your desire.

Enter FRANCISCUS.

Fran. [*sings.*] 'Down, down, down a-down a-down, and then
　　with a horse-trick,
　　To kick Latona's forehead, and break her bowstring.'

Lol. This is t'other counterfeit; I'll put him out of his　160

156. *Exit.*] *Dilke.*　　157. desire] *Q, Dilke, Dyce;* desert *Ellis (conj. Dyce).*
158. *sings.*] *Dilke.*

145–6.] An obvious allusion to III. iii. 143.

146. *fox-skin*] Sampson's suggestion that Antonio may be wearing a fox-skin garment is extremely unlikely; the phrase probably means nothing more than 'cunning disguise'. Cf. *The Whore of Babylon,* II. ii. 155–6:
　　To flea off this hypocrisie, tis time,
　　Least worne too long, the Foxes skinne be known.
　　　　　　　　　　　　　　　　　　(Dekker, II, 225).

159. *Latona*] A Latin form of the Greek Leto, daughter of the Titan Coeus and Phoebe, and mother of Apollo and Artemis by Zeus. In *Cynthia's Revels,* I. ii. 90 (Jonson, IV, 51) it is possible that Jonson uses the name to indicate Artemis or Diana, the daughter of Latona (see Herford and Simpson's note, IX, 494), and the same may have occurred here, in which case the 'bowstring' would belong to Diana's bow. The line is possibly another of Franciscus' concealed references to Isabella.

humour. [*Takes out letter and reads.*] 'Sweet lady, having
now cast off this counterfeit cover of a madman, I appear
to your best judgment a true and faithful lover of your
beauty.' This is pretty well for a madman.

Fran. Ha! What's that?   165

Lol. 'Chide those perfections in you, which have made me
    imperfect.'

Fran. I am discover'd to the fool.

Lol. I hope to discover the fool in you, ere I have done with
    you. 'Yours all, or one beside himself, FRANCISCUS.'   170
    This madman will mend sure.

Fran. What do you read, sirrah?

Lol. Your destiny, sir; you'll be hang'd for this trick, and
    another that I know.

Fran. Art thou of counsel with thy mistress?   175

Lol. Next her apron strings.

Fran. Give me thy hand.

Lol. Stay, let me put yours in my pocket first; [*puts away the
    letter*] your hand is true, is it not? It will not pick? I
    partly fear it, because I think it does lie.   180

Fran. Not in a syllable.

Lol. So; if you love my mistress so well as you have handled
    the matter here, you are like to be cur'd of your madness.

Fran. And none but she can cure it.

Lol. Well, I'll give you over then, and she shall cast your   185
    water next.

Fran. Take for thy pains past.   [*Gives him money.*]

---

161. *Takes . . . reads.*] Dilke.   162. cast off] *Dyce;* cast *Q.*   166. which
have] *Dyce;* which *Q.*   172. What do] *All eds.;* What? Do *Q.*
178–9. *puts . . . letter*] Dyce.   187. *Gives . . . money.*] Dilke.

---

162. *off*] Cf. l. 13 above, and also 'have' in l. 166 with 18 above.

172.] Lollio's reply seems to justify omitting the question-mark after
'What'.

177–9. *hand*] A similar pun on 'hand' as (i) hand; (ii) handwriting, letter,
is found in Rowley's *All's Lost by Lust*, II. vi. 101–3:

      Speake, is not this your hand?
    Dio. I have three then it should seeme,
    For I have two of my owne fingring.   (ed. Stork, p. 110).

Lol. I shall deserve more, sir, I hope; my mistress loves you,
    but must have some proof of your love to her.

Fran. There I meet my wishes.   190

Lol. That will not serve, you must meet her enemy and yours.

Fran. He's dead already!

Lol. Will you tell me that, and I parted but now with him?

Fran. Show me the man.

Lol. Ay, that's a right course now, see him before you kill him   195
    in any case, and yet it needs not go so far neither; 'tis but
    a fool that haunts the house and my mistress in the shape
    of an idiot; bang but his fool's coat well-favouredly, and
    'tis well.

Fran. Soundly, soundly!   200

Lol. Only reserve him till the masque be past, and if you find
    him not now in the dance yourself, I'll show you. In, in!
    My master!

Fran. He handles him like a feather. Hey!   [*Exit dancing.*]

Enter ALIBIUS.

Alib. Well said; in a readiness, Lollio?   205

Lol. Yes, sir.

Alib. Away then, and guide them in, Lollio;
    Entreat your mistress to see this sight.   [*Exit* LOLLIO.]
    Hark, is there not one incurable fool
    That might be begg'd? I have friends.   210

204. *Exit dancing.*] *Dilke.*   208. *Exit Lollio.*] *This ed.*

202ff.] The stage-business of these last dozen lines is not too clear, as Q
gives no exit for Lollio or Franciscus. Possibly some stage-directions were
omitted when the transcript from prompt-copy was made. 'My master'
(203) seems to be a warning of the approach of Alibius, though it could also
be an ironical description of Franciscus. The exit for Lollio at l. 208
gives him time to assemble the madmen behind the stage and lead them on.

205. *Well said*] A stock phrase, meaning 'well done' rather than 'well
spoken'; cf. v. i. 74 and 89.

209–10.] 'To beg a fool was to seek appointment as his guardian and thus
enjoy his estate' (Schelling). The phrase is very common; cf. *The Honest
Whore, Part I*, I. ii. 132: '. . . if I fret not his guts, beg me for a foole'
(Dekker, II, 12). In his reply (l. 211) Lollio may perhaps be alluding to
Antonio or Franciscus.

Lol. [*within.*] I have him for you, one that shall deserve it too.
Alib. Good boy, Lollio.

> [*Enter* ISABELLA, *then* LOLLIO *with Madmen and Fools.*]
> *The Madmen and Fools dance.*

'Tis perfect; well, fit but once these strains,
We shall have coin and credit for our pains.   *Exeunt.*

211. *within.*] *This ed.*   212.1. *Enter . . . Fools.*] *Dyce.*   213. perfect;
well, fit] *Dyce;* perfect well fit, *Q.*

Act V

Enter BEATRICE. *A clock strikes one.*

Bea. One struck, and yet she lies by't!—Oh my fears!
    This strumpet serves her own ends, 'tis apparent now,
    Devours the pleasure with a greedy appetite,
    And never minds my honour or my peace,
    Makes havoc of my right; but she pays dearly for't: 5
    No trusting of her life with such a secret,
    That cannot rule her blood to keep her promise.
    Beside, I have some suspicion of her faith to me
    Because I was suspected of my lord,
    And it must come from her, —hark, by my horrors,   10
    Another clock strikes two.   *Strikes two.*

Enter DE FLORES.

De F.   Pist, where are you?
Bea. De Flores?
De F.   Ay; is she not come from him yet?
Bea. As I am a living soul, not.
De F.   Sure the devil
    Hath sow'd his itch within her; who'd trust
    A waiting-woman?
Bea.   I must trust somebody.   15

Act v] *Dilke, Dyce;* ACTUS QUINTUS. *Q.*   11. *Strikes*] *Dilke; Strike Q.*

---

    1. *lies by't*] Presumably 'it' is the 'pleasure' of l. 3.
    1–25.] Sampson points out the resemblance between this part of the
play and v. i of Heywood's *A Maidenhead Well Lost* (*Dramatic Works,*
1874, IV, 152–3). The whole scene should be compared to the extracts from
Digges's *Gerardo* in Appendix A.

De F. Push, they are termagants,
　　Especially when they fall upon their masters,
　　And have their ladies' first-fruits; th'are mad whelps,
　　You cannot stave 'em off from game royal; then
　　You are so harsh and hardy, ask no counsel,　　　　20
　　And I could have help'd you to an apothecary's daughter,
　　Would have fall'n off before eleven, and thank'd you too.
Bea. Oh me, not yet? This whore forgets herself.
De F. The rascal fares so well; look, y'are undone,
　　The day-star, by this hand! See Phosphorus plain yonder. 25
Bea. Advise me now to fall upon some ruin,
　　There is no counsel safe else.
De F.　　　　　　　　　　Peace, I ha't now;
　　For we must force a rising, there's no remedy.
Bea. How? Take heed of that.
De F.　　　　　　　　　　Tush, be you quiet,
　　Or else give over all.
Bea.　　　　　　　Prithee, I ha' done then.　　　　30
De F. This is my reach: I'll set some part a-fire
　　Of Diaphanta's chamber.
Bea.　　　　　　　　How? Fire, sir?
　　That may endanger the whole house.
De F. You talk of danger when your fame's on fire?
Bea. That's true; do what thou wilt now.
De F.　　　　　　　　　　　　Push, I aim　　35
　　At a most rich success, strikes all dead sure;
　　The chimney being a-fire, and some light parcels
　　Of the least danger in her chamber only,
　　If Diaphanta should be met by chance then,
　　Far from her lodging (which is now suspicious),　　40
　　It would be thought her fears and affrights then

20. harsh] *Q, Dilke, Dyce;* rash *Bullen (conj. Dyce).*　　21. an] *Dilke;* a *Q.*
22. thank'd] *All eds.;* thank *Q.*　　25. Phosphorus] *All eds.;* Bosphorus *Q.*

25. *Phosphorus*] The morning-star. The compositor or transcriber mis-read 'h' as the bottom loop of a 'B' (cf. IV. ii. 54).
26. *fall upon some ruin*] Happen upon, or devise, some catastrophe.
28. *force a rising*] Create a disturbance to wake the house.

Drove her to seek for succour; if not seen
Or met at all, as that's the likeliest,
For her own shame she'll hasten towards her lodging;
I will be ready with a piece high-charg'd,   45
As 'twere to cleanse the chimney: there 'tis proper now,
But she shall be the mark.
Bea.   I'm forc'd to love thee now,
'Cause thou provid'st so carefully for my honour.
De F. 'Slid, it concerns the safety of us both,
Our pleasure and continuance.
Bea.   One word now, prithee;   50
How for the servants?
De F.   I'll despatch them
Some one way, some another in the hurry,
For buckets, hooks, ladders; fear not you;
The deed shall find its time, —and I've thought since
Upon a safe conveyance for the body too.   55
How this fire purifies wit! Watch you your minute.
Bea. Fear keeps my soul upon't, I cannot stray from't.

Enter ALONZO'S GHOST.

De F. Ha! What art thou that tak'st away the light
'Twixt that star and me? I dread thee not;
'Twas but a mist of conscience. —All's clear again.   *Exit.* 60
Bea. Who's that, De Flores? Bless me! It slides by;
                                        [*Exit* GHOST.]
Some ill thing haunts the house; 't has left behind it
A shivering sweat upon me: I'm afraid now.
This night hath been so tedious; oh, this strumpet!
Had she a thousand lives, he should not leave her   65
Till he had destroy'd the last. —List, oh my terrors!

59. 'Twixt] *Q, Brooke;* Betwixt *Dilke, Dyce.*   61.1. *Exit Ghost.] Dyce.*

---

45. *piece*] See G.
50. *continuance*] Beatrice's adultery has now become habitual.
65–6.] This may be an unconscious echo of Reynolds, p. 124: '. . . had he
a thousand liues, as he hath but one, he is ready, if shee please, to expose
and sacrifice them all at her command and seruice.'

    Three struck by Saint Sebastian's!   *Struck three o'clock.*

Within. Fire, fire, fire!

Bea. Already? How rare is that man's speed!

    How heartily he serves me! His face loathes one,   70

    But look upon his care, who would not love him?

    The east is not more beauteous than his service.

Within. Fire, fire, fire!

       Enter DE FLORES; *Servants pass over, ring a bell.*

De F. Away, despatch! Hooks, buckets, ladders; that's well

    said;

    The fire-bell rings, the chimney works; my charge;   75

    The piece is ready.   *Exit.*

Bea.   Here's a man worth loving—

             Enter DIAPHANTA.

    Oh, y'are a jewel!

Dia.   Pardon frailty, madam;

    In troth I was so well, I ev'n forgot myself.

Bea. Y'have made trim work.

Dia.   What?

Bea.   Hie quickly to your chamber;

    Your reward follows you.

Dia.   I never made   80

    So sweet a bargain.   *Exit.*

             Enter ALSEMERO.

Als.   Oh my dear Joanna.

    Alas, art thou risen too? I was coming,

    My absolute treasure.

Bea.   When I miss'd you,

    I could not choose but follow.

73.1. *De Flores; Servants*] Dilke; *Deflores servants: Q.*   76.1. *Enter Diaphanta.*] Dyce; *before Beatrice's speech in Q.*

   71.] Cf. Middleton's *Michaelmas Term*, v. i. 60: 'Did he want all, who would not love his care?' (Bullen, I, 313).

Als.   Th'art all sweetness!
    The fire is not so dangerous.
Bea.   Think you so, sir?   85
Als. I prithee tremble not: believe me, 'tis not.

        Enter VERMANDERO, JASPERINO.

Ver. Oh bless my house and me!
Als.   My lord your father.

        Enter DE FLORES *with a piece.*

Ver. Knave, whither goes that piece?
De F.   To scour the chimney. *Exit.*
Ver. Oh, well said, well said;
    That fellow's good on all occasions.   90
Bea. A wondrous necessary man, my lord.
Ver. He hath a ready wit, he's worth 'em all, sir;
    Dog at a house of fire; I ha' seen him sing'd ere now:
                    The piece goes off.
    Ha, there he goes.
Bea. [*aside.*]   'Tis done.
Als.   Come, sweet, to bed now;
    Alas, thou wilt get cold.
Bea.   '   Alas, the fear keeps that out;   95
    My heart will find no quiet till I hear
    How Diaphanta, my poor woman, fares;
    It is her chamber, sir, her lodging chamber.
Ver. How should the fire come there?
Bea. As good a soul as ever lady countenanc'd,   100
    But in her chamber negligent and heavy;
    She 'scap'd a mine twice.

93. of] *Q, Dyce, Bullen;* on *Dilke.*   94. aside.] *Dilke.*

    95.] The second hypermetrical 'alas' may be an accidental repetition (cf.
III. iii. 103), and possibly 'the fear keeps that out' was intended as an aside.
    102. *mine*] Diaphanta twice narrowly escaped an accident of some sort;
the exact meaning is not clear. Beatrice's 'twice' may be an allusion to the
fact that Diaphanta successfully passed the virginity test, and was not
detected by Alsemero when she took Beatrice's place.

Ver.   Twice?
Bea.   Strangely twice, sir.
Ver. Those sleepy sluts are dangerous in a house,
     And they be ne'er so good.

Enter DE FLORES.

De F.   Oh poor virginity!
     Thou hast paid dearly for't.
Ver.   Bless us! What's that?   105
De F. A thing you all knew once—Diaphanta's burnt.
Bea. My woman, oh, my woman!
De F.   Now the flames
     Are greedy of her; burnt, burnt, burnt to death, sir!
Bea. Oh my presaging soul!
Als.   Not a tear more!
     I charge you by the last embrace I gave you   110
     In bed before this rais'd us.
Bea.   Now you tie me;
     Were it my sister, now she gets no more.

Enter Servant.

Ver. How now?
Ser. All danger's past, you may now take your rests, my
     lords; the fire is throughly quench'd; ah, poor gentle-   115
     woman, how soon was she stifled!
Bea. De Flores, what is left of her inter,
     And we as mourners all will follow her:
     I will entreat that honour to my servant,
     Ev'n of my lord himself.
Als.   Command it, sweetness.   120
Bea. Which of you spied the fire first?

104. *Enter De Flores.*] Q, Dilke, Dyce; *Enter De Flores with the body of Diaphanta. Tatlock.*

104.] Tatlock's emendation has a certain plausibility; if it were accepted, 'that' and 'thing' (105–6) would refer to the body carried in by De Flores. But there is nothing in the rest of the scene to make this interpretation inevitable, and ll. 54–5 above weigh against it.

De F.   'Twas I, madam.

Bea. And took such pains in't too? A double goodness!
    'Twere well he were rewarded.

Ver.   He shall be;
    De Flores, call upon me.

Als.   And upon me, sir.

                         Exeunt. [*Manet* DE FLORES.]

De F. Rewarded? Precious, here's a trick beyond me!   125
    I see in all bouts, both of sport and wit,
    Always a woman strives for the last hit.   *Exit.*

[v. ii]

                         Enter TOMAZO.

Tom. I cannot taste the benefits of life
    With the same relish I was wont to do.
    Man I grow weary of, and hold his fellowship
    A treacherous bloody friendship; and because
    I am ignorant in whom my wrath should settle,   5
    I must think all men villains, and the next
    I meet (whoe'er he be) the murderer
    Of my most worthy brother. —Ha! What's he?

                Enter DE FLORES, *passes over the stage.*

    Oh, the fellow that some call honest De Flores;
    But methinks honesty was hard bested   10
    To come there for a lodging, —as if a queen
    Should make her palace of a pest-house.
    I find a contrariety in nature
    Betwixt that face and me: the least occasion
    Would give me game upon him; yet he's so foul,   15

124.1. *Manet De Flores.*] *Dyce.*

---

v. ii. 9ff.] Tomazo's change of attitude towards De Flores is certainly
rather sudden, though the dramatists are aware of this (see ll. 38–42 below).
Perhaps it is meant to indicate that the other characters in the play are beginning to see through De Flores, and thus prepare us for v. iii.

15. *give me game*] The meaning is not too clear; Schelling suggests
'cause me to fight with him'.

One would scarce touch him with a sword he loved
And made account of; so most deadly venomous,
He would go near to poison any weapon
That should draw blood on him; one must resolve
Never to use that sword again in fight,   20
In way of honest manhood, that strikes him;
Some river must devour't, 'twere not fit
That any man should find it. —What, again?

Enter DE FLORES.

He walks a' purpose by, sure, to choke me up,
To infect my blood.

De F.   My worthy noble lord!   25
Tom. Dost offer to come near and breathe upon me? [*Strikes him.*]
De F. A blow!   [*Draws his sword.*]
Tom.   Yea, are you so prepar'd?
I'll rather like a soldier die by th'sword,
Than like a politician by thy poison.   [*Draws.*]
De F. Hold, my lord, as you are honourable.   30
Tom. All slaves that kill by poison are still cowards.
De F. [*aside.*] I cannot strike; I see his brother's wounds
Fresh bleeding in his eye, as in a crystal.
[*To Tom.*] I will not question this, I know y'are noble;
I take my injury with thanks given, sir,   35
Like a wise lawyer; and as a favour,
Will wear it for the worthy hand that gave it.
[*Aside.*] —Why this from him, that yesterday appear'd
So strangely loving to me?

16. touch him] *Dilke;* touch *Q.*   18. near] *Dyce, Bullen;* ne're *Q;* ne'er
Dilke.   26. *Strikes him.*] *Dilke.*   27. *Draws . . . sword.*] *Dilke.*
29. *Draws.*] *Dilke.*   32. *aside.*] *Dilke.*   38. *Aside.*] *Dilke.*

18. *near*] Dyce's reading is far more likely to be right than Dilke's; Q has
'ne're' at l. 42, where it can only mean 'near'. 'He' is De Flores.
28–9.] Cf. Middleton's *The Phoenix*, I. vi. 71–2: 'Would he die so like a
politician and not once write his mind to me?' (Bullen, I, 132).
33. *Fresh bleeding*] Perhaps alluding to the belief that a murdered man's
congealed wounds began to bleed again if the murderer came near the
corpse; cf. *R 3*, I. ii. 55ff.

Oh, but instinct is of a subtler strain,   40
Guilt must not walk so near his lodge again;
He came near me now.   *Exit.*

Tom. All league with mankind I renounce for ever,
Till I find this murderer; not so much
As common courtesy but I'll lock up: 45
For in the state of ignorance I live in,
A brother may salute his brother's murderer,
And wish good speed to th'villain in a greeting.

> *Enter* VERMANDERO, ALIBIUS *and* ISABELLA.

Ver. Noble Piracquo!
Tom.   Pray keep on your way, sir,
I've nothing to say to you.
Ver.   Comforts bless you, sir.   50
Tom. I have forsworn compliment; in troth I have, sir;
As you are merely man, I have not left
A good wish for you, nor any here.
Ver. Unless you be so far in love with grief
You will not part from't upon any terms,   55
We bring that news will make a welcome for us.
Tom. What news can that be?
Ver.   Throw no scornful smile
Upon the zeal I bring you, 'tis worth more, sir.
Two of the chiefest men I kept about me
I hide not from the law, or your just vengeance.   60
Tom. Ha!

42. near] *Dyce, Bullen;* ne're *Q;* ne'er *Dilke.*   53. any] *Q, Dilke;* for any
Dyce, Bullen.   60. law, or] *Q, Dilke, Dyce;* law of *Bullen.*

54-5.] Possibly an echo of *The Duchess of Malfi*, v. ii. 252-3:
> Are you so farre in love with sorrow,
> You cannot part with part of it? (Webster, II, 112-13).

60. *law, or*] Bullen's emendation is unnecessary. Even as late as the Jacobean period, many believed that private vengeance, provided it was 'just',
was a permissible equivalent to going to law, though James's official policy
was directly opposed to this. Vermandero offers Tomazo a choice; he can
either hand his brother's murderers over to the law to undergo trial and
punishment, or take private vengeance on them himself.

Ver. To give your peace more ample satisfaction,
    Thank these discoverers.

Tom.   If you bring that calm,
    Name but the manner I shall ask forgiveness in
    For that contemptuous smile upon you: 65
    I'll perfect it with reverence that belongs
    Unto a sacred altar.   *[Kneels.]*

Ver.   Good sir, rise;   *[Raises him.]*
    Why, now you overdo as much a' this hand,
    As you fell short a' t'other. Speak, Alibius.

Alib. 'Twas my wife's fortune (as she is most lucky   70
    At a discovery) to find out lately
    Within our hospital of fools and madmen
    Two counterfeits slipp'd into these disguises;
    Their names, Franciscus and Antonio.

Ver. Both mine, sir, and I ask no favour for 'em.   75

Alib. Now that which draws suspicion to their habits,
    The time of their disguisings agrees justly
    With the day of the murder.

Tom.   Oh blest revelation!

Ver. Nay more, nay more, sir— I'll not spare mine own
    In way of justice— they both feign'd a journey   80
    To Briamata, and so wrought out their leaves;
    My love was so abus'd in't.

Tom.   Time's too precious
    To run in waste now; you have brought a peace
    The riches of five kingdoms could not purchase.
    Be my most happy conduct; I thirst for 'em: 85
    Like subtle lightning will I wind about 'em,
    And melt their marrow in 'em.   *Exeunt.*

---

65. upon] *Q, Baskervill;* I cast upon *Dilke;* I threw upon *Dyce.*   67.
Kneels.] *Dilke.*   67. *Raises him.*] *Dyce.*   81. Briamata] *Dyce; Bramata Q.*

---

80. *both*] Apparently an oversight; according to IV. ii. 7–8 one of them
pretended to be going to Valencia.

85. *thirst*] Cf. II. ii. 133.

86–7.] Cf. *Bussy D'Ambois,* IV. ii. 188–9:
    A politician must like lightning melt
    The very marrow, and not taint the skin. (Chapman, *Tragedies,* 57)

[v. iii]

Enter ALSEMERO *and* JASPERINO.

Jas. Your confidence, I'm sure, is now of proof.
        The prospect from the garden has show'd
        Enough for deep suspicion.
Als.   The black mask
        That so continually was worn upon't
        Condemns the face for ugly ere't be seen—   5
        Her despite to him, and so seeming-bottomless.
Jas. Touch it home then: 'tis not a shallow probe
        Can search this ulcer soundly, I fear you'll find it
        Full of corruption; 'tis fit I leave you;
        She meets you opportunely from that walk: 10
        She took the back door at his parting with her.

                                        Exit JASPERINO.

Als. Did my fate wait for this unhappy stroke
        At my first sight of woman? —She's here.

                    Enter BEATRICE.

Bea. Alsemero!
Als.   How do you?
Bea.   How do I?

---

v. iii. 3. *black mask*] De Flores' ugliness.

5–6.] Line 6 is a little abrupt; possibly a line or two of text has dropped out accidentally between ll. 5 and 6.

7–9.] Compare Sidney's remark on 'Tragedy, that openeth the greatest wounds, and sheweth forth the Vlcers that are couered with Tissue . . .' (*An Apology for Poetry*, in *Elizabethan Critical Essays*, ed. Gregory Smith, 1904, I, 177).

10.] Dyce points out that the later part of this scene, with its references to Alsemero's closet, takes place in the same part of the castle as IV. i, but suggests that this line may indicate that the earlier part of the scene is supposed to take place elsewhere. But the scene does not allow for a change of locality, and in any case there is no need for it. Alsemero's closet is merely a small room in which he keeps his medical supplies and papers, and it could easily be near the door leading out into the castle grounds. Alsemero and Jasperino, having watched a meeting between Beatrice and De Flores in the garden, come into the castle and wait for her to overtake them.

14ff.] Compare the three paragraphs in Reynolds, pp. 134–6, beginning, 'Hee is no sooner departed . . .'

Alas! How do you? You look not well.   15

Als. You read me well enough, I am not well.

Bea. Not well, sir? Is't in my power to better you?

Als. Yes.

Bea.   Nay, then y'are cur'd again.

Als. Pray resolve me one question, lady.

Bea.   If I can.

Als. None can so sure. Are you honest?   20

Bea. Ha, ha, ha! That's a broad question, my lord.

Als. But that's not a modest answer, my lady:
Do you laugh? My doubts are strong upon me.

Bea. 'Tis innocence that smiles, and no rough brow
Can take away the dimple in her cheek.   25
Say I should strain a tear to fill the vault,
Which would you give the better faith to?

Als. 'Twere but hypocrisy of a sadder colour,
But the same stuff; neither your smiles nor tears
Shall move or flatter me from my belief: 30
You are a whore!

Bea.   What a horrid sound it hath!
It blasts a beauty to deformity;
Upon what face soever that breath falls,
It strikes it ugly: oh, you have ruin'd
What you can ne'er repair again.   35

Als. I'll all demolish, and seek out truth within you,
If there be any left; let your sweet tongue
Prevent your heart's rifling; there I'll ransack
And tear out my suspicion.

Bea.   You may, sir,

15–16.] Cf. the play of words on 'well' at I. i. 22–3.

26. *vault*] See G., and cf. *Lr.*, v. iii. 258–9:
     Had I your tongues and eyes, I'd use them so
     That heaven's vault should crack.

36–9.] Cf. Rowley's *All's Lost by Lust*, III. i. 36–9:
     O that thine eyes were worth the plucking out,
     Or thy base heart, the labour I should take
     In rending up thy bosome; I should but ope
     A vault to poyson me (detested wretch).   (ed. Stork, p. 114).

'Tis an easy passage; yet, if you please,   40
Show me the ground whereon you lost your love:
My spotless virtue may but tread on that,
Before I perish.

Als.   Unanswerable!
A ground you cannot stand on: you fall down
Beneath all grace and goodness, when you set   45
Your ticklish heel on't; there was a visor
O'er that cunning face, and that became you:
Now impudence in triumph rides upon't;
How comes this tender reconcilement else
'Twixt you and your despite, your rancorous loathing,   50
De Flores? He that your eye was sore at sight of,
He's now become your arm's supporter, your
Lip's saint!

Bea.   Is there the cause?

Als.   Worse: your lust's devil,
Your adultery!

Bea.   Would any but yourself say that,
'Twould turn him to a villain.

Als.   'Twas witness'd   55
By the counsel of your bosom, Diaphanta.

Bea.   Is your witness dead then?

Als.   'Tis to be fear'd
It was the wages of her knowledge; poor soul,
She liv'd not long after the discovery.

Bea.   Then hear a story of not much less horror   60
Than this your false suspicion is beguil'd with;
To your bed's scandal, I stand up innocence,

61. with;] *Dyce, Bullen;* with, *Q.*

___

43. *Unanswerable*] i.e. The 'ground' of his accusation.
48.] Perhaps imitated by Nathaniel Richards in *The Tragedy of Messal-lina*, ll. 438–9:
        ... the divels vaulting schoole; where lust
    In triumph rides or'e shame and innocence.
                                (ed. Skemp, Louvain, 1910, p. 25).
62.] i.e. In answer to your bed's scandal, I stand up (set up, put forward)

Which even the guilt of one black other deed
Will stand for proof of: your love has made me
A cruel murd'ress.

Als.   Ha!

Bea.   A bloody one;   65
I have kiss'd poison for't, strok'd a serpent:
That thing of hate, worthy in my esteem
Of no better employment, and him most worthy
To be so employ'd, I caus'd to murder
That innocent Piracquo, having no   70
Better means than that worst, to assure
Yourself to me.

Als.   Oh, the place itself e'er since
Has crying been for vengeance, the temple
Where blood and beauty first unlawfully
Fir'd their devotion, and quench'd the right one;   75
'Twas in my fears at first, 'twill have it now:
Oh, thou art all deform'd!

Bea.   Forget not, sir,
It for your sake was done; shall greater dangers
Make the less welcome?

Als.   Oh, thou shouldst have gone
A thousand leagues about to have avoided   80
This dangerous bridge of blood; here we are lost.

Bea. Remember I am true unto your bed.

Als. The bed itself's a charnel, the sheets shrouds
For murdered carcasses; it must ask pause
What I must do in this, meantime you shall   85
Be my prisoner only: enter my closet;   *Exit* BEATRICE.
I'll be your keeper yet. Oh, in what part
Of this sad story shall I first begin? —Ha!

---

innocence. . . It is possible, however, that 'To your bed's scandal' should
be linked with l. 61 (Q has commas after 'with' and 'scandal').

72–6.] Cf. I. i. 1–12.

76. *'twill have it now*] The place is determined to have vengeance now.

79–81.] i.e. You should have made a detour of a thousand leagues rather
than cross over to your goal by means of murder.

Enter DE FLORES.

> This same fellow has put me in. —De Flores!
>
> *De F.* Noble Alsemero?
>
> *Als.*   I can tell you   90
> News, sir; my wife has her commended to you.
>
> *De F.* That's news indeed, my lord; I think she would
> Commend me to the gallows if she could,
> She ever lov'd me so well; I thank her.
>
> *Als.* What's this blood upon your band, De Flores?   95
>
> *De F.* Blood? No, sure, 'twas wash'd since.
>
> *Als.*   Since when, man?
>
> *De F.* Since t'other day I got a knock
> In a sword and dagger school; I think 'tis out.
>
> *Als.* Yes, 'tis almost out, but 'tis perceiv'd, though.
> I had forgot my message; this it is: 100
> What price goes murder?
>
> *De F.*   How, sir?
>
> *Als.*   I ask you, sir;
> My wife's behindhand with you, she tells me,
> For a brave bloody blow you gave for her sake
> Upon Piracquo.
>
> *De F.*   Upon? 'Twas quite through him, sure;
> Has she confess'd it?
>
> *Als.*   As sure as death to both of you,   105
> And much more than that.
>
> *De F.*   It could not be much more;
> 'Twas but one thing, and that—she's a whore.

88.1. *Enter De Flores.*] *This ed.; after l. 89 in Q.* 107. that—] *Dyce,
Bullen;* that *Q.*

---

89. *put me in*] Probably meaning, as Schelling suggests, 'given me the
cue'; cf. *The Revenger's Tragedy,* I. iii. 143 (Tourneur, *Works, ed. cit.,* p. 92).
    95.] Cf. Middleton's *A Mad World, My Masters,* III. ii. 109: 'How comes
your band bloody, sir?' (Bullen, III, 302). The hint for the incident may
have been a metaphor in Middleton's *A Chaste Maid in Cheapside,* II. ii.
133–4:
> . . . this is like a murderer
> That will outface the deed with a bloody band.
(Bullen, V, 41). Possibly a topical allusion lies behind both references.

Als. It could not choose but follow; oh cunning devils!

How should blind men know you from fair-fac'd saints?

Bea. within. He lies, the villain does bely me!   110

De F. Let me go to her, sir.

Als.   Nay, you shall to her.

Peace, crying crocodile, your sounds are heard!

Take your prey to you, get you in to her, sir. *Exit* DE FLORES.

I'll be your pander now; rehearse again

Your scene of lust, that you may be perfect   115

When you shall come to act it to the black audience

Where howls and gnashings shall be music to you.

Clip your adult'ress freely, 'tis the pilot

Will guide you to the Mare Mortuum,

Where you shall sink to fathoms bottomless.   120

---

108. It] *Dilke, Dyce;* I *Q, Baskervill.*

---

112. *crying crocodile*] Cf. Nashe's *Pierce Penilesse His Supplication*: 'Enuie is a Crocodile that weepes when he kils' (*Works*, ed. McKerrow, I, 184). McKerrow comments, 'This fable is, of course, of constant occurrence, but seems to have been unknown to the classical writers. The phrase is well explained in *A Brief Collection out of S. Munster*, 1574, fol. 90v, "The teares of a Crocodile: That is when one doth weepe with his eyes withoute compassion, and not with his hart and minde"' (*ibid.*, IV, 112). See R. R. Cawley, *The Voyagers and Elizabethan Drama* (1938), pp. 52ff.

116–17.] Cf. Rowley's *All's Lost by Lust*, II. i. 107–10:

It is not love you seeke;
But an Antipathy as dissonant
As heaven and hell, the musique of the spheares,
Comparde with gnashings, and the howles below.

(ed. Stork, p. 99).

118. *pilot*] Cf. *All's Lost by Lust*, The Argument, 6–8: '. . . whilst hee sailes in these lustfull thoughts, Lothario, (a Gentleman of better fortunes than condition) is his Pilot, steering his wickednesse on' (ed. Stork, p. 77). See also the Prologue, 17–19 (p. 79).

119. *Mare Mortuum*] The Dead Sea. For l. 120, cf. *Purchas His Pilgrimes*: 'A man can hardly sinke to the bottom if he would' (ed. Maclehose, 1906, VII, 462). Possibly Alsemero also has in mind the bottomless pit of hell. For an account of contemporary beliefs about the Dead Sea, see R. R. Cawley, *op. cit.*, pp. 128–30. The use of a Latin phrase might be compared to *All's Lost by Lust*, I. i. 36–8:

They come to sacrifice their blouds to us,
If that be red, a *mare rubrum*,
Wee'le make so high to quench their silver moones. (ed. Stork, p. 82).

Enter VERMANDERO, ALIBIUS, ISABELLA, TOMAZO,
FRANCISCUS, *and* ANTONIO.

Ver. Oh, Alsemero, I have a wonder for you.
Als. No, sir, 'tis I, I have a wonder for you.
Ver. I have suspicion near as proof itself
　　For Piracquo's murder.
Als. 　　　　　　　　Sir, I have proof
　　Beyond suspicion for Piracquo's murder.　　　　　　125
Ver. Beseech you hear me; these two have been disguis'd
　　E'er since the deed was done.
Als. 　　　　　　　　I have two other
　　That were more close disguis'd than your two could be,
　　E'er since the deed was done.
Ver. You'll hear me! —these mine own servants—　　　130
Als. Hear me; —those nearer than your servants,
　　That shall acquit them, and prove them guiltless.
Fran. That may be done with easy truth, sir.
Tom. How is my cause bandied through your delays!
　　'Tis urgent in blood, and calls for haste;　　　　135
　　Give me a brother alive or dead:
　　Alive, a wife with him; if dead, for both
　　A recompense, for murder and adultery.
Bea. within. Oh, oh, oh!
Als. 　　　　　　　　Hark, 'tis coming to you.
De F. within. Nay, I'll along for company.
Bea. within. 　　　　　　　　Oh, oh!　　　　140
Ver. What horrid sounds are these?

126. two] *Q, Dilke, Dyce;* who *Bullen.*　　135. blood] *Q, Baskervill;* my
blood *Dilke, Dyce.*　　136. alive] *Q, Schelling;* or alive *Dilke, Dyce.*

126. *two*] Probably Vermandero points directly at Antonio and Franciscus.
138. *adultery*] It would be a blemish on the play if Tomazo is intended to
refer to Beatrice's adultery with De Flores, for at this point he knows nothing of their relationship. The only explanation seems to be that he regards
Beatrice as Alonzo's 'wife' (see l. 137), and considers her marriage to Alsemero to be a kind of adultery.
139.] i.e. Tomazo's recompense.

Als. Come forth, you twins of mischief!

      Enter DE FLORES *bringing in* BEATRICE [*wounded*].

De F. Here we are; if you have any more
    To say to us, speak quickly, I shall not
    Give you the hearing else; I am so stout yet,   145
    And so, I think, that broken rib of mankind.
Ver. An host of enemies enter'd my citadel
    Could not amaze like this: Joanna! Beatrice! Joanna!
Bea. Oh come not near me, sir, I shall defile you:
    I am that of your blood was taken from you   150
    For your better health; look no more upon't,
    But cast it to the ground regardlessly:
    Let the common sewer take it from distinction.

142.1. *wounded*] Dilke.   150. am that] *Q, Dilke, Dyce, Bullen;* that am
Ellis; that was *Neilson, Tatlock.*   153. sewer] *All eds.;* shewer *Q.*

---

146. *rib of mankind*] Beatrice; an obvious allusion to Genesis, ii. 21–3. Cf.
Glapthorne's *Wit in a Constable,* I. i: 'That rib of mans flesh should be
Clare...' (*Plays,* 1874, I, 175).

150. *am that*] Ellis's emendation would turn Beatrice into a Changeling,
a child who has been stolen from her father. But attractive though this
reading is, it has no real justification, for Q makes perfect sense, and
Ellis's reading obscures the meaning of ll. 151–3. A further proof of Q's
authenticity is the catchword on 12ʳ, 'I am'. Lines 150–1 might be expanded to 'I am that infected part of your blood which was taken from you /
For your better health . . .' Vermandero is imagined as holding the con-
tainer of bad blood which has been purged from him, uncertain what to do
with it. Beatrice tells him not to debate the problem any more ('look no
more upon't'), but to throw the blood ('it') to the earth, whence it will run
into the common sewer. For the purging of bad blood as an equivalent for
death, cf. *The Duchess of Malfi,* II. v. 34–6:

    We must not now use Balsamum, but fire,
    The smarting cupping-glasse, for that's the meane
    To purge infected blood, (such blood as hers:)

(Webster, II, 65–6) and *The White Devil,* v. vi. 105–6 (*ibid.,* I, 187).

152. *cast . . . ground*] There may possibly be a faint echo here of the Old
Testament laws governing burnt-offerings and sacrifices, as in Deutero-
nomy, xii. 16: 'Only ye shall not eat the blood; ye shall pour it upon the
earth as water'.

153. *common sewer*] See G. Rowley uses the phrase in *A New Wonder,
A Woman Never Vexed,* I. i (said of a son who uses his father's wealth to
support a dissolute uncle):

       . . . he's the conduit-pipe

Beneath the stars, upon yon meteor
Ever hung my fate, 'mongst things corruptible;   155
I ne'er could pluck it from him: my loathing
Was prophet to the rest, but ne'er believ'd;
Mine honour fell with him, and now my life.
Alsemero, I am a stranger to your bed,
Your bed was cozen'd on the nuptial night,   160
For which your false bride died.

Als.   Diaphanta!

De F. Yes; and the while I coupled with your mate
At barley-brake; now we are left in hell.

Ver. We are all there, it circumscribes here.

---

155. hung] *Dyce, Bullen;* hang *Q, Dilke.*   164. here] *Q;* us here *All eds.*

That throws it forth into the common sewer.
(ed. Dilke, *Old English Plays*, 1815, v, 241). Cf. also *The Honest Whore, Part I*, II. i. 324–6:

> . . . for your body,
> Its like the common shoare, that still receiues
> All the townes filth.   (Dekker, II, 35–6).

distinction] See G. Beatrice's wish to lose her separate identity might be compared to Faustus' desire for oblivion:

> O soul, be changed into little water-drops,
> And fall into the ocean, ne'er be found!

(Marlowe, *Dr Faustus*, v. ii. 189–90; ed. Boas, 1932, p. 173).

154–5.] A deliberate contrast is intended between 'stars' and 'meteor' (i.e. De Flores). In Elizabethan cosmology the stars were pure, fixed, and eternal; meteors belonged to the sublunary world of change and decay, and were transitory, of evil omen, and the result, or indication, of corruption, as in *All's Lost by Lust*, III. i. 20–1:

> . . . thou bundle of diseases,
> The store-house of some shaggy meteor . . .

(ed. Stork, p. 114). The same contrast can be found elsewhere; cf. *The Humorous Lieutenant*, IV. viii:

> I am above your hate, as far above it,
> In all the actions of an innocent life,
> As the pure Stars are from the muddy meteors.

(Fletcher, II, 358). Cf. also Dekker and Middleton's *The Roaring Girl*, III. ii. 102–4 (Dekker, III, 179; Bullen, IV, 71).

155.] Cf. II. i. 36.

163. *barley-brake*] See III. iii. 165.

164.] Helen Gardner (see Introduction, p. liv) believes this to be an echo of Marlowe's *Dr Faustus*, II. i. 122–4:

> Hell hath no limits, nor is circumscrib'd

De F. I lov'd this woman in spite of her heart;   165
    Her love I earn'd out of Piracquo's murder.

Tom. Ha! My brother's murderer!

De F.   Yes, and her honour's prize
    Was my reward; I thank life for nothing
    But that pleasure: it was so sweet to me
    That I have drunk up all, left none behind   170
    For any man to pledge me.

Ver.   Horrid villain!
    Keep life in him for further tortures.

De F.   No!
    I can prevent you; here's my penknife still.
    It is but one thread more, [*stabs himself*] —and now 'tis cut.
    Make haste, Joanna, by that token to thee: 175
    Canst not forget, so lately put in mind,
    I would not go to leave thee far behind.   *Dies.*

Bea. Forgive me, Alsemero, all forgive;
    'Tis time to die, when 'tis a shame to live.   *Dies.*

Ver. Oh, my name is enter'd now in that record   180
    Where till this fatal hour 'twas never read.

Als. Let it be blotted out, let your heart lose it,

---

174. *stabs himself*] *Dilke.*   175. thee:] *Dilke;* thee. *Q;* thee, *Dyce.*
176. mind,] *Q, Dilke;* mind; *Dyce.*

    In one self place; but where we are is hell,
    And where hell is, there must we ever be.
                    (ed. Boas, 1932, p. 86).

165.] Cf. Webster and Rowley's *A Cure for a Cuckold*, III. iii. 29: 'I do love you in spight of your heart' (Webster, III, 64).

175–7.] The exact syntax of these lines is hard to determine, and they could be punctuated and interpreted in a variety of ways. The 'token' seems to be the wound De Flores has just given himself, which will remind Beatrice that he is unwilling to be parted from her.

180. *record*] The heavenly record of human deeds and misdeeds; cf. *The Witch of Edmonton*, I. i. 200–2:

    And shall I then for my part
    Unfile the sacred Oath set on Record
    In Heaven's Book?

(Dekker, IV, 356) and *The Spanish Gipsy*, V. i. 91–2: '. . . that white book above, which notes the secrets / Of every thought and heart' (Bullen, VI, 215).

And it can never look you in the face,
Nor tell a tale behind the back of life
To your dishonour; justice hath so right   185
The guilty hit, that innocence is quit
By proclamation, and may joy again.
Sir, you are sensible of what truth hath done;
'Tis the best comfort that your grief can find.

Tom. Sir, I am satisfied, my injuries   190
Lie dead before me; I can exact no more,
Unless my soul were loose, and could o'ertake
Those black fugitives that are fled from thence,
To take a second vengeance; but there are wraths
Deeper than mine, 'tis to be fear'd, about 'em.   195

Als. What an opacous body had that moon
That last chang'd on us! Here's beauty chang'd
To ugly whoredom; here, servant obedience
To a master sin, imperious murder;
I, a suppos'd husband, chang'd embraces   200
With wantonness, but that was paid before;
Your change is come too, from an ignorant wrath
To knowing friendship. Are there any more on's?

Ant. Yes, sir; I was chang'd too, from a little ass as I was, to
a great fool as I am, and had like to ha' been chang'd to   205
the gallows, but that you know my innocence always
excuses me.

---

193. thence] *Q, Baskervill;* hence *Dilke, Dyce.*

186–7.] i.e. The innocent have been cleared of suspicion by public proclamation of the truth; cf. *Northward Ho,* v. i. 294: 'Victorie wife thou art
quit by proclamation' (Dekker, III, 73).

193.] If Tomazo is looking at the bodies of Beatrice and De Flores, as the
context suggests, 'thence' is quite appropriate.

black fugitives] The damned souls of Beatrice and De Flores; cf. Reynolds, p. 137: '. . . whiles their soules flye to another world, to relate what
horrible and beastly crimes their bodies haue committed in this'.

201. *wantonness*] i.e. Diaphanta.

before] Earlier, by the death of Diaphanta.

202. *Your*] Tomazo's.

206. *innocence*] As Dyce points out, a pun is intended: (i) guiltlessness;
ii) idiocy.

Fran. I was chang'd from a little wit to be stark mad,
  Almost for the same purpose.

Isa.   Your change is still behind,
  But deserve best your transformation: 210
  You are a jealous coxcomb, keep schools of folly,
  And teach your scholars how to break your own head.

Alib. I see all apparent, wife, and will change now
  Into a better husband, and never keep
  Scholars that shall be wiser than myself.   215

Als. Sir, you have yet a son's duty living,
  Please you, accept it; let that your sorrow
  As it goes from your eye, go from your heart;
  Man and his sorrow at the grave must part.

EPILOGUE

Als. All we can do to comfort one another,   220
  To stay a brother's sorrow for a brother,
  To dry a child from the kind father's eyes,
  Is to no purpose, it rather multiplies:
  Your only smiles have power to cause re-live
  The dead again, or in their rooms to give   225
  Brother a new brother, father a child;
  If these appear, all griefs are reconcil'd.

                Exeunt omnes.

FINIS.

EPILOGUE.] *Q; added to Alsemero's final speech in Dyce, Bullen.*

---

209. *still behind*] Yet to come.
224. *Your only smiles*] Only your smiles (those of the audience).

APPENDIX A
The Sources

(i) *God's Revenge Against Murder*

(The text given here is from the 1621 quarto edition of Reynolds's book. A few minor misprints have been silently corrected, and certain contractions expanded. The page-numbers of the 1621 edition have been inserted into the text for ease of reference.)

In *Valentia* (an ancient and famous Cittie of *Spaine*) there dwelt one *Don Pedro de Alsemero*, a noble young Cauallier, whose father, *Don Iuan de Alsemero*, beeing slayne by the Hollanders in the Sea-fight at *Gibralter*, he resolued to addict himselfe to Nauall & sea actions, thereby to make himselfe capeable to reuenge his fathers death: a braue resolution, worthy the affection of a sonne, and the generositie of a Gentleman!

(107) To which end he makes two viages to the West-Indies, from whence he returnes flourishing and rich, which so spred the sayles of his Ambition, and hoysted his fame from top to top gallant, that his courage growing with his yeeres, he thought no attempt dangerous enough, if honourable, nor no honour enough glorious, except atchieued and purchased by danger. In the actions of *Alarache* and *Mamora*, hee shewed many noble proofes and testimonies of his valour and prowesse, the which he confirmed and made good by the receit of eleuen seuerall wounds, which as markes and Trophees of Honour, made him famous in *Castile*.

Boyling thus in the heate of his youthfull blood, and contemplating often on the death of his father, he resolues to goe to *Validolyd*, and to imploy some Grando either to the King or to the Duke of *Lerma*, his great Fauorite, to procure him a Captains place and a Companie vnder the Arch-duke *Albertus*, who at that time made bloody warres against the Netherlanders, thereby to draw them to obedience: but as he beganne this sute, a generall truce of both sides layd aside Armes, which (by the mediation of *England* and *France*) was shortly followed by a peace, as a mother by the daughter: which was concluded at the *Hage* by his Excellency of *Nassaw* and *Marquis Spinola*, being chiefe Commissioners of either partie. *Alsemero* seeing his hopes frustrated, that the keyes of peace had now shut vp the temple of warre, and that muskets, pikes and corslets that were wont to grace the fields, were now rusting by the walles, hee is irresolute what course to (108) take, resembling those fishes who delight to liue in cataracts and troubled waters, but die in those that are still and quiet: for he spurnes at the pleasures of the Court, and refuseth to haunt and frequent the companies of Ladies: and so not affecting, but rather disdaining the pompe, brauerie and vanitie of Courtiers, he withdrawes himselfe from *Validolyd*, to *Valentia*, with a noble and generous intent to seeke warres abroad, sith hee could finde none at home, where being ariued, although he were often inuited into the companies of the most Noble and Honourable Ladyes both of the Citty and Country: yet his thoughts ranne still on the warres, in which Heroike and illustrious Profession, hee conceiued his chiefest delight and felicity: and so taking order for his lands and affaires, hee resolues to see *Malta* that inexpugnable Rampier of *Mars*, the glorie of Christendome, and the terrour of Turkie, to see if he could gaine any place of command and honour either in that Iland, or in their Gallies; or if not, he would from thence into *Transiluania*, *Hungarie*, and *Germanie*, to inrich his iudgement and experience, by remarking the strength of their castles and Citties, their order and discipline in warre, the Potencie of their Princes, the nature of their Lawes and customes, and all other matters worthie the obseruation both of a Traueller and a Souldiour: and so building many castles in the ayre, he comes to *Alicant*, hoping to finde passage there for *Naples*, and from thence to ship himselfe vpon the *Neopolitan* Gallies for *Malta*.

(109) There is nothing so vaine as our thoughts, nor so vncertaine as our hopes: for commonly they deceiue vs, or rather wee our selues in relying on them, not that God is any way vniust: (for to thinke so, were impiety:) but that our hopes take false obiects, and haue no true foundation, and to imagine the contrary, were folly: the which *Alsemero* findes true: for heere the winde doth oppose him, his thoughts fight and vanquish themselues, yea and the prouidence of God doth crosse him in his intended purposes, and giues way to that hee least intendeth:

For comming one morning to our Ladies Church at *Masse*, and being on his knees in his deuotion, hee espies a young Gentlewoman likewise on hers next to him, who being young, tender and faire, he thorow her thinne vaile discouered all the perfections of a delicate and sweet beautie, she espies him feasting on the dayties of her pure and fresh cheekes; and tilting with the inuisible lances of his eyes, to hers, he is instantly rauished and vanquished with the pleasing obiect of this Angelicall countenance, and now he can no more resist either the power or passion of loue.

This Gentlewoman (whose name as yet wee know not) is young and fayre, and cannot refraine from blushing, and admiring to see him admire and blush at her. *Alsemero* dies in conceit with impatiency, that hee cannot enioy the happinesse and meanes to speake with her, but hee sees it in vaine to attempt it, because shee is ingaged in the company of many Ladies, and he of many Caualiers: (110) but Masse being ended, hee enquires of a good fellow Priest who walked by, what shee was, and whether she frequented that Church, and at what houre. The Priest informes him, that shee is *Don Diego de Vermandero's* daughter: hee being Captaine of the Castle of that City, that her name was *Dona Beatrice-Ioana*, and that shee is euery morning in that Church and Place, and neere about the same houre.

Alsemero hath the sweetnesse of her beautie so deepely ingrauen in his thoughts, and imprinted in his heart, that hee vowes *Beatrice-Ioana* is his Mistresse, and hee her seruant: yea, heere his warlike resolutions haue end, and strike sayle. And now hee leaues *Bellona* to adore *Venus*, and forsakes *Mars*, to follow *Cupid*: yea, so feruent is his flame, and so violent his Passion, as hee can neither giue nor take truce of his thoughts, till hee bee againe made happie with her sight, and blessed with her presence.

The next morne (as Louers loue not much rest) *Alsemero* is stirring very timely, and hoping to finde his Mistresse: no other Church will please him but our Ladies, nor place, but where he first and last saw her: but she is more zealous then himselfe; for shee is first in the Church, and on her knees to her deuotion, whom *Alsemero* gladly espying, he kneeles next to her: and hauing hardly the patience to let passe one poore quarter of an houre, he (resoluing as yet to conceale his name) like a fond Louer, whose greatest glory is in complements and courting his Mistresse, he boords her thus:

(111) Faire Lady, it seemes, that these two mornings my deuotions haue beene more powerfull and acceptable then heretofore, sith I haue had the felicity to be placed next so faire and so sweet a Nimph as your selfe, whose excellent beautie hath so sodainely captiuated mine eyes, and so secretly rauished my heart, that he which heretofore reiected, cannot now resist the power of loue; and therefore hauing ended my deuotions, I beseech you excuse me, if I beginne to pray you to take pittie of mee: sith my flame is so feruent, and my affection so passionate, as either I must liue yours, or not die mine owne.

Beatrice-Ioana could not refraine from blushing vnder her vaile, to see an vnknowne Cauallier boord her in these termes in the Church: and as she gaue attentiue eare to his speech, so shee could not for a while refraine from glancing her eye vpon the sprucenesse of his person, and the sumptuousnesse of his apparell: but at last, accusing her owne silence, because shee would giue him no cause to condemne it, she with a modest grace, and a gracefull modestie, returnes him this answere:

Sir, as your deuotions can neither bee pleasing to God, nor profit-able to your soule, if in this place you accompt it a felicity to inioy the sight of so meane a Gentlewoman as my selfe, so I cannot repute it to affection but flattery, that this poore beauty of mine (which you vniustly paint foorth in rich prayses) should haue power either to captiuate the eyes, or which is more, to rauish the heart of so Noble a Cauallier as your selfe. Such victories are reserued for those Ladies, who are as much your (112) equall, as I your inferiour: and therefore directing your zeale to them, if they finde your affection such as you professe to mee, no doubt but regarding your many vertues, and merits, they will in honour grant you that fauour which I in modestie am constrained to deny you.

Alsemero (though a nouice in the art of Loue) was not so ignorant and cowardly to bee put off with her first repulse and refusall, but rather seeing that the perfections of her minde corresponded with those of her beautie, hee resolues now to make triall of his wit and tongue, as heeretofore hee had done of his courage and sword: and so ioynes with her thus:

It is a prettie Ambition in you, sweet Lady, to disparage your beautie, that thereby it may seeme the fayrer; as the Sunne, who appeares brighter by reason of the nights obscuritie: and all things are best, and more perfectly discerned by their contraries: but I can-not commend, and therefore not excuse your policy, or rather your dis-respect, to slight and poast me ouer from your selfe, whom I loue, to those Ladies I neither know nor desire, which in effect is to giue mee a cloude for *Iuno*. No, no, it is onely to you, and to no other that I present and dedicate my seruice: and therefore it will be an ingrati-tude as vnworthy my receiuing, as your giuing, that I should bee the obiect of your discourtisie: sith you are that of my affection.

To these speeches of *Alsemero*, *Beatrice-Ioana* returnes this reply:

(113) It is not for poore Gentlewomen of my ranke and complexion, either to be ambitious, or politike, except it bee to keepe themselues from the snares of such Caualliers as your selfe, who (for the most part) vnder colour of affection, ayme to erect the trophees of your desires vpon the tombs of our dishonours; only I so much hate ingra-titude, as you being to me a stranger, charitie and common courtesie commands me to thanke you for the proffer of your seruice; the which I can no other way either deserue or requite, except in my deuotions & prayers to God, for your glory and prosperitie on earth.

As she had ended this her speech, the Priest ends his Masse; when *Alsemero* arising, aduanced to lift her vp from kneeling, and so with his Hat in his hand, (sequestring her from the crowd of people, who nowe began to depart the Church) he speakes to her to this effect:

Fayre Lady, as I know you to bee the Lady *Beatrice-Ioana*, daughter to the noble knight *Don Diego de Vermandero*, Captaine of the Castle of this Cittie: so I being a stranger to you, I admire that you offer so voluntary an iniurie to your iudgement and my intents, as to peruert my affection and speeches to a contrarie sence: but my inno-cencie hath this consolation, that my heart is pledge for my tongue, and my deeds shall make my words reall. In the mean time, sith you will giue me no place in your heart, I beseech you lend me one in your Coach, & bee at least so courteous as to honour me, in accepting my company to conduct you home to your fathers Castle.

(114) *Beatrice-Ioana*, calling to minde the freenesse of her speeches, and the sharpnesse of his answere, not blushing for ioy, but now looking pale for sorrow, repents her selfe of her errour, the which shee salues vp the best she could in this reply:

Noble Sir, when I am acquainted aswell with your heart as with your speeches, I shall then not onely repent, but recant mine errour, in iudging your selfe by others; in the meane time, if I haue any way wronged your merits and vertues; to giue you some part of satis-faction, if you please to grace mee with your company to the Castle, (although it bee not the custome of *Alicant*) I doe most kindly and thankfully accept thereof: when *Alsemero* giuing her many thanks, and kissing his hand, he takes her by the arme, & so conducts her from the Church to her Coach.

It is both a griefe and a scandall to any true Christians heart, that the Church ordained for thankes-giuing and Prayer vnto God, should be made a Stewes, or at least, a place for men to meet and court Ladies: but in all parts of the Christian World, where the Romane religión reigneth, this sinfull custome is frequently practised, especially in *Italy* and *Spaine*, where, for the most part, men loue their Courtizans better then their God: and it were a happines for *France*, if her Popish Churches were freed of this abomination, and her people of this impiety. But againe to our Historie.

We will purposely omit the conference which *Alsemero* and *Beatrice-Ioana* had in the Coach, and allow them by this time arriued to the Castle: (115) where first her selfe, then the Captaine her father, thanke him for his honour and courtesie: in requitall whereof, hee shewed him the rarities and strength of his Castle, and after some speeches and complements betweene them, he was so happie as to kisse *Beatrice-Ioana*, but had not the felicitie to entertain her: and so he departs, his Lacky attending him with his Gennet to the counter-scarfe. So home he rides to his lodging, where, whiles the winde holds contrary, wee will a little leaue him to his thoughts, and they to resolue in what sort he might contriue his sute for the obtain-ing of his newe and fayre Mistris *Beatrice-Ioana*, and likewise her selfe, to muse vpon the speeches and extraordinarie courtesie, which this vnknowne Cauallier afforded her, and beginne to speake of *Don Alonso Piracquo*, a rich Cauallier of the Cittie, who vnknowne to

Alsemero, was his riuall and competitor, in likewise seeking and courting *Beatrice-Ioana*, for his Mistris and wife.

This *Piracquo* being rich both in lands and money, and descended of one of the chiefest and Noblest families of *Alicant*, by profession a Courtier, and indeed (to giue him his dew) a Cauallier indued with many braue qualities and perfections, was so highly beloued, respected and esteemed in that Cittie, as the very fayrest and noblest young Ladies were, with much respect & affection, proffered him in marriage by their parents: but there was none either so precious or pleasing to his eye, as was our *Beatrice-Ioana*, whome he obserued for beauty to excell others, and for maiestie and grace to surpasse (116) her selfe, and indeede hee could not refraine from louing her, nor be perswaded or drawne to affect any other: so as he settled his resolution either to haue her to his wife, or not to be the husband of any. Yea, he is so earnest in his sute, as scarce any one day passeth, but he is at the Castle.

Vermandero thinkes himselfe much honoured of him, in seeking his daughter, yea, he receiues him louingly, and entertaines him courteously; as knowing it greatly for her preferment, & aduancement: and so giues *Piracquo* many testimonies of his fauour, and many hopes that he shall preuaile and obtaine his Mistris. But *Beatrice Ioana* stands not so affected to him, rather shee receiues him coldly; and when he beginnes his sute to her, shee turnes the deafe eare, and neuer answereth him, but in generall tearmes: only not peremptorily to disobey her parents, she seemes to be pleased with his company, and yet secretly in her heart wisheth him farther from her.

But *Piracquo* flattering him selfe in his hope, and as much doating on *Beatrice-Ioana's* beautie, as hee relies on her fathers constant affection to him, hee is so farre from giuing ouer his sute to her, as hee continueth it with more earnestnesse and importunitie, and vowes that he will forsake his life ere his Mistris: but sometimes wee speake true, when wee thinke wee iest: yet he findes her one and the same: for although shee were not yet acquainted with *Alsemero*, yet shee made it the thirteenth article of her Creede, that the supreme power had ordained her another husband, and not *Piracquo*: (117) yea at that very instant, the remembrance of *Alsemero* quite defaced that of *Piracquo*, so that shee wholly refus'd her heart to the last, of purpose to reserue and giue it to the first: as the sequell will shew.

Now by this time *Vermandero* had notice, & was secretly informed of *Alsemero's* affection to his daughter, and withall, that she liked him farre better then *Piracquo*: which newes was indeed very distastefull and displeasing to him, because he perfectly knew that *Piracquo's* meanes farre exceed that of *Alsemero*. Whereupon considering that hee had giuen his consent, and in a manner ingaged his promise to

Piracquo: he, to preuent the hopes, and to frustrate the attempts of *Alsemero*, leaues his Castle to the command of *Don Hugo de Valmarino* his sonne, and taking his daughter *Beatrice-Ioana* with him, hee in his Coach very sodainely and secretly goes to *Briamata*: a fayre house of his, tenne leagues from *Alicant*: where he meanes to soiourn, vntill he had concluded and solemnized the match betwixt them: But he shall neuer be so happy, as to see it effected.

At the newes of *Beatrice-Ioana's* departure, *Alsemero* is extremely perplexed & sorrowfull, knowing not whether it proceed from her selfe, her father, or both; yea, this his griefe is augmented, when hee thinkes on the suddennesse thereof, which he feares may bee performed for his respect and consideration: the small acquaintance and familiarity he hath had with her, makes that hee cannot condemne her of vnkindnesse: yet sith he was not thought worthy (118) to haue notice of her departure, hee againe hath no reason to hope, much lesse to assure himselfe of her affection towards him: hee knowes not how to resolue these doubts, nor what to thinke or doe in a matter of this nature and importance: for thus hee reasoneth with himselfe; if hee ride to *Briamata*, he may perchance offend the father; if hee stay at *Alicant*, displease the daughter; and although hee bee rather willing to runne the hazzard of his enuy, then of her affection, yet hee holds it safer to bee authorised by her pleasure, and to steere his course by the compasse of her commands: Hee therefore bethinkes himselfe of a meanes to auoyde these extremes, and so findes out a Channell to passe free betwixt that *Sylla* and this *Carybdis*; which is, to visit her by letters: he sees more reason to embrace, then to reiect this inuention, and so prouiding himselfe of a confident messenger, his heart commands his pen to signifie her these few lines:
[He writes to Beatrice and receives a non-committal reply, but a second letter convinces her that his affection is genuine.]

(121) *Beatrice-Ioana* seeing *Alsemero's* constant affection, holds it now rather discretion, then immodesty to accept both his seruice and selfe, yea, her heart so delights in the agreeablenesse of his person, and triumphs in the contemplation of his vertues, that shee either wisheth her selfe in *Alicant* with him, or hee in *Briamata* with her: but considering her affection to *Alsemero* by her fathers hatred, and her hatred to *Piracquo*, by his affection; she thinks it high time to informe *Alsemero* with what impatiencie they both endeuour to obtaine her fauour and consent: hoping that his discretion will interpose and finde meanes to stop the progresse of these their importunities, and to withdraw her fathers inclination from *Piracquo*, to bestowe it on himselfe: but all this while she thinks her silence is an iniurie to *Alsemero*, and therefore no longer to be vncourteous to him, who is so kinde to her, shee verie secretly conueyes him this Letter:

(122) As it is not for earth to resist heauen, nor for our wills to contra-
dict Gods prouidence, so I cannot deny, but now acknowledge, that if
euer I affected any man, it is your selfe: For your Letters, protestations,
and vowes, but chiefly your merits; and the hope, or rather the assurance
of your fidelitie, hath wonne my heart from my selfe to giue it you; but
there are some important considerations and reasons, that enforce mee
to craue your secresie herein, and to request you as soone as conueniently
you may, to come priuately hither to mee: for I shall neuer give content
to my thoughts, nor satisfaction to my minde, till I am made ioyfull with
your sight, and happie with your presence: in the meane time manage this
affection of mine, with care and discretion, and whiles you resolue to
make Alicant your Malta, I will expect and attend your comming with
much longing and impatiencie, to Briamata.

BEATRICE-IOANA.

It is for no others but for Louers to iudge how welcome this Letter
was to *Alsemero*, who a thousand times kissed it, and as often blest the
hand that wrote it; he had, as we haue formerly vnderstood, beene
twice in the Indies: But nowe in his conceit, hee hath found a farre
richer treasure in *Spaine*: I meane his *Beatrice-Ioana*, whom he
esteemes the ioy of his life, and the life of his ioy: But shee will not
prooue so: he is so inamored of her beautie, and so desirous to haue
the felicitie of her presence: as the winde comming good, the ship
sets sayle for *Malta* and hee (to giue a colour for his stay) (123)
feignes himselfe sicke, fetcheth backe his Trunkes, and remayneth in
Alicant: and so burning with desire, to see his sweetely deare and
dearely sweete Mistris, he dispatcheth away his confident messenger
to *Briamata* in the morning, to aduertise her, that he will not fayle to
bee with her that night at eleuen of the clocke.

Beatrice-Ioana is rauished with the ioy of this newes, and so pro-
uides for his comming. *Alsemero* takes the benefit of the night, and
shee giues him the aduantage of a posterne dore, which answeres to a
Garden, where *Diaphanta* her waiting Gentlewoman attends his
arriuall. He comes: she conducts him secretly thorow a priuate
gallery, into *Beatrice-Ioana's* chamber; where (richly apparelled)
shee verie courteously and respectiuely receiues him. At the beginning of their meeting they want no kisses: which they second with
complements, and many louing conferences, wherein she relates him
Piracquo's importunate sute to her, and her fathers earnestnesse, yea,
in a manner, his constraint, to see the match concluded betwixt them:
he being for that purpose there, in her fathers house; againe, after
shee hath alleadged and shewne him the intirenesse of her affection to
himselfe, with whome shee is resolued to liue and dye, shee lets fall
some darke and ambiguous speeches, tending to this effect, that
before *Piracquo* be in another World, there is no hope for *Alsemero* to

inioy her for his wife in this. Lo here the first plot and designe of a lamentable and execrable murther: which we shall shortly see acted and committed.

(124) There needes but halfe a word to a sharpe and quicke vnderstanding. *Alsemero* knowes it is the violence of her affection to him, that leades her to this dis-respect, and hatred to *Piracquo*, and because her content is his: yea, rather it is for his sake, that shee will forsake *Piracquo*, to liue and dye with him; Passion and affection blinding his Iudgement, and beautie triumphing and giuing a lawe to his conscience: he freely proffereth himselfe to his Mistris, vowing, that he will shortly send him a challenge, and fight with him, yea, had he a thousand liues, as he hath but one, he is ready, if shee please, to expose and sacrifice them all at her command and seruice. *Beatrice-Ioana* thankes him kindly for his affection & zeale, the which she sayth shee holds redoubled by the freenesse of his proffer: but being loth that he should hazard his owne life, in seeking that of another, shee coniures him by all the loue he beares her, neither directly nor indirectly to intermeddle with *Piracquo*: but that he repose and build vpon her affection and constancie: not doubting, but shee will so preuaile with her father, that he shall shortly change his opinion, and no more perswade her to affect *Piracquo*, whome shee resolutely affirmes, neither life nor death shall enforce her to marry. And to conclude, although shee affirme, his presence is dearer to her then her life; yet the better and sooner to compasse their desires, shee praies him to leaue *Alicant*, and for a while to returne to *Valentia*, not doubting but time may worke that, which perchance haste, or importunitie may neuer. Thus (125) passing ouer their kisses, and the rest of their amorous conference, he assured of her loue, and shee of his affection, hee returnes for *Alicant*, packes vp his baggage which hee sends before, and within lesse then foure dayes, takes his iourney for *Valentia*: where wee will leaue him a while, to relate other accidents and occurrences: which (like riuers into the Ocean) fall within the compasse of this History.

This meeting, and part of *Alsemero's* and *Beatrice-Ioana's* conference at her fathers house of *Briamata*, was not so secretly carried and concealed, but some curious or trecherous person neere him, or her, ouer-heare and reueale it: which makes her father *Vermandero* fume and bite the lippe; but hee conceales it from *Piracquo*: and they still continue their intelligence and familiarity: *Vermandero* telling him plainely, that a little more time shall worke and finish his desire; and that sith his request cannot preuayle with his daughter, his commands shall: But he shall misse of his ayme.

There is not so great distance from *Briamata* to *Alicant*, but some of the Noblest of the city are aduertised hereof: and one among the rest, in great zeale and affection to *Piracquo*, secretly acquaints *Don*

Tomaso Piracquo his younger brother therewith, being then in the citie of *Alicant*: who hearing of this newes, whereof hee imagined his Brother was ignorant, loth that hee should any longer perseuere in his present errour, and to preuent his future disgrace, hee, like a faithfull and honest brother, takes occasion from *Alicant* to (126) write him this ensuing Letter to *Briamata*:

Being more ielous of your prosperity, then of mine owne; & knowing, it many times falls out, that louers lose the cleerenes & solidity of their iudgement, in gazing and contemplating on the Roses and Lillies of their Mistresses beauties: I desirous to preuent your disgrace, thought my selfe bound to signifie you, that I heere vnderstand by the report of those, whose speeches beare their perswasion with them, that your sute to Beatrice-Ioana *is in vayne, and shee vnworthy of your affection, because she hath already contracted her selfe to* Alsemero *your riuall: I am as sorry to bee the Herald of this newes, as glad and confident, that as shee hath matched your inferiour, so you are reserued for her better: Wherefore, Sir, recall your thoughts, tempt not impossibilities, but consider that the shortest errours are best; and though you loue her well, yet thinke that at your pleasure you may finde variety of beauties, whereunto hers deserues not the honour to doe homage. I could giue no truce to my thoughts, till I had aduertised you hereof, and I hope either the name of a brother, or your owne generositie will easily procure pardon for my presumption.*

THOMASO PIRACQVO.

Piracquo, notwithstanding this his brothers Letter of counsell and aduice, is so farre from retyring in his sute, as he rather aduanceth with more violence and zeale: and as many mens iudgements are dazled and obscured a little before their danger and misfortune, when indeed they haue most need to haue them sound and cleere: so he is not capable (127) to bee disswaded from re-searching his Mistresse, but rather resembleth those Saylors, who are resolute to indure a storme, in hope of faire weather: but hee had found more security, and lesse danger, if hee had embraced and followed the counsell that his Brother gaue him. For *Beatrice-Ioana* seeing shee could not obtaine her desire in marrying *Alsemero*, e're *Piracquo* were remoued, doth now confirme that which formerly she had resolued on, to make him away, in what manner or at what rate soeuer. And now, after shee had ruminated, and runne ouer many bloody designes: the diuell, who neuer flies from those that follow him, proffers her an inuention as execrable as damnable. There is a Gallant young Gentleman, of the Garison of the Castle, who followes her father, that to her knowledge doth deepely honour, and dearely affect her: yea, she knowes, that at her request he will not sticke to murther *Piracquo*: his name is

Signiour Antonio de Flores: shee is resolute in her rage, and approues him to be a fit instrument to execute her will.

Now, as soone as *Vermandero* vnderstands of *Alsemero's* departure to *Valentia*, he with his daughter and *Piracquo* returnes from *Briamata* to *Alicant*: where, within three dayes of their arriuall, *Beatrice-Ioana*, boyling still in her reuenge to *Piracquo*, which neither the ayre of the Country, nor City, could quench or wipe off, shee sends for *de Flores*, and with many flattering smiles, and sugered speeches, acquaints him with her purpose and desire, making him many promises of kindenesse (128) and courtesies, if hee will performe it.

De Flores hauing a long time loued *Beatrice-Ioana*, is exceeding glad of this newes, yea, feeding his hopes with the ayre of her promises, hee is so caught and intangled in the snares of her beautie, that hee freely promiseth to dispatch *Piracquo*; and so they first consult, and then agree vpon the manner how, which foorth-with wee shall see performed, to which end, *de Flores* insinuates himselfe fairely into *Piracquo's* company and familiarity, as hee comes to the Castle; where watching his hellish opportunitie, he one day hearing *Piracquo* commend the thicknesse and strength of the Walles, told him that the strength of that Castle consisted not in the Walles, but in the *Casemates* that were stored with good ordnance to scoure the ditches. *Piracquo* very courteously prayes *de Flores* to be a meanes that he may goe downe and see the *Casemates. De Flores* like a bloody Fawkner, seeing *Piracquo* already come to his lure, tells him it is now dinner time, and the bell vpon ringing: but if hee please, hee himselfe will after dinner accompany him, and shew him all the strength and rarities of the Castle. Hee thankes *de Flores* for this courtesie, and accepts heereof, with promise to goe. So hee hies in to dinner, and *de Flores* pretending some businesse, walkes in the Court.

Whiles *Piracquo* is at dinner with *Vermandero*, *de Flores* is prouiding him a bloody banquet in the East *Casemate*, where, of purpose hee goes, and hides a naked Sword and Ponyard behinde the doore. Now dinner being ended, *Piracquo* findes (129) out *de Flores*, and summons him of his promise: who tells him hee is ready to waite on him: so away they goe from the Walles, to the Rauellins, Sconces and Bulwarkes, and from thence by a Posterne to the ditches: and so in againe to the *Casemates*, whereof they haue already viewed three, and are now going to the last, which is the Theater, whereon wee shall presently see acted a mournfull and bloody Tragedy. At the descent hereof *de Flores* puts off his Rapier, and leaues it behinde him, trecherously informing *Piracquo*, that the descent is narrow and craggie. See heere the .policy and villany of this diuellish and trecherous miscreant.

Piracquo not doubting, nor dreaming of any Treason, followes his example, and so casts off his Rapier: *De Flores* leades the way, and hee followes him: but, alas poore Gentleman, hee shall neuer returne with his life: they enter the Vault of the *Casemate*: *de Flores* opens the doore, and throwes it backe, thereby to hide his Sword and Ponyard: Hee stoopes and lookes thorow a Port-hole, and tells him, that that Peece doth thorowly scowre the ditch. *Piracquo* stoopes likewise downe to view it, when (O griefe to thinke thereon!) *de Flores* steppes for his weapons, and with his Ponyard stabbes him thorow the backe, and swiftly redoubling blow vpon blow, kills him dead at his feete, and without going farther, buries him there, right vnder the ruines of an old wall, whereof that *Casemate* was built. Loe heere the first part of this mournefull and bloody Tragedy.

(130) *De Flores* (like a gracelesse villaine) hauing dispatched this sorrowfull businesse, speedily acquaints *Beatrice-Ioana* heerewith, who (miserable wretch) doth heereat infinitly reioyce, and thankes him with many kisses; and the better to conceale this their vilde and bloody murther, as also to cast a mist before peoples conceits and iudgements, shee bids him (by some secret meanes) to cause reports to be spred: first, that *Piracquo* was seene gone foorth the Castle gate; then, that in the City hee was seene take boate, and went (as it was thought) to take the ayre of the sea. But this wit of theirs shall proue folly: for though men as yet see not this murther, yet God in his due time will both detect and punish it.

By this time *Piracquo* is found wanting, both in the City and Castle; so these aforesayd reports runne for current, all tongues prattle hereof: *Vermandero* knowes not what to say, nor *Piracquo's* brother and friends what to doe herein: they euery houre and minute expect newes of him, but their hopes bring them no comfort, and amongst the rest, our diuellish *Beatrice-Ioana* seemes exceedingly to grieue and mourne heereat. *Don Tomaso Piracquo* with the rest of his friends, search euery corner of the City, and send scouts, both by land and Sea, to haue newes of him. *Vermandero* the Captaine of the Castle doth the like, and vowes that next his owne sonne, hee loued *Piracquo* before any man of the world: yea, not onely his friends, but generally all those who knew him, exceedingly weepe and bewayle the absence, and losse of (131) this Cauallier; for they thinke sure he is drowned in the Sea.

Now in the middest of this sorrow, and of these teares, *Beatrice-Ioana* doth secretly aduertise her louer *Alsemero* heereof, but in such palliating tearmes, that thereby shee may delude and carry away his iudgement, from imagining, that shee had the least shadow, or finger heerein; and withall prayes him to make no long stay in *Valentia*, but to come away to her to *Alicant*. *Alsemero* wonders at this newes, and to please his faire Mistresse, beleeues part thereof, but will neuer beleeue all; but hee is so inflamed with her beautie, as her remembrance wipes away that of *Piracquo*: when letting passe a little time, hee makes his preparations for *Alicant*: but first hee sends the chiefest of his Parents to *Vermandero*, to demaund his Daughter *Beatrice-Ioana* in marriage for him, and then comes himselfe in person, and in discreete and honourable manner courts her Parents priuately, and makes shew to seeke her publikely.

In fine, after many conferences, meetings and complements, as *Alsemero* hath heretofore wonne the affection of *Beatrice-Ioana*; so now at last, hee obtaines likewise the fauour and consent of *Vermandero* her father. And heere our two Louers, to their exceeding great content, and infinite ioy, are vnited, and by the bond of marriage of two persons made one; their Nuptialls being solemnized in the Castle of *Alicant*, with much Pompe, State, and Brauery.

(132) Hauing heeretofore heard the conference that past betwixt *Alsemero* and *Beatrice-Ioana* in the Church; hauing likewise seene the amorous Letters that past betwixt them, from *Alicant* to *Briamata*, and from *Briamata* to *Alicant*; and now considering the pompe and glory of their Nuptialls; who would imagine that any auerse accident could alter the sweetnesse and tranquillity of their affections, or that the Sunne-shine of their ioyes should so soone bee eclipsed, and ouertaken with a storme? But God is as iust as secret in his decrees. [After three months Alsemero becomes violently and unreasonably jealous of Beatrice, and removes her from Alicant to Valentia. His behaviour causes her to lose all affection for him. Vermandero becomes anxious about them, and sends letters to them both by De Flores.]

(133) *De Flores* is extremely ioyfull of this occasion, to see his old Mistris *Beatrice-Ioana*, whom he loues dearer then his life: he comes to *Valentia*, and finding *Alsemero* abroade, and shee at home, deliuers her her fathers Letter, and salutes and kisseth her, with many amorous embracings and dalliances, (which modestie holds vn-worthy of relation:) (134) shee acquaints him with her husbands ingratitude: he rather reioyceth, then greeues hereat, and now reuiues his old sute, and redoubleth his newe Kisses: shee consider-ing what he hath done for her seruice, and ioyning therewith her hus-bands ielousie, not onely ingageth her selfe to him for the time present, but for the future, and bids him visit her often. But they both shall pay deare for this familiarity and pleasure.

Alsemero comes home, receiues his fathers Letter, sets a pleasing face on his discontented heart, and bids him welcome: and so the next day writes backe to his father *Vermandero*, and dispatcheth *de Flores*, who for that time takes his leaue of them both, and returnes for *Alicant*.

Hee is no sooner departed, but *Alsemero* is by one of his spies, a wayting Gentlewoman of his wiues, whom hee had corrupted with

money, aduertized, that there past many amorous kisses, and dalliances betweene her Mistris and *de Flores*: yea, shee reueales all that
either shee sawe or heard; for shee past not to be false to her Lady, so
shee were true to her Lord and Master. And indeede this waiting
Gentlewoman was that *Diaphanta*, of whom we haue formerly made
mention, for conducting of *Alsemero* to her Ladyes chamber at
Briamata. *Alsemero* is all fire at this newes: he consults not with
iudgement, but with passion, and so, rather like a deuill, then a man,
flyes to his wiues chamber, wherein furiously rushing, hee with his
sword drawne in his hand, to her great terrour and amazement
deliuers her these words:

(135) Minion (quoth he) vpon thy life, tell mee what familiaritie
there hath nowe past betwixt *de Flores*, and thy selfe: whereat shee,
fetching many sighs, and sheading many teares, answeres him, that
by her part of heauen, her thoughts, speeches and actions haue no
way exceeded the bonds of honour, and chastitie towards him; and
that *de Flores* neuer attempted any courtesie, but such as a brother
may shew to his own natural sister. Then quoth he, whence proceeds
this your familiarity? Whereat shee growes pale, and withall silent.
Which her husband espying, Dispatch, quoth he, and tell mee the
truth, or else this sword of mine shall instantly finde a passage to thy
heart. When loe, the prouidence of God so ordained it, that shee is
reduced to this exigent and extremity, as she must bee a witnesse
against her selfe, and in seeking to conceale her whoredome, must
discouer her murther; the which she doth in these words:

Know, *Alsemero*, that sith thou wilt enforce mee to shew thee the
true cause of my chaste familiarity with *de Flores*, that I am much
bound to him, & thy selfe more, for he it was, that at my request, dispatched *Piracquo*, without the which (as thou well knowest) I could
neuer haue enioyed thee for my husband, nor thou me for thy wife:
And so shee reueales him the whole circumstance of that cruell
murther, as wee haue formerly vnderstood: the which shee coniures,
and prayes him to conceale, sith no lesse then *de Flores* and her owne
life depended thereon, and that shee will dye a thousand deaths, before consent to defile his bed, or (136) to violate her oath and promise
giuen him in marriage.

Alsemero both wondering and grieuing at this lamentable newes,
sayes little, but thinks the more: and although he had reason, and
apparance to beleeue, that shee who commits murther, will not sticke
to commit adultery, yet vpon his wiues solemne oaths and protestations, he forgets what is past; onely hee strictly chargeth her, no
more to see, or admit *de Flores* into her company; or if the contrary,
he vowes hee will so sharply bee reuenged of her, as he will make her
an example to all posteritie.

[Beatrice continues to be unfaithful, however, and Alsemero prepares a trap for her by pretending to go away when De Flores next comes to the house. He hides in a bedroom, and waits until Beatrice and De Flores are in the act of adultery, and then, unable to contain himself, rushes out and shoots and stabs them both. They are immediately killed. Alsemero is arrested, but released after Diaphanta has testified to the repeated infidelity of Beatrice. The murder of Piracquo is still concealed.

Thomaso is convinced that Alsemero and Beatrice are responsible for the death of his brother:

. . . hee raiseth this resolution, that hee is not worthie to bee a Gentleman, nor of the degree and title of a brother, if hee craue not satisfaction for that irreparable losse which hee sustaineth in that of his brother . . . (140)

He challenges Alsemero, who accepts the challenge, but at the appointed place kills Thomaso by a base and cowardly trick. He tries to flee, but is caught and condemned, and at his execution reveals the truth concerning the death of Piracquo. His body is thrown in the sea, the bodies of Beatrice and De Flores are dug up, burnt, and their ashes thrown in the air, and the body of Piracquo is given honourable burial.]

(ii) *Gerardo The Unfortunate Spaniard*

(The following passages are taken from pages 95–7 and 105–7 of Digges's book. They describe the events on the wedding night of Roberto and Isdaura, who has lost her virginity to the Biscayner (see Introduction, pp. xxxiii–iv) and is forced to substitute her maid Julia. The second extract is from a letter written by the wife to her husband some time after the events narrated in it have taken place.)

At length the prefixed day came, together with the wished night, in which hauing to my vnspeakable ioy reaped from my Bride the sweet fruit, amorously passing the rest of it, at length (our bodies in each others Armes enterlaced) we fell asleepe. But not long were our weary limmes laid to soft rest, when my Wife with her hands and sudden affrighting shriekes awoke mee, and lowd lowd cries raised mee to the helpe of her Fathers house, that was now all on a light flame; at which I was so astonisht, that without so much as a question, taking my night-gowne, I nimbly leapt out of the Chamber, vvhere the smoake and sparkles of the vntamed element, that euen now mounted vp to it's owne Sphere, euen blinded me; and running vvhere the flame was greatest, I might see my Father and Mother gotten thither, and the rest of the house also, by which time the Bels had giuen their accustomed signall of the danger; whereupon (the neighbourhood and Citie all in a confused vproare) vvith their helpe, the mercilesse flames vvere soone humbled. All our house vvas nothing but noise, vvringing and wailing; in midst of vvhich, I might most lowdly heare my wiues scrieches, that, fearing lest some disaster had befalne her, finding her quickly out by the eccho of her shrill cries, I might view her supported by her Mother, hauing falne in a deepe swoune into her Armes, not farre from a deep Well, about vvhich, diuers of the seruants were gotten together vvith much stirre; vvhereupon, seeing my *Isdaura* in so sad plight, my torment increast, and the more, vvhen they told me the cause of her sudden dismaying, no lesse vvofull then the lamentable end of the vnhappie *Biscayner*; for a handsome discreet maid-seruant of hers, following his vnluckie fate, a little before I came, hauing been earnest to draw water to quench the fire (whether vvith some fright or other accident falling in) in an instant (there being no meanes to saue her) vvas drowned: and beeing within a vvhile after drawne up, my Wife and Mothers moanes were againe renued, and so extremely, in respect of their loue to the poore Wench brought vp from a child by them, that I thought it impossible to comfort them, especially for me, that in such cases needed it as vvell, as much my selfe.

But time cured in them their griefes, though with mee they are still present; neither can I forget those propheticall boadings of my vvretched marriage (which thus accomplished) . . .

My misfortunes so stopped not, rather with your comming they increast, in such manner, that but for feare of hell fire, I had sacrificed mine owne life, seeing my selfe so neere a knowne infamy. But the comfort of a maid of mine, changed that desperate imagination; one, that was my companion from a child, and as then Secretary to my most hidden thoughts: though this (as being of so great consequence) I feared to make knowne vnto her; but shee perceiuing my extreme vexation, wondred much, (as thinking I had now most reason to be ioyfull) and so with louing intreaties requested the cause of my griefe, and I (for now necessitie had no law with me) making choice of *Iulia* for a dead lift, satisfied of her true affection, told her the occasion of my distraction, but without any mention of the *Biscayner*, laid my dishonour to anothers charge, relying wholly vpon her person for my liues remedy; and so with the pitifullest reasons that the necessity of the time would permit me, I reduced her to my will, preparing her to make good my defect, with the integritie of her honesty, which (I nothing doubted) but was entire. *Iulia* could not but refuse the danger, aswell for her losse, as other vncertainties of the successe. But to free me (out of her loue) from such a strait, made her shut her eyes; and so my plot tooke effect: for hauing the night of our marriage, placed

Iulia behind our bed Curtaines, and faining modestie, commanded the lights to be put out, darknesse fauoring, and *Iulia* supplying my roome; neither was the deceit knowne, nor you perceiued the exchange.

Not long after, she belike either wearied, or taken with the sweet of so much pleasure, contrary to the order I had giuen, fell asleepe, and now I knew not which in mee was most, my iealousie or feare, and my rage increased the more, when (hearing the Clocke strike three) I saw so little memory in her of my danger. This and the difficulty of waking her, without being perceiued by you, made me vndergo as desperate a course, as that of the *Biscayner*: for without better aduice, or more delay, beginning at the dining roomes Tapistry, with a Torch, I by chance found lighted, I set it all on fire, til it was almost consumed; and hoping that with the vprore, (my Father and the whole house raised) you would take no notice of ought but my cries, embracing you closely, and crying, Fire, fire: you awoke, and frightfully leapt out of your bed and the chamber; leauing me with *Iulia*, and so sensible of the mischiefe, that (by her neglect) I was forced to, that I was ready to haue runne her thorow with your sword. This iust anger of mine was furthered with the remembrance of what might hereafter ensue, to thinke I should haue her a Corriual in my desires, and (taking her to be too shallow a vessel for my secrets) the matter at least was doubtfull, and I like to become a slaue to her litle constancie, which necessity had made me subiect to. This sorrowful thought still pursued me, whilst you and the rest of the Family were quenching the violent flames; and so vnder colour of helping, taking *Iulia* by the hand, we went downe, vvhere the seruants were hastily drawing vvater; and as they went and came, laying hold vpon a fit opportunity, to be free from the confusion I was in, bidding *Iulia* draw me a little water; whilst she vvas performing it, with a small push I toppled her into the deepe Well; where giuing her leaue awhile to struggle with her last agonie, when I supposed her to be thoroughly dead, dissembling my cruell ingratitude, crying out vvith fained teares, aswell to my parents, as your selfe and the rest, I made *Iulia's* misfortune as casuall, and my sorrow to bee true, infallibly beleeued. This diuellish act, this horrid sinne, is that which now lights to her shame, and heauy dishonour, on your vnfortunate vvife, vvho hath euer truly loued and obeyed you, as Heauen can witnesse.

APPENDIX B
Lineation

All departures from the quarto are recorded here, together with a few editorial alterations which have not been accepted in the present text. The presence of so much mislineation in an otherwise clean text is difficult to explain; it is noticeable, however, that in most cases two half-lines are printed as one, or a line and a half as a single line, which suggests that the compositor of the quarto was anxious to save space.

[I. i]

36–9. Lover . . . way.] *Dyce;* Lover . . . Stoick / Was . . . mother / Nor . . . beauty, / I and . . . way *Q.*

49. 'Tis . . . Aquarius.] *Dyce;* Tis . . . day, / It . . . *Aquarius. Q.*

90–2. I meant . . . top-sail.] *Dyce; prose in Q.*

153–4. Oh . . . ended ?] *Dilke; one line in Q.*

169–70. Alsemero; not . . . Alsemero ?] *Dyce; one line in Q.*

171–3. He . . . truth.] *Dyce;* He . . . speaks / A . . . truth. *Q.*

217–18. He's . . . sir.] *Dyce; one line in Q.*

219–20. As fast . . . else.] *Dyce; one line in Q.*

231–3. Here's . . . fingers] *Dyce;* Here's . . . Now / I . . . tan'd / In . . . fingers *Q.*

[I. ii]

30–1. You . . . into't.] *Dyce;* You . . . by, / One . . . into't. *Q.*

33–4. Must . . . home.] *Dyce; one line in Q.*

84–5. Ay . . . patient.] *This ed.; one line in Q.*

86–90.] *Dyce;* And . . . commodious, / To . . . sick / And . . . are / But . . . pieces / That . . . charge / Of . . . necessaries / Fully defrayed. *Q, Dilke.*

92–3. Sir . . . hands.] *Dyce;* Sir . . . somthing, / The . . . hands. *Q.*

97–8. His . . . Tony.] *Dyce;* His . . . half / To . . . *Tonie. Q.*

104–5. Well . . . height,] *Dyce; one line in Q.*

122–3. Oh . . . enough.] *Dyce;* Oh . . . shorter / Will . . . enough. *Q.*

173–4. Yes . . . Tony.] *Dilke;* Yes . . . say't; / Once . . . *Tonie. Q.*

206–8. There's . . . for't.] *Dilke;* Theres . . . mad-man, / Was . . . Permasant, / Lost . . . for't. *Q.*

[II. i]

9–10. Than . . . choose] *This ed.; one line in Q.*

52–3. Again . . . me] *Dilke; one line in Q.*

56–7. Soft . . . now.] *Dyce; one line in* Q.
57–8. The . . . toad-pool!] *Dyce; one line in* Q.
60–1. My lord . . . you.] *Dilke; one line in* Q.
61–2. What . . . thee.] *Dilke; one line in* Q.
64–5. Let . . . all.] *Dyce; one line in* Q.
66–7. Signor . . . Tomazo de Piracquo—] *Dilke; one line in* Q.
69–70. The said . . . Tomazo—] *Dyce; one line in* Q.
73–4. My lord . . . out.] *Dyce; one line in* Q.
74–5. Is . . . by?] *Dyce; one line in* Q.
75–6. It . . . still.] *Dyce; one line in* Q.
76–7. So . . . ways] *Dilke; one line in* Q.
122–3. May . . . sirs.] *Q; May . . . ever / Meet . . . sirs. Dyce.*
142–3. Nay . . . enough.] *Dilke; one line in* Q.

[II. ii]

5–6. This . . . cabinets,] *Dilke; one line in* Q.
12–13. W'are . . . borrow] *Dilke; one line in* Q.
25–6. Pray . . . happy?] *Dilke; prose in* Q.
48–9. I do . . . side] *Dilke; one line in* Q.
51–2. As thrifty . . . opens.] *Dyce; one line in* Q.
63–4. One . . . royal.] *Dilke; one line in* Q.
69–70. And . . . De Flores.] *Dyce; one line in* Q.
72–3. What . . . physician;] *Dilke; one line in* Q.
75–6. Not . . . pimple,] *Dilke; one line in* Q.
77–8. Which . . . this?] *Dyce; one line in* Q.
79–80. Turn . . . perceiv't.] *Dyce; one line in* Q.
81–2. Her . . . amber.] *Dyce; one line in* Q.
83–4. I'll . . . fortnight.] *Dilke; one line in* Q.
85–6. Yes . . . other.] *Dilke; one line in* Q.
86–7. 'Tis . . . to me.] *Dilke; one line in* Q.
87–8. When . . . unpleasing;] *Dilke; one line in* Q.
89–90. It . . . experience.] *Dilke; one line in* Q.
90–1. I was . . . on't.] *Dilke; one line in* Q.
93–4. It . . . employment.] *Dilke; one line in* Q.
94–5. 'Twould . . . it.] *Dilke; one line in* Q.
96–7. I would . . . to.] *Dilke; one line in* Q.
97–8. We . . . De Flores!] *Dilke; one line in* Q.
98–9. How's . . . De Flores!] *conj. Dyce; one line in* Q.
101–2. There . . . on't.] *conj. Dyce; one line in* Q.
106–7. For . . . bosom.] *Dyce; one line in* Q.
109–10. Oh . . . one] *Dilke; prose in* Q.
112–13. Then . . . sight.] *Dilke; one line in* Q.
113–14. Oh . . . wishes.] *Dilke; prose in* Q.
115–16. In . . . that.] *Dilke; one line in* Q.
116–17. Put . . . you.] *Dilke; one line in* Q.
120–1. If . . . employed] *Dilke; one line in* Q.
124–5. This . . . such] *Dilke; one line in* Q.
127–8. Possible . . . thee:] *Dilke; one line in* Q.
130–2. That . . . ravishes.] *Dilke; prose in* Q.
134–5. His . . . more.] *Dilke; one line in* Q.

135–7. How . . . rewarded.] *Dilke;* How . . . me! / Never . . . rewarded. *Q.*
141–3. When . . . country.] *Dilke; prose in Q.*
144–5. I shall . . . time,] *Dilke; one line in Q.*
146–7. Oh . . . already,] *Dilke; one line in Q.*
157–8. Thou . . . castle?] *Dilke; one line in Q.*
159–61. And if . . . lord.] *Dilke; prose in Q.*
162–4. I'm . . . me.] *Dilke; prose in Q.*

[III. i]

9–10. Here . . . purpose.] *Dyce; one line in Q.*

[III. ii]

1–2. All . . . on.] *Dilke; one line in Q.*
2–3. I am . . . house] *Dilke; one line in Q.*
10–14. Ay . . . awhile.] *Dyce; prose in Q.*
15–16. De Flores . . . put on?] *Dilke; one line in Q.*
16–17. Do . . . you.] *Dilke; one line in Q.*

[III. iii]

2–3. To . . . to me,] *Bullen;* To . . . If you / Keep . . . me, *Q.*
29–31. If I . . . fool.] *Dilke;* If . . . shew / You . . . may / Call . . . fool. *Q.*
45–7. For . . . neither.] *Dilke;* For . . . Mistress, / He . . . first / The
. . . Chambermaid, / Yet . . . neither. *Q.*
48–52. Hail . . . poesie.] *Dilke; prose in Q.*
54–6. Oh . . . kneels.] *Dilke; prose in Q.*
63–4. Didst . . . poet?] *Dyce; one line in Q.*
68–9. Yes . . . ago.] *Dyce; prose in Q.*
79–85. Luna . . . sheep.] *Dilke; prose in Q.*
89–90. *Sweet . . . thee.*] *Dilke; one line in Q.*
110–11. Hark . . . order.] *Dyce; prose in Q.*
122–3. Oh . . . all] *Dilke; one line in Q.*
124–8. The . . . in.] *Q;* The . . . poet, / Catches . . . knowledge, / Yet
. . . mystery, / Into . . . in. *Dilke.*
138–9. Take . . . within] *Dilke; one line in Q.*
140–2. When . . . enough.] *Dilke;* When . . . mean time / Keep . . .
enough *Q.*
147–8. And . . . morning.] *Dyce;* And . . . Valentine / To morrow
morning. *Q.*
152–3. If . . . something.] *Dyce; prose in Q.*
154–6. Ay . . . six?] *Dilke;* I, thank . . . begins / To . . . is / Five . . .
six? *Q.*
158–9. What . . . seven?] *Dilke;* What . . . is / One . . . seven? *Q.*
166–8. Again . . . together.] *Dilke;* Agen . . . home! / I . . . together. *Q.*
172–3. How . . . alone] *Dilke; one line in Q.*
178–80. How . . . that—] *Dilke;* How . . . *Lipsius?* / He's . . . harder /
Questions . . . that— *Q.*
181–2. What . . . smile,] *Dilke; one line in Q.*
191–2. Of fear . . . lunatics,] *Dilke; one line in Q.*
226–7. 'What . . . smile,] *Dyce; one line in Q.*

233–7. Becomes . . . on't.] *Dilke;* Becomes . . . more / Foolish . .
Lacedemonian. / Let . . . thing / About . . . on't. *Q.*
247–8. Fie . . . that.] *Dyce;* one line in *Q.*
275–6. Y'have . . . commodity.] *Dyce; prose in Q.*

[III. iv]

29–30. Why . . . heart-strings.] *Dyce; prose in Q.*
48–50. It . . . recompense.] *Dilke; prose in Q.*
50–1. No . . . then!] *Dilke; prose in Q.*
60–1. 'Tis . . . florins:] *Dilke;* one line in *Q.*
68–9. I could . . . rate,] *Dilke;* one line in *Q.*
73–4. You . . . do.] *Dilke;* one line in *Q.*
89–90. How . . . well.] *Dilke;* one line in *Q.*
90–1. What . . . us.] *Dilke;* one line in *Q.*
94–5. Take . . . us.] *Dilke;* one line in *Q.*
97–8. I have . . . pain,] *Dilke;* one line in *Q.*
101–2. Oh . . . lose] *Dilke;* one line in *Q.*
104–5. I would . . . deed.] *Dilke;* one line in *Q.*
105–6. Soft . . . act] *Dilke;* one line in *Q.*
124–5. I cannot . . . modesty.] *Dilke;* one line in *Q.*
125–6. Push . . . modesty?] *Dilke; prose in Q.*
160–1. The . . . me;] *Dyce;* one line in *Q.*

[IV. i]

30–2. 'If . . . glass C—'] *Dilke;* If . . . not, / Give . . . C. *Q.*
33–5. Where's . . . not.'] *Dilke;* Wher's . . . child, / She . . . not *Q.*
51–2. Where . . . bedtime.] *Dyce; prose in Q.*
57–8. Would . . . madam.] *Q;* Would . . . cause / To . . . madam. *Dyce.*
83–4. You . . . me.] *Dilke;* one line in *Q.*
103–4. And . . . it.] *Dilke;* one line in *Q.*
112–13. As if . . . another.] *Dilke;* one line in *Q.*
115–16. Ay . . . by't.] *Dilke;* one line in *Q.*
117–18. It . . . now.] *Dyce;* It . . . *Diaphanta* / I . . . now. *Q.*
120–1. I'll . . . business.] *Dilke; prose in Q.*
121–2. I shall . . . burthen.] *Dyce;* one line in *Q.*
122–3. About . . . gently,] *Dyce;* one line in *Q.*

[IV. ii]

3–4. Nor . . . and who.] *Neilson;* Nor . . . absent? / Tell . . . who. *Q.*
7–8. Some . . . Valencia.] *Dyce;* Some . . . *Briamata,* / Th'other . . .
Valentia. Q.
17–18. Y'are . . . here.] *Dyce;* one line in *Q.*
33–4. 'Tis . . . you] *Dyce;* one line in *Q.*
35–6. The best . . . on.] *Dilke;* one line in *Q.*
43–4. Oh purely . . . him,] *Dilke;* one line in *Q.*
60–1. 'Twill . . . Sir!] *Dilke;* one line in *Q.*
67–8. Your . . . strangers.] *Dilke;* one line in *Q.*
68–9. Time . . . business:] *Dilke;* Time . . . acquainted; / This . . .
businesse. *Q.*
73–4. You . . . sir.] *Dilke;* one line in *Q.*

74–5. Fear . . . meeting.] *Dilke; one line in Q.*
85–6. This . . . slowness.] *Dilke; one line in Q.*
97–8. Still . . . her.] *Dilke; one line in Q.*
104–5. Such . . . earth,] *Dilke; one line in Q.*
110–11. Done . . . secret,] *Dilke; one line in Q.*
133–4. Sir . . . composition.] *Dilke; one line in Q.*
143–4. Ha . . . lord.] *Dilke; one line in Q.*

[IV. iii]

87–8. Ay . . . la la.] *Dyce;* I . . . out, / Vault . . . la la. *Q.*
94–6. Marry . . . caper.] *Dilke;* Marry . . . yeomandry / Itself . . .
    stiffened, / There . . . caper. *Q.*
98–100. Very . . . Tony ?] *Dilke;* Very . . . high, / Has . . . agen, /
    You . . . *Tony* ? *Q.*
102–8. Hey . . . clue.] *Dyce;* Hey . . . way, / He . . . *Icarus,* / More . . .
    moons; / He's . . . up, / Thou . . . lower / Labyrinth . . . Clue. *Q.*

[V. i]

14–15. Hath . . . woman ?] *Dilke; one line in Q.*
29–30. Tush . . . all.] *Dilke; one line in Q.*
31–2. This . . . chamber.] *This ed.; one line in Q.*
32–3. How . . . house.] *This ed.; one line in Q.*
35–6. Push . . . sure;] *Dyce; one line in Q.*
50–1. One . . . servants ?] *Dilke; one line in Q.*
51–2. I'll . . . hurry,] *Dilke; one line in Q.*
76–7. Here's . . . jewel!] *Dyce; one line in Q.*
79–80. Hie . . . you.] *Dyce; one line in Q.*
80–1. I never . . . bargain.] *Dyce; one line in Q.*
83–4. When . . . follow.] *Dyce; one line in Q.*
84–5. Th'art . . . dangerous.] *Dyce; one line in Q.*
94–5. Come . . . cold.] *Dyce; one line in Q.*
104–5. Oh poor . . . for't.] *Dilke; one line in Q.*
107–8. Now . . . sir!] *Dilke;* Now . . . are / Greedy . . . sir. *Q.*
109–11. Not . . . us.] *Dilke;* Not . . . embrace / I . . . us. *Q.*
114–16. All . . . stifled!] *This ed.;* All . . . Lords, / The . . . Gentle-
    woman, / How . . . stifled! *Q.*
123–4. He . . . upon me.] *Dilke; one line in Q.*

[V. iii]

14–15. How do I . . . well.] *Dilke; one line in Q.*
39–40. You . . . please,] *Dilke; one line in Q.*
52–3. He's . . . saint!] *Dilke; one line in Q.*
53–4. Worse . . . adultery!] *Dyce; one line in Q.*
55–6. 'Twas . . . Diaphanta.] *Dilke; one line in Q.*
90–1. I can . . . you.] *Dyce; one line in Q.*
172–3. No . . . still.] *Dyce; one line in Q.*
209–10. Your . . . transformation:] *Dilke; one line in Q.*
214–15. Into . . . myself.] *Dilke;* Into . . . Scholars / That . . . self. *Q.*

Glossary

Note: Where there appears to be a deliberate ambiguity or play on words, the meanings are distinguished as (*a*) and (*b*).

ABLE vb: make capable for (a post, office, etc.); warrant, vouch for, I. ii. 130 [cf. *Lr.*, IV. vi. 172].

ACCIDENT: event, incident, IV. i. 0.7; symptom, IV. i. 112.

ADDITION: title, rank, II. i. 99.

ADULTERY: person with whom adultery has been committed, V. iii. 54 [not in this sense in *O.E.D.*].

ALLIANCE: kindred, family, IV. ii. 34.

AMAIN: violently, with full force, II. i. 58.

AMAZING adj.: amazed, astonished, III. iii. 117 [not in this sense in *O.E.D.*].

AMBER: ambergris; possibly adjectival, 'sweet-scented', II. ii. 82 [cf. Milton, *Samson Agonistes*, l. 720: 'An Amber sent of odorous perfume'].

AMOROUSLY adj.: lovely, lovable, II. ii. 75 [not in this sense in *O.E.D.*].

ANSWER vb: answer for, justify, IV. ii. 11.

ANTIC: clown, grotesque figure, IV. iii. 125.

APPROVE: confirm, prove, III. ii. 23.

ARCTIC sb.: North Pole, III. iii. 217.

ART: skill, learning, II. ii. 46–7.

ARTICLE: term, condition, I. i. 162.

AUNT: implying 'woman of easy morals', III. iii. 99 [cf. Middleton's *Michaelmas Term*, II. iii. 25 (Bullen, I, 247)].

BAIT vb: harass, torment, II. i. 32.

BAND: neck-band, collar, V. iii. 95.

BANKER: labourer who makes banks of earth, dykes, etc., III. iii. 213 [not rec. before 1795 in *O.E.D.*].

BARLEY-BRAKE: a country game, V. iii. 163 [see Commentary].

BAUBLE: stick surmounted by a carved head with ass's ears, carried by the court fool or jester (possibly used here with an indecent implication), III. iii. 103.

BEADLE: minor parish officer, I. ii. 128.

BEDLAM: lunatic asylum, III. iii. 21; mad person, IV. iii. 126 [cf. *Lr.*, III. vii. 103].

BEHOLDING adj.: indebted, obliged, I. i. 157.

BESHREW vb: curse, IV. i. 71 [cf. *Oth.*, IV. iii. 78].

BESTED pa. pple: bestead, in difficulty, V. ii. 10.

BID pa. pple: invited, I. i. 206.

BLAST sb.: breath, puff of air, II. ii. 25.

BLOOD: sensual desire, II. ii. 146, III. iv 100, V. i. 7, etc.

BOARD vb: accost, approach, I. i. 91; put on board, I. i. 47.

BOUNCE bang, the noise of a gun, III. iii. 109.

BOUND adj : (*a*) indebted, under an obligation, I. i. 218, II. i. 153; (*b*) fastened, tied, I. i. 218.

BOUNDEN adj.: with the same meanings as *bound*, III. iii. 247.

BRAVELY: splendidly, lavishly, II. ii. 143.

BRING (ON): ? lead forward; ? persuade, convince, II. i. 108 [see Commentary].

BUCKLER: small round shield used for defence, I. ii. 66.

BY-BET: ? side-bet, IV. i. 88 [see Commentary].

CAPARISONS: clothes, IV. iii. 134.

CAPCASE: small travelling case, wallet, III. iv. 44.

CAPER: leap, lively movement in dancing, IV. iii. 96-8.

CASEMENT: window, window-recess, III. ii. 6.

CAST sb.: throw of the dice, II. ii. 139 [cf. *R3*, v. iv. 9].

CAST vb (in *cast water*): examine (urine), IV. iii. 185 [cf. *Mac.*, v. iii. 50-1].

CAT-WHORE: term of abuse, I. ii. 202 [not in *O.E.D.*].

CAUSE sb.: charge, accusation, III. iv. 54, v. iii. 53 [cf. *Lr.*, IV. vi. 111].

CENSURER: judge, critic, II. i. 107.

CHALDEAN: a native of Chaldea, hence a soothsayer, astrologer, IV. ii. 112 [see Book of Daniel, Chapter ii].

CHALLENGE vb: claim, demand, III. iv. 138, IV. i. 78, IV. ii. 102.

CHARGE sb.: expenses, I. ii. 89; explosive charge (of powder and shot), v. i. 75 [second meaning not rec. in *O.E.D.* before 1653].

CHECK vb: restrain, rebuke, I. i. 76.

CHOPS: jaws, mouth, II. i. 84.

CIRCUMSCRIBE: encircle, encompass, v. iii. 164; ? confine, restrict, IV. i. 112.

CLIP vb: embrace, v. iii. 118.

COME (*near*): make a thrust which nearly reaches the target (in fencing); fig., get near the truth, make a penetrating remark, v. ii. 42.

COMFORTABLE: comforting, reassuring, I. ii. 43.

COMMODIOUS: beneficial, useful, I. ii. 86.

COMMON SEWER: also in the form 'common shore', both forms used frequently in 17th and 18th cent.; *O.E.D.* derives the phrase not from 'sewer' (though it generally came to mean this) but more probably from 'shore', ' "the common shore" being originally the "no-man's-land" by the water-side, where filth was allowed to be deposited for the tide to wash away', v. iii. 153.

COMPOSITION: medicine, preparation of mixed ingredients, IV. ii. 134.

COMPOUND vb: mix, combine, I. i. 144.

CONCEIT: whim, fancy, III. iii. 195.

CONCEIVE vb: understand, I. ii. 32.

CONDUCT sb.: escort, guide, v. ii. 85; safe-conduct, paper with directions, II. i. 3.

CONSTABLE: parish officer appointed to keep the peace, I. ii. 126.

COST: expenditure, I. ii. 120.

COUNTENANCE vb: favour, patronize, v. i. 100.

COZEN vb: cheat, deceive, II. i. 128, v. iii. 160.

CRAG: neck, I. ii. 198.

CRITICAL (in *critical day*): decisive, crucial (a term frequently used in contemporary medicine and astrology), I. i. 49.

CRYSTAL: crystal-glass, ball of glass, v. ii. 33.

CUCKOO (*what you call't*); ? cuckoo pintle-root, I. i. 150 [see Commentary].

CUDS: corruption of 'God's' (a mild oath), IV. i. 53.

DELIVER: speak of, describe, IV. ii. 118.

DESPITE sb.: object of scorn or contempt, V. iii. 50.

DIE sb.: sing. of 'dice', IV. i. 16.

DISCOVER: reveal, disclose, I. i. 150, III. iii. 143, IV. ii. 14, etc.

DISMANTLE: strip, unclothe, IV. iii. 22 [cf. *Lr.*, I. i. 220].

DISTASTE vb: dislike, disrelish, I. i. 118.

DISTINCTION: the condition of being distinct or separate, V. iii. 153.

DOG (*at*): skilled in, adept at, V. i. 93 [cf. *Tw. N.*, II. iii. 63–4].

DOUBT vb: fear, suspect, I. i. 26, III. iv. 92.

DUCAT: gold coin used in various continental countries. Coryat gives its equivalent in English money as 3s. 4d.; other authorities give higher figures, III. iv. 43, IV. i. 74, 126.

ENVY sb.: ill-will, malice, II. ii. 16.

EXCEPTIOUS: captious, prone to take exception, II. i. 125.

FAG sb.: end, conclusion, III. iii. 257.

FAITHFULLY: confidently, truthfully, II. ii. 118, IV. ii. 11.

FARTHEST (in *at farthest*): ? least successful, farthest away from the goal, I. i. 88 [cf. *The Maid in the Mill*, IV. i: 'I am at farthest/ In my counterfeit' (Fletcher, VII, 49). Not in *O.E.D.*].

FAULT: misprint, defect, II. i. 109, 111.

FIGURE: (*a*) dance-figure, set of movements in dancing, IV. iii. 100; (*b*) shape, appearance (with play of words on both meanings), IV. iii. 101.

FIND: find out, understand, I. i. 75, II. ii. 25.

FIT vb: ? make suitable, prepare, IV. iii. 50, 213.

FLORIN: gold coin first issued at Florence in 1252, III. iv. 61.

FORM sb.: school-class, I. ii. 148, 162.

FORWARD adj.: eager, II. i. 24; pert, precocious, I. ii. 178, III. iii. 133.

FOX-SKIN: cunning disguise, IV. iii. 146 [see Commentary].

GAME (in *give game*): ? quarry, target, V. ii. 15 [see Commentary].

GET (*up*): mount (a horse, etc.), III. iii. 56.

HABIT: dress, clothes, I. ii. 55, III. iii. 142.

HAND: handwriting, IV. iii. 179.

HAPPILY: haply, perhaps, II. ii. 59.

HARD adj.: ugly, repellent, II. ii. 88. adv.: severely, V. ii. 10.

HARDNESS: ugliness, II. ii. 92.

HEADBOROUGH: a parish officer whose duties were very similar to those of the constable, I. ii. 128.

HEAVY: ? clumsy, sluggish, IV. i. 50, V. i. 101.

HOME adv.: forcibly, deeply, to the point, III. iv. 87, V. iii. 7.

HONEST: chaste, virtuous, IV. i. 118, V. iii. 20.

HONESTY: chastity, IV. i. 98.

HONOUR sb.: bow or curtsy (in dancing), IV. iii. 90–8.

HORSE-TRICK: buffoonery, rough behaviour (imitating the movements of a performing horse), IV. iii. 158 [cf. Middleton, Massinger and Rowley's *The Old Law*, III. ii. 86–93 (Bullen, II, 183–4)].

ILL-FAC'D: evil-looking, ugly, II. i. 53.

ILL-SET: with many misprints (referring to the setting-up of type), II. i. 110.

INCONTINENTLY: immediately, IV. i. 49.

INFINITE sb.: infinite number (of people, etc.), I. i. 119.

INJURY: insult, II. i. 151, V. ii. 35.

INNOCENCE: (a) guiltlessness, IV. ii. 79, V. iii. 24, 62; (b) simplicity, silliness (with play of words on both meanings), V. iii. 206.

IULAN adj.: youthful, boyish (applied to the first growth of the beard), I. i. 175 [see Commentary].

JUSTICE: justice of the peace, magistrate, I. ii. 130, IV. i. 126.

KINDLY adv.: (a) affectionately; (b) appropriately, according to kind, IV. iii. 47 [used here with both meanings].

LACEDEMONIAN: lit. a Spartan; fig. ? one whose speech is concise and to the point, III. iii. 235 [see Commentary].

LARGELY: generously, widely, at length, III. iv. 9.

LAY (in *lay my hand*): (a) place, put; (b) make a bet, III. iii. 237 [used here with both meanings].

LAY: ? become calm, die down, IV. i. 117.

LOATHE: inspire loathing in, V. i. 70.

LOOK: look for, seek, IV. i. 56, 57.

LUGG vb: pull by the hair or ears (hence tease, worry), II. i. 81.

LYCANTHROPI: those suffering from wolf-madness, III. iii. 84 [see Commentary].

MAGNIFICO: a magistrate of Venice; transf. a person in high authority, I. ii. 121.

MATCH: agreement, compact, III. iii. 32 [cf. *Tp.*, II. i. 34].

MINE: ? explosion, fire, V. i. 102.

MORRIS: morris-dance, grotesque dance, IV. iii. 65.

MURDERER: small cannon loaded with shot, I. i. 223.

MYSTERY: art, skill, III. iii. 127; secret, IV. i. 39.

NICE: fastidious, IV. iii. 60.

NIGGET: idiot, fool, III. iii. 102.

OPACOUS: opaque, shadowed, obscured, V. iii. 196.

OPPORTUNEFUL: timely, convenient, III. iii. 116.

ORISONS: prayers, I. i. 34.

OVERLAY vb: weigh down, oppress, IV. ii. 56.

OWE: own, IV. i. 67.

PARLOUS: dangerously cunning, shrewd (contracted from 'perilous'), I. ii. 162, III. iii. 128.

PARTICIPATE: partake, share, III. iii. 18.

PASSIONS: feelings, emotions, II. i. 54; displays of emotion, outbursts, IV. ii. 109.

PELT: skin, I. i. 232.

PENNYWORTH: bargain, I. i. 18.

PERMASANT: parmesan cheese, I. ii. 202–3, 207.

PHYSNOMY: physiognomy, face, II. ii. 76.

PICK-HAIR'D: ? with hard, bristly hair and beard, II. i. 40 [not in *O.E.D.*].

PIECE: young woman, girl, IV. i. 54; fowling-piece, gun, V. i. 45, 76, etc.

PINCHING adj.: niggardly, restricted, II. i. 117.

PINFOLD: a place for confining stray sheep or cattle, III. iii. 8.

PIT-HOLE: cant term for 'grave', IV. i. 63 [cf. *The Honest Whore, Part I*, V. ii. 298: 'I am dead, put me I pray into a good pit-hole' (Dekker, II, 84)].

PIZZLE: bull's penis, used as a whip, IV. iii. 62.

PLEASURE: sensual pleasure, II. i.

133, II. ii. 86, 150, III. iv. 115, 161, 168, V. i. 3.

POP (in *pop i' th' lips*): kiss (with punning allusion to *poppy*), I. i. 148 [not in *O.E.D.*].

POPPY: opium prepared from poppy-seeds, I. i. 149 [cf. *Oth.*, III. iii. 330].

POSTERN: side-door, back-door, III. i. 2.

POUNDED: impounded, confined as a stray, III. iii. 10.

PRAISE vb: appraise, value, IV. i. 105.

PRESENCE: demeanour, appearance, I. i. 98.

PRESENT adj.: immediate, III. iii. 194.

PRESENTLY: immediately, III. iii. 36.

PRETEND: offer, IV. ii. 90.

PREVENT: forestall, anticipate, I. i. 186, IV. ii. 97, V. iii. 173.

PROMONTS: promontories, I. i. 166.

PROPER: handsome, admirable, III. iii. 23, 60.

PRUNE vb: preen, adorn (used of a bird cleaning and oiling its feathers), II. ii. 74.

PUMPS: dancing-shoes, slippers, I. i. 233.

PURCHASE sb.: prize, reward, III. iii. 240.

PUSH-PIN: a child's game, I. ii. 175 [see Commentary].

PUT (*case*): grant, suppose that, II. ii. 66.

PUT (*down*): defeat in an argument (but with an obvious double meaning), III. iii. 210–11 [cf. *Ado*, II. i. 292–5].

PUT (*in*): advance a claim, II. ii. 60; ? give the cue, V. iii. 89.

PUT (*on*): incite, provoke, IV. ii. 85.

QUESTION: conversation, discussion, I. ii. 43.

RANGER: gamekeeper, keeper of the royal park, IV. i. 60.

REACH sb.: scheme, device, V. i. 31.

RECEIPT: recipe, means towards, III. iv. 168.

REFULGENT: shining, gleaming, III. iv. 17.

REMEMBER: devise, II. i. 24.

RESOLVE vb: answer (a question, problem), IV. ii. 108, V. iii. 19.

RESPECT sb.: esteem, regard, I. i. 135.

REVERSION: the right of succeeding to an estate, place, etc., IV. iii. 120.

RIDE vb: have intercourse with, IV. iii. 86, 151.

ROUND-PACK'D: ? plump, IV. ii. 51 [see Commentary].

SADDER: darker, more dismal, V. iii. 28.

SAINT: used to mean both patron-saint and lover, I. i. 155, V. iii. 53 [second sense not rec. in *O.E.D.* though common in period].

SALUTE vb: greet, I. i. 59, IV. ii. 55, V. ii. 47.

SCONCE: small fort or earthwork, III. i. 3.

SCRUTINOUS: examining, searching, III. iii. 124.

SERVE (*turn*): be of use, I. ii. 59, 127, 136; make use of, II. ii. 69.

SET (*on*): attack, IV. ii. 16.

SEWER: see *Common sewer*.

SHAPE sb.: dress, costume, III. iii. 119, 187, 193, etc.

SHOUGH: exclamation to scare off birds, etc. (mod. 'shoo!'), IV. iii. 102.

SHREWD: severe, malicious, I. ii. 26, 57.

SHROUD vb: shelter, conceal, III. iii. 119, III. iii. 167.

SIMPLE sb.: plant or herb used as medicine, I. i. 149.

SLEIGHT: trick, device, IV. i. 45.

SOCKETS: fingers of a glove, I. i. 234 [this sense not in *O.E.D.*].

STALL vb: ? forestall, I. i. 97 [see Commentary].

STANDING adj.: stagnant, II. i. 58.

STATE: position, circumstance, I. ii. 139; dignity, ceremony, IV. i. o.5.

STILL adv.: constantly, always, I. i. 102, 236, I. ii. 30, 144, etc.

STRANGE: cold, unfriendly, III. iv. 90.

SUSPECT sb.: suspicion, III. iv. 86; cause of suspicion, III. ii. 26.

SUTLER: camp-follower selling provisions to soldiers, II. ii. 64 [cf. *H 5*, II. i. 116].

SWEET adj.: clean, wholesome, I. ii. 95, 116.

TERMAGANT: an imaginary deity supposed to be worshipped by the Mohammedans, of a violent, overbearing nature; transf. a fierce, shrewish woman, V. i. 16.

THIRDS: 'a third of the proceeds of captures, or of certain fines, forfeitures, etc., of which two thirds were due to the king' (*O.E.D.*), IV. iii. 36.

THROUGHLY: thoroughly, V. i. 115.

TICKLISH: fickle, unreliable, V. iii. 46.

TOUCH'D: tainted, corrupted, IV. ii. 107.

TOY: caprice, trifle, I. i. 197.

TRAP vb: put on trappings, harness, I. i. 30.

TREADINGS: movements, actions, I. ii. 39.

TRUE: honest, trustworthy, I. ii. 152, IV. i. 45, 80, 105, etc.

URGE vb: provoke, incite, III. iv. 141, IV. i. 94.

VALENTINE: lover chosen on St Valentine's day, III. iii. 148.

VAULT sb.: the arch of the sky, V. iii. 26 [cf. *Tp.*, V. i. 43].

VENTURER: one who took a share in the risks and expenses of a commercial voyage and received a share of the profits in return, I. i. 90.

VIAL: phial, bottle, IV. i. 21.

WAITING adj.: meaning uncertain, IV. iii. 1 [see Commentary].

WANT vb: fail to achieve, lack, need, I. i. 69, 133, 219, 220, etc.

WARD sb.: guard, position of defence (in fencing), I. ii. 61.

WATER sb.: lotion, preparation, II. ii. 83, IV. i. 31, 36, 47; urine, IV. iii. 186.

WELL-FAVOUREDLY: soundly, severely, IV. iii. 198.

WIRE: whip of wire, I. ii. 201 [cf. *Ant.*, II. v. 65].